PRAISE FOR *SISTER OF SILENCE*

"In *Sister of Silence*, author Daleen Berry gently guides us through the dark corridors of her life, so that we can emerge in the light, as she has courageously done, with a sense of hope, authenticity and courage. *Sister of Silence* is a brave book, written from the heart. It's a must read for the brave-hearted."

—Asra Q. Nomani
Author of *Standing Alone: An American Woman's Struggle for the Soul of Islam*

"*Sister of Silence* is a powerful and moving story that will touch your soul." —Rick Shartzer

"*Sister of Silence* speaks for all of us who couldn't, or didn't, have the words to express what we were going through. So many women just stay in abusive situations and never speak out. Thank you for being their voice, Daleen!"

—Lori Green Supinski

"New book from an incredible person. Worth checking out."

—Jerry Toppins

"Great book! I hope everyone gets a chance to read it. I wish you much success and look forward to your next book."

—Rayne Hutson

"The first paragraph had me. I honestly could not put it down, and several f..... sking to borrow it. I'm so glad ıgth, determination, and cour- omen will see themselves in it."

—Patty Strahin Markley

SISTER OF SILENCE

A MEMOIR

DALEEN BERRY

Foreword by Kenneth V. Lanning

Nellie Bly Books
Morgantown, West Virginia

Nellie Bly Books
Morgantown, W.Va.

First Nellie Bly Books trade paperback edition 2011
Nellie Bly Books and design are registered trademarks.

Manufactured in the United States of America

Library of Congress Control Number: 2010934361
ISBN 978-0-6153-8860-1 (alk. paper)

Nellie Bly Books can arrange for Ms. Berry to speak at your live
event. Special discounts for bulk purchases for educational, gift
purposes, or as premiums for increasing magazine subscriptions
or renewals are available. Book excerpts can also be created to
fit specific needs. For information or to book an event, please
contact Nellie Bly Books at 888-241-5534, or send an email to:
contact@nellieblybooks.com.

DEDICATION

For my four sweet grapes,
because without you
there would be no story.

ACKNOWLEDGEMENTS

I'm eternally grateful to my Creator, who has never left my side, who gave me the amazing gift of being a wordsmith, and my greatest blessings: my four "sweet grapes."

It was those same sweet grapes who gave me a reason to live. Their lives made my own meaningful, and they taught me more about love than I ever could have learned otherwise.

Warm appreciation goes to the men and women in blue during my early journalism days, who taught me how to ask the right questions.

Linda and Delbert Benson saw something within my words that I didn't, and their unswerving faith led me down a different path.

I'm indebted to Ken Lanning, who graciously gave of his time and expertise and, most of all, his endorsement.

Julie Sexstone, who showed me how to dig deeply enough to find my story, deserves heartfelt thanks.

So do my dear friends Boyd and Lennoe, who told me I had a story to tell in the first place.

Deep gratitude to Deb Beazley, who believed my story could help other victims, and whose enthusiasm was contagious.

Darron Padilla deserves a big hug because his own certainty that Oprah would love it made me wipe away the dust and kept me moving forward.

I came to know more fully what Wanda Toppins, my sister in silence, went through, thanks to the generosity of her stepson, Jerry, who patiently answered my questions.

Like Wanda, I had help in the form of wonderful friends who sheltered my children and me when we were at the breaking point, and I would be remiss in not thanking (or remembering, as the case may be) Butch and Shirley.

Heartfelt appreciation to the many authors who have supported me: Richard Currey, who bestowed a great honor upon my work; Julie Gregory, who saw the raw beauty in my story; John Searles, who graciously helped me get one foot in Oprah's door; and Asra Nomani, who led by example.

I'm most grateful to my editor, Arlene Robinson, whose advice helped hone my skills.

More thanks than she will ever know go to Jackie Campbell, who graciously took time from her very busy academic schedule to help me.

Jeannette Walls' incredibly kind words gave me the courage to do just that, when she said urged me to finish writing this book.

Hugs go to Lisa Jan, Hilda Heady, Fran Kirk, Teresa Neel, Scott Radabaugh, Troy Helmick, Pete and Shirley Vuljanic, and Steve and Nina Calvert for just being there, to Rick Shartzer, who taught me about inner warrior, and to anyone else I may have overlooked along my journey.

Finally, I must thank my parents, who, in spite of their flaws, gave me all they could—which, as it turns out, was more than enough.

FOREWORD

In the United States, society's historical attitude about sexual victimization of children can generally be summed up in one word: *denial*. Most people do not want to hear about it and would prefer to pretend such victimization does not happen. Today, however, that's difficult when stories and reports about child sexual abuse and exploitation occur daily.

Especially during the 1950s and 1960s, the primary focus in the limited literature and discussions on sexual victimization of children was on "stranger danger"—the dirty old man in the wrinkled raincoat approaching an innocent child. If one could not totally deny the existence of child sexual victimization, one could describe it in simplistic terms of good and evil. The investigation and prevention of this "stranger danger" are more clear-cut. We immediately know who the good and bad guys are, what they look like, and that the danger is external. Although no longer the primary focus of literature and training, "stranger danger" remains a disproportionate concern for our society.

The criminal sexual assault of an adult is, by definition, almost always violent. The criminal sexual assault of a child may or may not be violent. In the U.S., however, it's common to view or even legally define sexual victimization of children as violent—even if many cases do not meet common definitions of violence (i.e., threats, force). Although emotionally understandable, this often creates confusion and unrealistic evidentiary expectations. Many laypeople and even professionals, who hear terms such as "sexual assault" or "rape" applied to children, seek out or expect evidence of physical violence even when the law may not require it. Often in response to atypical, highly publicized, violent sexual assaults of children, laws requiring sex offender registration and community notification were passed in the U.S. to protect society from these "sexually violent predators." Only later was it "discovered" that many of the most persistent and prolific child molesters have typically used seduction (not violence) and are, therefore, not adequately covered by these laws.

In reality, sexual victimization of children involves varied and diverse dynamics. It can range from one-on-one intrafamilial abuse to multi-offender/multi-victim extrafamilial sex rings, or from stranger abduction of toddlers to prostitution of teenagers. The often forgotten piece in the puzzle of the sexual victimization of children is "acquaintance molestation." This seems to be the most difficult manifestation of the problem for society and even professionals to face. People seem more willing to accept a sinister stranger from a different location or father/stepfather from a different socioeconomic background as a child molester than a clergy member, next-door neighbor, law enforcement officer, pediatrician, teacher, or a volunteer who has access to children. Society seems to have a problem dealing with any sexual victimization case in which the adult offender is not completely "bad," or the child victim is not completely "good." The idea that child victims could simply behave like human beings and respond to the attention and affection of offenders, by voluntarily and repeatedly returning to an offender, is a troubling one.

Stranger offenders can use trickery to initially lure their child victims, but tend to control them more through confrontation, threats of force, and physical force. Interfamilial offenders tend to control their victims more through their private access and family authority. Acquaintance child molesters, although sometimes violent, tend to control their victims through the grooming or seduction process. This process not only gains the victim's initial cooperation, but also decreases the likelihood of disclosure and increases the likelihood of ongoing, repeated access. Acquaintance offenders with a preference for young victims (younger than age twelve) are more likely to also spend time seducing the potential victim's parents or caretakers, to gain their trust and confidence. An acquaintance molester who uses violence will likely, and quickly, be reported to law enforcement. But an acquaintance molester who seduces his victims *without violence* can sometimes go unreported for thirty years or more.

One of the unfortunate outcomes of society's preference for the "stranger-danger" concept is that it has a direct impact on intervention into many acquaintance molestation cases. It is what I call "say no, yell and tell" guilt. This is the result of societal attitudes and prevention programs that focus only on "unwanted" sexual activity and tell potential child victims to avoid sexual abuse by saying no, yelling, and telling. This technique might work well with the stranger lurking behind a tree, but children who are seduced and actively participate in their victimization often feel guilty and blame themselves because they did not do what they were "supposed" to do. These seduced and, therefore, compliant victims may sometimes feel a need to describe their victimization in more socially acceptable but inaccurate ways that relieve their guilt.

Society's lack of understanding and acceptance of the reality of compliant child victims often results in:

1. Victims who fail to disclose and even deny their sexual victimization.

2. Incomplete, inaccurate, distorted, even contradictory victim disclosures when they do happen.

3. A lifetime of victim shame, embarrassment, and guilt.

4. Offenders having access to numerous victims over an extended period of time.

5. Ineffective prevention programs that not only do not prevent victimization, but also make the first four problems worse.

Awareness and prevention programs that focus on recognizing evil sexual "predators" and "pedophiles" and advise victims to "say no, yell and tell" decrease the likelihood of victim disclosure and increase the victims' shame and guilt. What are the long-term emotional and psychological consequences for child victims who are exposed to prevention and awareness programs that seem to deny the reality of their victimization or who must distort, misrepresent, and lie about what actually happened to them in order to have it accepted as "real" victimization?

Advice to prevent sexual exploitation of children by adult acquaintances is very complex and difficult to implement. Children younger than age twelve tend to listen to prevention advice but often to not understand it. Children older than age twelve tend to understand it, but often no longer listen to it. How do you warn children about offenders who may be their teachers, coaches, clergy members, neighbors, or Internet "friends"? Or whose only distinguishing characteristics are: they will treat the children better than most adults, listen to their problems and concerns, and fill their emotional, physical and sexual needs? Will parents, society, and professionals understand when the victimization is discovered or disclosed? Much prevention advice simply does not distinguish to which types of sexual victimization it applies. The right to "say no" and "good touch/bad touch" would be applied differently to a stranger, parent, teacher, physician or Internet acquaintance.

At an early age, children learn to manipulate their environment to get what they want. Almost all children seek attention and affection. Children, especially adolescents, typically find pornography online because they are looking for it, not because they made a mistake. They are moving away from the total control of parents and trying to establish new relationships outside the family. Ask any adult what the number one thing on their mind was when they were adolescents, and the answer is always the same: sex. Yet parents seem to want to believe their children are asexual.

Most acquaintance-exploitation cases involve seduced or compliant victims. Although applicable statutes and investigative or protective priorities may vary, the sexual activity is **not** the victim's fault even if the child:

- Did not say "no"
- Did not fight
- Actively cooperated
- Initiated the contact
- Did not tell
- Accepted gifts or money
- Enjoyed the sexual activity

Society must also remember that many children, especially those victimized through the seduction process, often:

- Trade sex for attention, affection, or gifts
- Are confused over their sexuality and feelings
- Are embarrassed and guilt-ridden over their activity
- Describe their victimization in socially acceptable ways
- Minimize their responsibility and maximize the offender's
- Deny or exaggerate their victimization

Seeming disagreements and differences of opinion often result from confusion over definitions. Some experts say pedophiles can be treated; others claim they cannot. Some people say there is a connection between missing children and child pornography; others say there is not. Some people say communities should be notified when sex offenders move into a neighborhood; others say it's an unproductive violation of privacy. This is not simply a matter of opinion.

Referring to the same thing by different names and different things by the same name also creates confusion. For example, the same fifteen-year-old can be referred to as a "baby," "child," "youth," "juvenile," "minor," "adolescent," "adult," or (as in one forensic psychological evaluation) "underage adult." A father who coerces, a violent abductor, an acquaintance who seduces, a child-pornography collector, or an older boyfriend can all be referred to as a "child molester" or "pedophile."

In communication, definitions are crucial to understanding. The problem is that when we use basic or common terms, we rarely define them. What is the difference between the sexual abuse of children and sexual exploitation of children? What is the difference between child molestation and child rape? What does it mean when the newspaper states a child was the victim of "indecent assault;" a child was "sodomized;" or an offender was convicted of "indecent liberties" or "lewd and lascivious conduct" with a child; or was "contributing to the delinquency of a minor?" Should statistics on violence against women include cases involving the "rape" of female children?

There's clearly a conflict between the law and society's viewpoint, when it comes to defining a *child*. Many people using the term *sexual abuse of children* have a mental image of children age twelve or younger. The main problem, therefore, is often with the thirteen- to seventeen-year-old age group. Those are the child victims who most likely look, act, and have sex drives like adults, but who may or may not be considered children under some laws and by society. There can be national, cultural, and ethnic variations in attitudes about who is a child. Pubescent teenagers can be viable sexual targets of a much larger population of sex offenders.

This complex problem can be viewed from three major perspectives: personal, political, and professional. The *personal* perspective encompasses the emotional—how the issues affect individual needs and wants. The *political* perspective encompasses the practical—how the issues affect getting elected, obtaining funding or pay, and attaining status and power. The *professional* perspective encompasses the rational and objective—how the issues affect sexually victimized children and what is in their best interests. Often these perspectives overlap or are applied in combination. Because most of us use all three, sometimes which perspective is in control may not be clear.

In this book, Daleen Berry openly tells the unique story of her victimization from her personal perspective. Her victimization may be both like and unlike that of any other child victims in a wide variety of ways. Although all the dynamics of her victimization cannot be generalized to all sexually abused children, they provide important insights into the complex and diverse reality of such victimization. Because it is a story that in many ways does not easily fit common stereotypes, it represents an important contribution to a better understanding of the issue. Most important, her story is ultimately one of survival and hope for victims. Her story is well worth telling and worth hearing.

Kenneth V. Lanning
Former Supervisory Special Agent
FBI's Behavioral Science Unit

"The present contains nothing more than the past, and what is found in the effect was already in the cause."
—Henri Bergson

CHAPTER ONE

White knuckles clenched the crib rail as I stood looking down at my newborn. Leaning over, I lifted the sleeping bundle and held it against my breast, feeling the softness of new skin as he pulled tiny legs up against his body. The small silky head turned as he continued breathing slow and evenly, and I felt the whisper of his warm breath against the pillow my neck provided.

Cradling him lovingly, I slowly walked over to the open window, held out my arms, and let go.

"You haven't had any thoughts of harming yourself, have you? Or anyone else?"

My throat seemed to close up so tight that any words just stuck there, leaving me unable to speak.

"Mrs. Leigh?"

I looked into the well-meaning eyes of my family doctor and shrugged.

"No! I'm just tired, that's all. I feel kind of blah. You know, like a cloud hanging over me. That's it. No, no, nothing like that."

He continued writing in my chart, then looked up and gave me an understanding smile. "I don't really think you need an antidepressant. You just need some more help at home. Tell your husband to pitch in and give you a break now and then.

Have an occasional glass of wine to help you relax. After all, you're only twenty-two and you have four little ones to take care of, not to mention a house and a husband. It isn't unreasonable to think you would need some help."

As always, my smile came easily, and I nodded. "Of course that's it. I'm sure you're right."

He turned toward the door, but then looked back at me. "Better yet, why don't you hire a sitter and you and your husband go away for a long weekend?"

Then he was gone.

I hung my head, ashamed of my blatant lies. Grappling with his words, I remembered the last "long weekend." It had led to a fourth baby, so there was no way that was going to happen. But I was also confused because he had totally ignored my concerns about Eddie: "I'm exhausted because my husband wants to have sex all the time. Do you think he might have an addiction?" My doctor, who had just come to our community fresh out of medical school, had only laughed: "Men would have sex with a tree, if they could," he said, discounting Eddie entirely and focusing only on my lingering feelings of sadness.

I wondered what he would've done had I told the truth. That since the birth of my first, that same scene had repeated itself in my mind, over and over again, leaving me afraid to venture too close to any open windows while holding a baby in my arms. The thought would come to me at the oddest moment, with such intensity I was sure I was going crazy, that I was crazy to harbor such insane ideas.

Hurt my baby? What kind of a mother would do that? What's wrong with me, anyway, that I would even consider such a thing? What does it mean? What does that say about me, about my ability to be a mother, to care for my children?

The pervasive thoughts remained for many years, for the entire time my four children were too helpless to care for themselves: too innocent to protect themselves from a mother whose mind was invaded by so many evil thoughts that, had she acted on them, it would have instantly put an end to their lives. Yet, I never told another human being about them. Ever. I was terrified of the consequences. Afraid something was wrong with me. Scared they would lock me up in some place where medication turned the minds of crazy people to mush, leaving them defenseless against orderlies in starched coats and nurses with long needles and little pink and blue pills.

I remembered Dr. Towson's suggestion to have a drink. But I never needed a glass of wine to get me through those mental minefields, when the wrong thought threatened to blow my world to smithereens; somehow I just did what I was supposed to, instead of killing us all. It was at night, when he came to me, that I needed the alcohol to drown out what happened whenever he touched me. And it was those times, all those perverse touches that made me feel like a tiny insect caught and held fast, being squished inside a little child's clenched fist—it was those times that drove me to stand before my baby's crib, waging a war within not to do the unthinkable.

Some people's problems begin with a shot of whisky or a bottle of rum. Mine began before my birth, inside a beer can. And then another. And another. After I was born, it took me about seven years to realize my father's drinking colored our family's life in every possible way: the beer he consumed was more important than we were. By 1972, the beer had become a dangerous tool that turned him from a sensitive, mild-mannered man into a monster. I was fortunate. I saw it happen only once, in a scene that played out before me as a child. I locked it carefully away, where it stayed until it was released as a painful memory years later.

Mom had kept dinner waiting on the stove when Daddy didn't come home. Again. I suspected she knew he was sitting at a beer joint somewhere, so after she packed us off to bed, leaving his dinner warming on the back burner, she went to sleep herself. The screaming woke me up.

"Get outta bed and make me sumpin' that duzen taste like burnt toast!"

My father's voice came from the room next to mine.

"Dale, stop it. Please, you're hurting me!" Those were my mother's cries. There were other noises, too, sounds of moving around, but I laid there with my eyes closed, too terrified to even move.

"I deserve sumpin' better'n that crap downstairs," Daddy yelled. "I work hard all day long and all I won' is a halfway decent meal when I come home!"

Though terrified, I had to see what was happening. I slid from beneath the heavy blankets and quilts that Mom had piled upon me and peeked around the corner of my bedroom door. Through the darkness, I could just make out my father's hand, buried beneath the dark silky strands of my mother's beautiful hair, as he pulled her toward the stairway. The echo of their voices moved along with them, past the faded, peeling wallpaper and out of my sight.

I tiptoed across the old and cracked Linoleum, and watched the breath that came from my mouth turn into a delicate mist, as I slowly, stealthily, crept toward the stairwell on my tiptoes, afraid that a single step would lead to a creaking floorboard and give me away. When I looked down, Mom was in front of my father, crying as he followed close behind, his hand clamped tightly around her arm. I don't know what frightened me more: her crying, or the realization that she could slip and tumble down the stairs any second.

When they had disappeared into the kitchen, I sat on the

stairs. "I hate you, I hate you, I hate you," I sobbed softly, my face framed between the two blackened stair dowels that my tiny hands were clenching, my body trembling from fear as well as the frigid night air that cloaked our cold brick home.

I heard his yelling continue until it gradually grew softer and then stopped altogether. I could picture him sitting there, eating whatever Mom had hastily whipped up, while she patiently waited for him to finish so she could carry his dishes to the sink. I wanted to see for myself that she was all right, yet I was too afraid to go down the stairs. But I was determined not to return to my room. If he tried to hurt her again, I was going to make him stop. I didn't know how, but I would do anything I could to protect Mom: Mom, who would hold me as I sobbed, thanks to yet another middle of the night ear infection, gently blowing her warm breath into my affected ear to ease the pain, until we arrived at the hospital. I would do whatever it took, even if that meant beating him off with my bare hands.

My toes turned numb as I sat there for what seemed like hours before they came into the living room. My parents looked like they were at someone's funeral. They were sad and silent, with Daddy's arm around my mother, trying to comfort her.

My sobs had stopped, but in their place, a few hiccups remained, and I guess that's what caused Mom to turn in my direction.

"Daleen, what are you doing out of bed? It's freezing in here and you're going to be ill!" Rising, she hurried up to me, and the next thing I knew, I was clinging to her as she carried me back down the stairs.

"I want you to divorce him," I said as my tears began flowing again. "I don't want him to hurt you anymore."

"Shh, there, it's all right," she cooed. "Your father didn't hurt me. I'm fine."

By then we were on the couch and I was on her lap. When she whispered my words to my father, he tried to put his arm around me but I pulled away and clung even tighter to Mom. He leaned back heavily. "I'm so sorry, Neelad," he whispered, using the pet name he had given me.

"There now, it's all right. Everything's fine now," Mom said.

I glanced his way. In the pale living room light, he did seem different. He no longer looked mean and frightening, like he had when I first woke up. He even smiled.

"I'm sorry if I scared you, Honey. I didn't mean to." His words were quiet and I could smell his horrible beer breath.

I buried my face against Mom again.

"Will you be all right now? We're coming to bed, and everything'll be fine, I promise." As she spoke, she brushed the hair back from my eyes. I nodded and looked into her flushed face, her own stormy blue eyes rimmed with red.

"I'm taking her back to bed, Dale," she told my father, who rose onto unsteady feet to follow us. Upstairs, Mom tucked me in with a kiss against my forehead. "Remember, God will protect us," she whispered against my ear.

A few minutes later I heard them both get into bed. Everything grew quiet then, but I laid there praying in the dark. "Please God, let her divorce him," I asked, over and over again.

Dad went to work in Washington, DC, soon afterward: I think he was ashamed of what he'd done that night. I wondered if he was also afraid his drinking might lead to a repeat performance, so I was happy when he left, knowing he wouldn't hurt my mother any more. But I was nine at the time and blissfully ignorant of how his void would be filled, just four years later, by a force that would change me forever.

That's when I entered junior high school, surrounded by unfamiliar faces during an era when school consolidation was becoming a national trend. In spite of being shy and subdued, I excelled academically, and somehow found my place during that period when adolescence is the most difficult. In my West Virginia History class, I was selected to enter the statewide Golden Horseshoe Contest. In English, I received regular praise from my teacher for my essays and short stories. I was proud of my accomplishments, but not wanting to be noticed, I pretended they were no big deal. I never wanted to draw attention to myself, but sometimes I just couldn't help it.

With spring near, I began to study for the county spelling bee. As the winner for my school, I would compete against students from several other schools. More than anything else, I wanted to win, so I grilled myself over and over again. That night, with my parents and two sisters in the audience watching, I was the only student standing when the last word was given out. I spelled it correctly—becoming the county winner, taking home a $50 savings bond, and having my photo in the local newspaper.

I felt a huge sense of achievement, and realized that with hard work and enough time, anything was possible. I knew I won because spelling was important to me, and I had been willing to give up my free time for it.

My parents were both very proud of me, but I think Dad, who drove three hours from work to be there, was the proudest. Spelling and grammar had always been important to him. He always corrected our misspelled words and improper grammar, he taught us to play Scrabble, and he instilled in his daughters the attitude that nothing is impossible.

"Even though you're a girl, you can succeed if you want something badly enough, and you can be whatever you want to be," Dad told me.

He was exceptional in countless ways, even in spite of his many other failures—one of those being his drinking. It had always been the great divide between my parents, making him unreliable when it came time to send money home, so Mom found a job as a waitress. Sometimes she took us (my sisters: Carla, and baby Jackie) with her to work.

When Jackie arrived in 1976, Carla was nine, but willingly gave up her position to help take care of our baby sister. But at twelve, I was preoccupied with my own plans, and didn't spend as much time with her. I thought Jackie was adorable and loved her dearly, especially when she began to coo and smile at me. I helped care for her when I had to, but I didn't spend all my free time playing with her like Carla did. An awkward adolescent, I thought a baby was just a necessary nuisance, and the last thing on my busy mind. I couldn't even foresee having any babies of my own for a very long time—if ever.

Sometimes after Carla and I got home from school, Mom would take us all with her on the thirty-minute drive to the restaurant. Once there, we would wander around the mall, pushing Jackie in her stroller. Most of the time, unless a diaper needed changed, all I had to do was oversee both my siblings. When the mall closed and Mom was busy cleaning her section in the restaurant, she would bring us desert for a treat and we would eat at one of the tables, waiting until her shift ended. Those were some of my favorite times with my mother. Even though the new job interfered with our social life and school studies, we managed. Instead of doing homework, Carla, who excelled socially but not academically, didn't mind running around the mall playing with Jackie. And I knew that, as the oldest, I had an obligation to make sure my mom could earn the income she desperately needed to pay the bills. So we did what we had to do.

The waitress job didn't last long, though, since Mom decided to advertise for boarders, instead. When two railroad workers rented rooms, Mom took our twin beds downstairs, along with her big double bed, turning the space we had once used as a music room into our bedroom. Then she bought a lock for the door—just in case.

In those days I was a skinny thirteen-year-old with a flat chest and beanpole legs. I wasn't tall, but people said I was because I looked like a pencil. My best feature was my hair, falling long and straight like a waterfall past my waist, where it pooled against the floor whenever I sat cross-legged. I knew Eddie Leigh, a family friend, liked my hair, too, because he was always touching it.

The rapes never would have happened had Dad been there. I think that's why I was such easy prey for Eddie, with whom my friendship began innocently, when I was just eight and he was fifteen. Eddie had been around since we first moved to West Virginia. Tall, all arms and legs, he walked so fast he looked like a moving cartwheel. Even though he wore a cocky attitude and sneered when he smiled, I didn't remember a time when he hadn't been nice to me. Our families went on social outings together, or we rode with Eddie's family to Bible meetings. We'd play hide and seek in their backyard with other neighborhood children, and more than once I vaguely remember being locked in their dark barn with those black eyes staring at me from between the door's wooden slats.

By the time I was eleven, Eddie began showing up at our house with a load of coal or firewood. Knowing Dad was gone and our finances were tight, he offered to drop some off. The first time, he took the gas money Mom gave him. But after that he always refused, gallantly telling Mom her fine cooking was payment enough. She really appreciated his help and was happy to let him join us for dinner, but I could tell by the way he acted he had a crush on her. Mom seemed flattered, but I thought that was weird and began feeling nervous whenever he was there.

The first time it happened, he was much older. At twenty, he stood six-foot-two and towered over me, and anyone who knew him said he wasn't happy unless he was tinkering under the roof of his beloved green Ford truck, which you could hear coming from a mile away. He wasn't much of a talker, unless it was about that truck, or some model he was building. Mostly he just smiled and acted charming, making coy comments that left me blushing. It wasn't so much what he said as how he said it. He might comment about the weather, then look at me and ask "Isn't that right?" with that grin on his face. When he nicknamed me "Legs," he was wearing that same grin while he told me his friend Rick had said I had legs like Angie Dickinson, clear up to my armpits. That was one of the times I caught him watching me with an odd expression. I turned away, embarrassed, as if I'd done something wrong.

Children's lives should be a mixture of fun and freedom from the pressures of adult life. Little about my life was either, unless you count the first few times I stayed with Eddie's sister, Kim. At nineteen, she was wild and daring, with a goofy, offbeat sense of humor. Though five years my senior, I had known Kim and Eddie since we began going to Bible meetings together years earlier.

Kim was always finding some mischief to get into, almost always without her parents' knowledge. One of the things she really liked was driving fast. I remember her racing along narrow country lanes in Eddie's blue Ford Falcon, her short black curls blowing across her face from the wind that whistled through the open windows.

"Kim, slow down!" I begged once, laughing.

"You just hold on there. We're gonna' see what this car really has," Kim said with a grin, shifting to take a sharp curve. "That Eddie thinks he can drive. Well, I'll show him I can make this thing go too!"

I'd been a visitor in their home for years, even staying overnight as a youngster, but by the time I turned thirteen, she'd come pick me up in that little car, and we'd fly the seven miles from my house, barely slowing for the curves. I was tossed from side to side, clutching the door handle while Kim tore the gear shifter from one gear to another as fast as any guy could, and the little car sped ever faster. Being with her made me feel less like a gangly adolescent and more like a sophisticated grownup.

And that's how we ended up together that terrible night in early spring 1977 when I was in eighth grade. The air outside was warm and fragrant from the scent of new vegetation that surrounded their little house, making it seem like it sat in the middle of a large forest. The house reminded me of the witch's cottage in "Hansel and Gretel," minus the candy decorations and gingerbread trim. Eddie and his parents had bedrooms downstairs, but Kim slept in the attic. To get there, we had to walk right by Eddie's bedroom.

I thought about how easily Kim had been able to talk Mom into letting me spend the night. Once I was there she made jokes about her parents, mocking them in voices that made me roll on the bed clutching my stomach. And we shared secrets, like the one she told me on the phone the day before, about how much Eddie liked me, and how he thought I was really pretty.

Twirling my pencil, I tried to do a few math problems, but my thoughts returned to Eddie while I sat cross-legged in the spare bedroom. It had been converted into an office, and I was working on my homework while the Beach Boys blasted from the stereo in Eddie's bedroom. Through open window screens came the sound of an occasional car, and the crunch of tires against gravel made me remember my promise to Mom.

"Yes, I'll finish my homework before I go to bed," I promised, conceding to her one condition in letting me go with Kim. "Don't I always?" I asked her in annoyance.

But once at Kim's, with Eddie home from work and just a few feet away, it was hard to concentrate. I stared out the window, preferring instead to daydream about him.

I couldn't believe someone as worldly as Eddie was interested in a wallflower like me, a mere kid of thirteen. He had a real job; he paid his own way in the world, made his own decisions, and didn't seem to have to account to his parents like Kim always did. He was an Adult!

Just then, Kim came bounding down her bedroom steps and burst into my thoughts, urging me with an impish grin to follow her. I jumped off the bed and ran after her. She wandered down the hallway and plopped down on her brother's bed. Eddie was sitting on the floor, working on one of his many model cars. I stood, not sure what to do, until she patted the bed beside her, indicating I should sit there. She started talking to Eddie, trying to say things that would get his attention and make him look up.

I watched while he glued together the plastic model of a classic '64 Mustang he'd probably spent hours working on, bantering with Kim or softly singing along to the music as he did so. Then, just as quickly as she'd breezed in, she breezed out again, leaving us alone together. I started to follow her when he stopped me, saying, "What's your rush?"

I struggled to say something, anything, before blurting out the first words that came to mind: "Do you know anything about algebra?"

I felt awkward and frozen, hovering like I might bolt at any moment, while trying to hide my nervousness. The question really wasn't so odd, I told myself. I'd been turning to him more and more, in response to the questions he started asking me about my parents, my classes, and what I liked doing in my spare time. I admired him, and now, standing there remembering what Kim had said yesterday, I just knew I was falling in love with him. And I was certain he loved me: why else would he show me so much attention?

I don't recall his answer because he wiped the glue from his fingers, leaned across the bed, and kissed me. I was so surprised I didn't know what to do. Only one other boy had kissed me before, and it had been more like a quick peck than a real kiss.

"Well, what do you think?" He seemed amused.

"I don't know," a voice I didn't recognize responded in a strained whisper. My head went down and I just stared at the floor.

"You can come to my room later tonight if you want, and we'll talk. Would you like that?"

I didn't say anything, and continued staring at the swirls in the dark green carpet.

"We'll just talk, that's all," he said.

I hesitated. Being in his bedroom when everyone else was sound asleep didn't feel right to me, and I knew his parents wouldn't approve. I must have said something, but I can't remember what, and quickly rushed out to find Kim.

It was just before bedtime a few hours later, and Kim and I were sitting at the old metal and Formica table playing cards while Mrs. Leigh finished cleaning the kitchen.

"Would you girls like some tea?" she asked, her arm poised above the teakettle.

"No, thank you," I said.

"Nah," Kim added.

"I know something you girls will like," Mrs. Leigh said,

her smile bright. With that—as if she'd just announced dinner was ready—she opened one of the kitchen cabinets and took out a glass bottle filled with a lovely red liquid. I watched while she mixed it with Coca-Cola, mesmerized by the movement inside the glass as the colors swirled together. Then she put two glasses before us.

"There you go," she said, "a sloe gin fizz."

It looked like the Shirley Temple my parents ordered for my sister and me on the rare occasions we dined out. I took a sip but my throat began burning. It tasted nothing like the 7UP and cherry juice that came in a Shirley Temple. I'd never had anything other than a small glass of wine with an occasional meal at home, so the idea of drinking something more "grown-up," especially one that Mrs. Leigh herself really liked, made me feel important. The drinks were accompanied with a teasing warning to not tell my mother. I promised, because I didn't want Mrs. Leigh to get mad at me. Besides, I didn't see what harm could come from such a delicious drink.

CHAPTER TWO

When the moon came up later that night and Kim went downstairs to the bathroom, I trailed along, as I usually did. We giggled and whispered as we opened the door at the bottom of the attic stairs, poking our heads around to see Eddie lying in his bed, one arm propped up under his head. I felt him watching us as we ran to the bathroom.

We were just opening the door to the attic bedroom when he asked if I was coming in. I looked at Kim, desperately wanting her to tell me to follow her upstairs. She just shrugged her shoulders and started back up the steps.

"Oh come on, I won't bite you," he teased, patting the bed. By then, I realized he was without a shirt, reading a magazine that featured the latest models in sports cars. I tentatively walked over, nervous about going into a man's bedroom. He was an Adult, after all.

I stood there, feeling like a deaf-mute and far more awkward than ever before. I wanted to turn and run but a fear he would think I was a child and wouldn't like me anymore, that he would laugh at me, or even worse—ignore me—glued my feet to the floor.

The hard vinyl floor was cold, so cold it made my toes curl up tight as I hesitantly took each step. I perched on the edge of the bed and tried to talk intelligently, but my thoughts were jumbled. He told me how pretty I was, and how much he liked my hair. Though clad in a long nightgown, I began shivering, and gooseflesh covered my arms and legs.

"Why don't you get under the covers, just to keep warm?" he asked in a sweet voice.

I bit my lip. My entire life had been one of strict religious upbringing: I knew what morals were, what good girls didn't do, and getting into bed with a grown man was on that list.

"Come on, I promise I won't touch you. Nothing will happen." He smiled.

I hesitated, feeling stupid and childish while he waited for me to do something. In one motion I quickly crawled onto the bed beside him, ignoring the screaming inside my brain.

This is wrong. Leave, now! Get out quickly!

For what seemed like a very long time, nothing happened. He didn't even touch me. Then he leaned over and kissed me gently, and I began to get warm. He smelled like fresh soap and deodorant, and I believed he was big enough to protect me from anything. He already had, by keeping an eye out for me at the basketball games I sometimes attended, scaring away any boys who tried to talk to me.

Though warmer, my shivers would not stop, and I clamped my teeth together to end their continuous chattering. Just then, he reached over and pulled the chain on the nightstand lamp, casting the room into darkness and deep shadows. He moved closer and pulled me toward him. I couldn't move a single muscle. My tongue felt paralyzed, and as his arms came around me, I was pushed under the blankets at the same time he pressed his body up against mine. I was afraid to move, even more afraid to breathe. My heart thumped so wildly inside my chest I knew he could hear it.

I'm in bed with Kim's brother. I'm in bed with Kim's brother …

The words kept vibrating inside my head, reminding me what I was doing was wrong, even as I pushed them far, far away. I knew his parents were sleeping, just as I knew they'd be mortified if they awoke and realized I was in bed with their son. They would think I was terrible!

"I have—have to g-g-go upstairs—to Kim. Now." My teeth chattered with each word, and in spite of the warmth seeping from his body into my own, I felt like I would never get warm.

"It's okay. Everyone's asleep," he whispered into the darkness. "We aren't doing anything wrong."

I could make out his face just inches from my own. His kisses became more persistent, and at first I enjoyed them. Still, I was confused by the feelings they seemed to be awaking in me. But those kisses soon became sloppy, and I tried to wipe away their wetness in a way he wouldn't notice. But he was in a hurry and blind to anything I said or did.

"No, stop it." I managed to push the words out in a whisper as I tried to turn my head away to get his tongue out of my mouth.

Fear filled me and I swung my legs to the floor, trying to raise my torso at the same time. He grabbed me and suddenly I was trapped beneath him, unable to move. He reached down and pulled up my nightgown and then, tugging at my panties, began trying to grope between my legs. I tried to press them tight together, but he used his knee to pry them apart, moving his legs between mine.

I just laid there, not moving. Part of me knew what was happening, yet the biggest part of me didn't want to, couldn't possibly believe it was happening. That's when a voice inside my head began speaking for me.

Oh God no!

I was forced back to reality by his movements. With one hand cupping my chin, he kissed me. At the same time I sensed he was using his other hand to do something beneath the covers.

He's taking off his shorts!

"Here, give me your hand." His breath was hot against my ear, and I couldn't stand to feel it. The smell of sweat reached my nose; its dampness clung to me and suddenly I felt like I was going to vomit. But I knew, had seen, how hot-headed he could be, and was more afraid of angering him by saying no again, so I slowly moved my hand, just a little. He guided it to the part of a man's body I'd never seen before, let alone touched. When I felt the hard thing there, I flinched and jerked my hand away. Seconds later, it was hurting me as he tried to push it into the small space down there. All the while, he kept telling me everything would be all right.

"I won't hurt you, I promise. I'll be careful, and it will feel so good, it really will. You'll see."

But it does hurt.

I stared at the ceiling, using an imaginary pencil to trace every single outline in the white tiles. Moonlight shining through the bedroom window illuminated them, and I tried not to miss one tiny squiggle.

Up and down, over and around, through a loop and crossed in the center. Up and down, over and around, through a loop and crossed in the center.

I traced the ceiling tiles at least a hundred times, paying no attention to whatever was happening with the people on the bed below.

But the pain became too real, ripping my mind away from the tiles.

"No, this is— This is wrong. We can't do this. Please don't!" I wasn't sure if I spoke the words out loud, or said them inside my head.

"Did I hurt you? I'm sorry. I didn't mean to hurt you."

It was over in what seemed like mere seconds. Still sore from what had just occurred, I didn't, couldn't move. My eyes wildly searched the tiles again.

Up and down, over and around, through a loop and crossed in the center. Up and down, over and around, through a loop and crossed in the center.

Then I felt a dead, suffocating weight on top on me.

I can't breathe. Help me. Please. I'm going to die.

"Eddie? Eddie!" My whisper was urgent. I couldn't stand to feel him there; I had to get away, before I died!

"What . . . what is it?" He mumbled. Then, as if he was waking up from a deep sleep, his eyes opened and he kissed me again, just the faintest touch against my swollen lips. I turned my head, wanting only to be out of that room, away from him and that horrible, pungent smell and everything that had taken place.

"I have to go! Please, let me up!" I told him. He rolled off and away from me. Then he reached down and pulled up my panties. I froze at the touch of his hands on my skin again. I wanted to run, but my limbs refused to cooperate. Instead, I slowly got out of the bed, tiptoeing to the door.

"Thank you," he said from where he lay.

Thank you? He was thanking me? For what?

Then he anxiously added, "You won't say anything to anyone about this, will you?"

I shook my head, unwittingly becoming a co-conspirator in the secrecy that would shroud my life for the next several years.

"That's good, because we'd both be in a lot of trouble." The sickening sound of his voice came from somewhere behind me. It seemed to reverberate from the walls, bouncing throughout my brain.

We'd both be in a lot of trouble . . . we'd both be in a lot of trouble . . . we'd both be in . . .

I left his bedroom without looking back, closing the door as I did so. Going into the bathroom, I gingerly wiped myself with toilet paper, hating the feel of the wetness down there. I was horrified at the red stain on the paper, and I stared at it dumbly.

The redness stayed there, but it made no sense. Instead, I saw red roses and a red house. The roses were at the bottom of four stone steps, hidden between two large Catawba trees and some shrubs at the edge of our property. I ran down the steps into the yard and lingered to touch the scarlet roses, the delicious fragrance wafting up into my nose and clinging there. I broke off some of the silky buds, bent to keep the low-hanging branches from smacking me across the face and emerged into the clearing of our yard with a small handful. I looked up to see our beautiful red brick house, bordered by my mother's beloved lavender lilac bushes on one side, dark green rhododendrons on the other, and the row of wispy ferns that grew from a thick blanket of moss that bordered the creek far below.

I looked down at the roses in my hand, thinking I would carry them inside for my mother, who would smile and place them in a Mason jar, when I realized they were bleeding. I looked at the roses again and saw bloody paper instead, and I closed my eyes tightly to keep from seeing it. Some part of me felt swollen and sore, but I couldn't figure out where it was.

Then I remembered. And realized how bad I was, to let it happen.

What have I done? I thought.

Tiptoeing up the stairs, I moved slowly so it wouldn't hurt so much. Easing myself into the twin bed beside Kim's, I turned toward the wall, curled up in a ball and wrapped my arms around myself.

I'm not a virgin anymore.

I saw myself on stage at the spelling bee, where I'd been

standing a few weeks ago. I stepped up to the microphone.

"*Virgin. Your word is 'virgin,' not that you would know it,*" a voice said.

I hesitated, wrapping a strand of hair around my finger. "*V-i-r-g-i-n. Virgin,*" I said solemnly, staring at the judges before me.

"*Intercourse. Your word is 'intercourse,'*" the same voice said.

"*Could I please have the definition?*" I whispered.

The voice was sharp. "*You have had sexual 'intercourse.' Now no one will ever want you.*"

I felt tears welling up behind my eyes and angrily wiped them away. "*Intercourse. I-n-t-e-r-c-o-u-r-s-e.*" I choked out.

I took first prize that night, but now the words tormented me, the judges passing judgment on me in a bizarre contest I couldn't win no matter what I did.

Hours later, after staring at the darkness, willing myself to block out the images floating around in my mind, of bodies and letters and stern, unsmiling faces, I finally fell asleep.

The next morning I woke up and looked around the room, feeling like I was going to be smothered by the big purple flowers on the walls. Memories from the previous night came flooding back, sweeping over me in one great, endless wave. I buried my face in my pillow, willing myself to smell nothing but the clean laundry scent of it.

Then the recollection was gone, and instead I was tracing the ceiling tile. But the memories became twisted and merged with my counting repetitions, and it happened again and again. Over and over. I tore myself away from the thoughts and closed my eyes in anguish.

I had given myself to a man whom I loved, but it had been wrong, because we weren't married. I felt soiled, dirty and disgusting.

I wanted to take a hot shower to wash his touch away, to

rid myself of his scent that still clung to me like a spider clings tenaciously to its web.

After breakfast, I went to the bathroom and stood staring at my reflection. The girl that peered back at me was no longer the same person. I began to tremble as I stood there, and I heard his voice as he placed my hand against his hard skin.

"You're so pretty. If only you weren't so pretty, you wouldn't do this to me . . . Look, you did this to me."

I squeezed my eyes shut, trying to block out the memory, wondering how I could have thought I loved him. *Oh why, why did it have to happen? Now I'll never be clean for another man, for the man I would've married.*

In that second, I knew what I had to do: I had to marry him, because I was damaged and not fit to be another man's wife. I had already been used.

"You have had sexual 'intercourse.' Now no one will ever want you," the voice from the previous night returned to taunt me.

The day passed slowly, but it did pass, as did each day after it. I learned to keep a smile on my face, freezing all emotions inside so no one could see them. I began living a lie, because the truth wasn't something I could face. The truth, I somehow sensed, would destroy me.

The first rape made the subsequent ones no easier; I began avoiding the mirror in the bathroom at home or, if I must, I would stare at the reflection, daring that girl to tell me how bad I was. Something inside me had snapped, which I didn't discern until years later. I began hanging out with the girls who had bad reputations, many of whom had boyfriends who were six, seven or even ten years older than they were. I also began smoking with them every morning before school, a short-lived practice that stopped after one pack of cigarettes, when I found I detested the aftertaste they left in my mouth. Other bad habits, like my self-loathing, were harder to break.

So after the rape, almost overnight, I become something I never had been: a rebellious adolescent who provoked the adults around me. It didn't last long, but its impact was so intense that the memories remain clearly and painfully imprinted on my mind to this day.

My new crowd, as well as some of the "good girls" who remained loyal friends, decided we were going to break the rules by wearing shorts on the last day of school. I packed a pair in my gym bag and changed from jeans once I got to the girls' restroom. But most of them backed out, so in the end only one other girl and I took a stand against the school's authority.

Attending school in a rural area where rule breaking wasn't tolerated, and where students were expected to show more than the usual amount of respect for teachers, was never a problem for me before that day. And on top of that, my mother had been, in a way, part of the educational establishment. She wasn't a teacher, but when money was in short supply, she'd worked part-time throughout the years as a substitute cook and janitor. Nonetheless, her role as an employee in the school system meant more was expected from her children. Until then that's all I'd ever given—and then some—in both my academic studies and my attitude toward my teachers and classmates.

But not so that day. The rebel within me fought to break loose, to fight back, and to make a statement about people in positions of authority. The first teacher I passed did a double take when he saw me, and ordered me straight to the office. Once there, the principal, Mr. Woodrow, wasted no time in ordering me to the locker room to change my clothes. He wanted to know why I would do something so unlike me, but I just glared past him out the window, refusing to speak. When

I got up to leave, he tried to say something else, but I brushed right past him.

As I left the office, Mr. Woodrow called out after me, "Do you hear me, Miss Berry?" I continued walking. I felt an arm reach out from behind and grab me, and I wheeled on him like a wild animal. Screaming. Kicking. Saying words I'd never thought, much less spoken.

"Mr. Hess, come here!" Mr. Woodrow yelled to a nearby teacher, and they both tried to restrain me.

"Let me go! Let me go!" I screamed at the top of my lungs. "You bastard! How dare you touch me? I hate you, you sonofabitch!"

The entire scene occurred within moments, but it felt like a lifetime, and I vaguely became aware that teachers were peering from their classrooms to see where all the commotion was coming from. Together, Mr. Woodrow and Mr. Hess finally managed to subdue me, and I found myself sitting in a chair in Mr. Woodrow's office, four strong arms making sure I couldn't move. They needn't have bothered, for all the fight had gone out of me and I sat there, unseeing, refusing to give way to the tears behind my eyes.

An hour later I sat in the car with my mother, and felt her disbelieving stare on me.

"Daleen, what's wrong with you? I hope you realize how much reproach this brings on God and your family. I would never have expected something like this from you."

I said nothing, for there was nothing to say. Not when I didn't even understand what had happened. Nor would I three months later when summer ended, school resumed, and the rebel within would escape once again.

CHAPTER THREE

I like to think I survived a nightmare that lasted thirteen years because I was surrounded by love and tenderness as a young child, sheltered by parents with reasonable expectations and moderate discipline. Their love stayed with me when I began to question the world and my own place in it, giving me a warm cocoon to curl up in. At the same time, with alcohol being such a strong force in our lives, that cocoon was bound to crack and wither away, just as the fragile remnants of a shell provide no protection once a newly hatched moth is free to roam on its own.

I loved hearing my parents tell the story about how we came to be a family. In 1961 my college dropout father was fifteen years her senior when he met the "California girl" who would become my mother. She wasn't tall, standing almost eye level with my father, but at fourteen, Eileen Freeman had a full figure. Her large, deep-set blue eyes matched Dad's, and she had pulled up her thick, brown hair into a chignon, making her look about eighteen. But her most distinguishing feature was probably a dark, oblong mole. No bigger than the end of her pinky finger, it lay just below her right eye, giving her an exotic look. Dad was smitten from the moment he met her. Mom said he refused to marry her until she was "grown up," but after he got drunk one night and said he would, she held him to his promise. That's why, when she was sixteen, they ran away to get married in Reno, Nevada, where she wasn't considered underage.

One year later and just few months before the youngest man ever to be elected president was assassinated, I was born in a hospital maternity ward without the benefit of air-conditioning, in what my mother has since said was the hottest August in the history of San Jose.

"I should know," she said laughing, "I lived through it. After you were born, the first thing I did was ask for a glass of water."

I never forgot what Mom told me about that day. A first-time father, Dad had been granted medical leave six weeks earlier from his job in Alaska, where he worked as an electronics engineer on the military's Distant Early Warning line. "I guess she's the youngest mother in here," Dad told the nurse on duty.

"Not by a long shot," the nurse replied. "There's a girl just fourteen down the hall having her second one."

Dad, who had always been a stickler for proper grammar and perfect spelling, had to complete the paperwork for my birth certificate. Nonetheless, Dale Berry's assiduous spelling failed him the night he became a parent. Mom told me the story over and over again, how he tried to write down my gender, crossing it out and respelling it, "D-o-t-t-e-r," before asking her how to spell the word.

Three days after I was born, my parents took me home to Sunnyvale. I still remember the story they told me, how when I was just two, I ran around in circles on the lawn, my blond hair bobbed short. My arms reached up toward the airplanes that flew above our heads, which they said I thought I could catch and hold in my hands.

My father, who had his private pilot's license and had dreamed of being an airline pilot, "thought you were just adorable," Mom said.

Dad couldn't live without the smell of jet fuel, and his feet were never planted on solid ground. The family joke later became that he must be part Gypsy, because he moved us from place to place every year or two. We would no sooner get settled in than Dad would be off, like a butterfly floating from one flower to the next in a big, open meadow. Thanks to a stint in Uncle Sam's Navy, by the time he married Mom, the only continent Dad hadn't seen was Australia.

Not long after I was born, we migrated from California to Wyoming, where the snowfalls were so deep that we would open our front door on winter mornings to find it piled higher than I was tall. Dad would take me to work with him, sitting me inside the circle of his arms, within the protective gating of the little snow cat he used to reach his work site.

In Wyoming, my father bought a grey Stetson cowboy hat that he took great pride in wearing, because, as my mother said, "That's what all the men in Wyoming wore then." His beloved hat later became a play toy for his two young daughters, in what was for me a testimony of the paternal feelings he showed when I was a little girl. But as the years passed, he was there less and less for all of us, as both his job and his booze took him away.

Wyoming was where I first remember seeing my father play his guitar. He would come home at night, sit down on the vanilla-colored Naugahyde couch next to the square metal warming stove in our living room, grab his guitar, and begin picking chords. Before long, he would start singing some country song from his own childhood.

One cold winter night, I sat, mesmerized, at his feet. He looked into my eyes and then, strumming his guitar, he sang the loveliest songs. After listening to his small repertoire, which included any number of tear-jerker tunes, I asked for more.

"Play me another one, Daddy," I begged.

"What would you like to hear?" he asked.

"Clementine," I said.

He grinned and twisted the white knobs at the end of the guitar, strumming a few times as he did so. "Oh my darlin', oh my darlin', oh my darlin', Clementine . . ." he began.

When he finished, I begged him to play "Red River Valley," and "You Are My Sunshine." By the time he sang all three songs, I had crawled up into a corner of the couch, and was growing sleepy.

Dad placed the guitar in its case and then turned to me, trying to sidestep the beer bottles that had taken my place on the floor at his feet.

"I think it's somebody's bedtime," he said, leaning down and hugging me. As he began to tickle me all over, I laughed, wriggling out of his grasp and running to my mother's chair, where she smiled at our antics as she sat crocheting.

Wyoming was a place of chuck wagons and horse riding trails, of men in cowboy hats and the wide-open spaces referred to by songwriters of long ago. It was the place where I saw my first Native American, resplendent in a full headdress.

We had just come out of J.C. Penney's, when I looked up and saw the largest man I had ever seen. Terrified, I grabbed my mother's leg.

"Mommy, will he scalp me?" I asked.

"Shhh," Mom's face was red as she tried to quiet me.

Either he didn't hear me or he pretended not to, and my embarrassed parents hurried to our car. "No, he won't hurt you," she assured me.

"Sometimes, it's better not to say certain things, for fear of hurting another person's feelings, or even making them angry," Daddy said.

After making sure my seatbelt was fastened, he closed the door and climbed into the driver's seat. As we pulled away from the curb, I watched the solemn-looking man standing there, unmoving. From where I sat, I could hear my father's quiet chuckle.

My sister Carla was born in Kemmerer not long after we moved there, and I was happy to have my own live baby doll. I would hop onto the couch and beg my mother to let me hold her. Then I would try to sing her some of my father's songs. She was a beautiful baby, and Mom would style her strawberry blonde hair so it formed a pretty little curl on top of her head, or Dad would pose us together on the couch, taking pictures with his old Rolodex camera. Later, he would come out of our little bathroom holding long strips of dark plastic that he would show us. All I could see were tiny black spots on the plastic, and I thought it was funny when Dad pointed to the spots and said they were really Carla and me.

The life I never should have lived began with an ill-fated American presidency, when I sat in the front seat of my mother's little black MG as we made the 2,500-mile journey from Kemmerer, Wyoming to Washington, DC, not long after President Richard Nixon took office. Dad transferred there after bidding on an open position within Western Union, where he then worked. I was five, Carla was two, and Dad's drinking was growing worse. Mom's loyalty remained undeterred; she seemed destined to fulfill the words of that ever-popular Tammy Wynette tune, "Stand by Your Man."

The long trek was the first of many things that would remind me of my Appalachian heritage, since it was made because of the strong family ties so common in that part of the country. The trip was also a sign of things to come, both in my mother's life and mine: that need for a woman to have more independence and freedom than was common at the time, made necessary by the men who wouldn't, or couldn't, be there themselves.

By then Dad was rarely home, content to spend his evenings at the local beer joints, while leaving us to fend for ourselves. My embarrassment began early, even as I struggled to do my part to keep up my parents' picture of a happy family. By West Virginia standards at least, we were considered middle class. With our own assorted vehicles, and the company vehicle my father drove, our neighbors seemed to think so. But the truth was, the income Dad earned meant little to his family waiting at home, since his penchant for alcohol stole away most of his paycheck. It was money we seldom saw, unless you counted the empty beer bottles lined up on the kitchen counter.

I still remember the fight caused by Dad's drinking, one night when I should've been sleeping, but instead found myself held captive to my parents' raised voices. I was in first grade; Carla was three. Mom had been taking night classes to get her long-delayed high school diploma. In the California of 1962, you see, pregnant girls didn't attend classes with everyone else. When Mom got "in the family way" three months after her teen marriage, a tutor was sent to her home. She dropped out of school entirely after I was born to take care of me.

One evening after she left for class, Daddy asked us if we wanted to go for a ride. "Yes!" we squealed. Going anywhere with him was a rare treat.

Climbing into a big Oldsmobile the color of a freshly filled swimming pool, we wound down the long dirt driveway, following the road running beside the mighty Cheat River. Our car had driven that exact route so many times, it could have found its own way to the beer joint where Daddy took us. The old coal dust-covered clapboard building sat next to the river, just a few doors down from the church where Carla and I once went to Sunday school. From time to time Daddy would take us there, or to other beer joints he frequented. Like the rest, it was loud and noisy and so hazy my eyes burned from the cigarette-smoke clouds that filled the place.

Daddy bought Carla and me each a soda, and his buddies gathered around and took turns pinching our cheeks. Two close friends of Daddy's stopped playing pool and came over to us. Luke and Levi were brothers in their late teens but who, when outfitted with cigarettes and beer cans, looked much older.

"How's Little Dale today?" Levi asked with a wink, using the nickname he'd given me.

Luke grinned at us, a cigarette dangling from the corner of his mouth. "You gals have such pretty hair, and you're so well-behaved."

Daddy only smiled while Luke patted our corn silk-colored heads and gave us each a quarter. Then he prompted, "What do you say?"

"Thank you," we said in unison, with matching grins.

I looked behind them to the shelves filled with bottles, and watched a bartender with a worn and wrinkled look hand Daddy a dark brown bottle that released a misty trail as its top was popped off. Daddy perched on a red vinyl-covered barstool next to a wiry old man whose eyes grew squinty when he released a puff of white smoke from his mouth. He reminded me of a shriveled walnut shell.

Daddy turned to me. "Hey Neelad, I have an idea. How about we play a game of pool?"

I hung back shyly. "I don't know how." I watched Levi and Luke, who had returned to the pool table behind us.

Daddy motioned to the pool cue that hung on the wall. "Well, I'll teach you. Come on, you'll really like it."

I climbed off the tall barstool and went over to stand next to Daddy. He held a small blue cube. "Here, you take it," he said, pressing it into my hand. "There, now rub it right here." He held the smaller end of the wooden stick toward me, and I rubbed the chalky stuff on the white tip. "That's good," he said, and then took the cube from me. I looked down and wrinkled my nose at my blue fingers.

"That'll come off," he laughed. "Don't worry about it." He placed the cue in my hands and then went behind me, showing me how to hold onto it.

"Hey, you're using the wrong hand," Levi yelled.

Daddy laughed. "She's a southpaw. A pretty good one, too." He put his hand over my own, and showed me how to run the stick along the edge of the table. Taking my right hand, he helped me form a hole between my thumb and forefinger, showing me how the stick could slide through, and move back and forth.

"Now, what you want to do is shoot one of these balls down into a pocket—that's the little holes in the corners and sides of the pool table." As he spoke, he picked up a stick and took aim. Just as I heard a sharp *crack*, the ball shot forward and into one of the holes. "Just like that," he said. "Now you try it."

Aware of an audience, I could barely hold the long stick still enough to do anything with it. But after a few tries, and with Daddy holding the heavier end, I managed to shoot one of the balls. It didn't go into a pocket, but it did scurry all over the table, even knocking against other balls.

Daddy was smoking, too, so as we played pool, Carla and I begged him to blow smoke rings for us. He laughed and said, "All right, just a few." Forming an O shape with his mouth, he produced the most magical, perfectly round wisps of smoke that escaped from his lips, floated a short distance away, and then vanished before our eyes, making us beg for more.

Then he walked over to the bar and ordered another beer. By then, we'd been there so long we were bored. I hated to interrupt him when he was talking or playing pool, but I wanted to go home. I knew Mom would be worried if she came home and couldn't find us.

I tugged gently at his shirtsleeve. "Daddy, when are we going home?"

He grinned. "As soon as I finish this one."

It was what he always said, and I never knew if that meant the one he was working on, or the next one. I turned away and tried to find something to do to keep from being bored.

Later that night I was upstairs with the new ballerina music box Daddy had won for me, and that's when I heard my parents downstairs. I'll never forget Mom's fiery voice as their words drifted up the stairs, like the smoke from one of Daddy's cigarettes.

"Dale, I can't believe you took our daughters to a beer joint again!" she hissed, unsuccessfully trying to keep her voice a whisper. Mom only talked to Daddy like that when he came home staggering and couldn't speak, the ever-present row of empty beer bottles his sole companions, or when he just sat at the kitchen table and stared straight ahead, ordering me or Mom to get him another beer from the fridge.

"Oh come on, Honey," he replied. "They like it. They had a good time." His words were slurred.

From upstairs, I opened and closed the music box lid, trying to watch the ballerina bend over and disappear each time, only to stand up and reappear when the lid opened again. I could hear their voices but only needed to imagine their faces; I listened to a scene I'd seen played out too many times before. My mother would have a stern, unsmiling expression, in direct contrast to the drunken, silly smile on my father's face.

"I don't care if they did like it," she said. "I do not want my daughters around those people. Those drunks!" I could picture her stormy blue eyes, and the way she would lean forward, shaking her finger at him.

"Wuz wrong wif' them?" Daddy asked. "They're my frenz."

Mom was probably shaking her dark head. "I think you need to choose better friends, Dale. Remember that time one of your *friends* dropped Carla on her head? Besides, you drove home afterward, and you know I hate it when you drink and drive! What if something happened? What if you wrecked the car and the girls were hurt?"

By then she was crying, and I heard Daddy's chair scrape across the floor as he stood, legs wobbly, and went over and put his arms around her.

"Hey Eileen, I'm sorry, Honey. I dint know it would make you so upset. I won' do it again. I promise."

But he did. The same thing would happen again the next week. And within a year or two, it grew even worse.

Throughout elementary school, Carla and I were together through good times and bad. Her tomboy tendencies made Carla a perfect "daddy's girl," which complimented my close relationship with Mom. In spite of the similar looks that declared us sisters—both fair-skinned, blue-eyed towheads—we were polar opposites. I liked to wear dresses, while Carla was happy in cut-offs and a tee shirt. I loved school, but Carla tried everything she could to escape it. I had a serious nature, while she was full of mischief. And on the way home from school, I took pains to walk around the puddles—while Carla jumped right in them, laughing as the muddy water stained her clothes.

That first summer, Dad often took us to the Western Union microwave station where he worked, and we'd play at a workbench in a room that had equipment as tall as the ceiling, a smell like that of baked electrical wires, and humming engines. Sometimes, Dad would take us outside and show us where to find nearby blackberry patches, so we could feast on the juicy black fruit. Other times, Mom would take Dad his lunch, and when he came out to greet us, he took turns tossing us up into the air, twirling us around like little airplanes. Then Mom would hand us plastic buckets and take us into the deeper woods, where the best blackberries were hidden from human eyes.

Our first few years in West Virginia were good, in spite of Dad's drinking problem, and one of the best things about moving there was getting to know my cousins. Anne and Jeannie wore pretty costumes and took tap dancing and ballet lessons. The first time we went to visit my grandmother in Charleston, the four of us dressed up in their costumes, pretending to be famous dancers.

Their basement served as our dance floor, and we pulled out the costumes from where they were stored in a corner. I found a pink leotard with a white tutu, but when I tried to wear the little black ballet slippers, my toes wouldn't stay pointed like my cousins' toes did.

"That's because we take ballet lessons," Jeannie said.

"When I grow up, I want to be a ballerina," I said.

"You can if you take lessons, too," Anne said.

Because I couldn't get my toes to work right, I donned a bright green sequined leotard with a matching hat and feathers sticking out, and some shiny black shoes with silver metal plates on the heels and toes. After trying to imitate my cousins' movements, I soon learned how to dance a few steps. I loved the loud clicking sound of the silver metal against the solid concrete floor, but what I enjoyed most was watching Jeannie and Anne perform for Carla and me, their feet making clickety-click movements as they danced together.

Afterward, as we left their house, I tugged on Mom's arm. "Can I please, please, please, take dance lessons like Anne and Jeannie?"

"We'll see," she said, leaving me clinging to the hope that someday I would get to dance.

In 1971, Dad and Mom bought an ancient two-story brick home for us in Independence. I liked to believe my parents bought it just for me, because someone had left an old, upright piano sitting in the downstairs hallway. Its ivory keys had long since yellowed, its varnished wood was as dark as the shadows where it sat, but when I placed my fingers on the keyboard, it sounded perfect. Mom couldn't read sheet music but could somehow play anyway, having learned some tunes many years before. She taught me to play and before long, I was tapping out songs on the old keys.

When Dad heard me playing, he said I was going to become a famous concert pianist. He promised he would some-day send me to a music conservatory. I would sit for hours on the little bench, trying to play the old, worn-out instrument. For years, just as I had with dancing, I begged for lessons, but there was never enough money.

So instead, I went outside to play, or stayed inside and read. After school, I would jump off the bus, eager to explore on my way home. Mom always waited for us at the bus stop. Then she and Carla walked home while I dawdled behind. I walked down the narrow country lane on my own. It was a short walk, made longer by the presence of a general store and post office in a gray-shingled building. Inside, I bought pieces of nickel candy from Mr. Edwards, the elderly shop owner who shuffled slowly around, helping me remove the lids from the candy jars that sat atop glass display cabinets. He also sold ice cream and all kinds of household and garden items in the comfortable but dusty old shop, and I would slowly wander around savoring my sweet as I peered closely at everything there.

His son worked in the post office next door. Tom was the postmaster and he sorted mail in a room barely big enough to turn around in, but which had the most lovely, little brass boxes from floor to ceiling. There was row upon row of them, except where a small window opened in the center. That was where customers bought stamps or leaned over the narrow ledge, eager to share neighborhood news.

Each brass box had its own small window, and an even smaller brass knob with a pointer that turned around a numbered dial to unlock the boxes. I loved turning the little knob and opening its tiny, hinged door, to find someone had sent me a letter of my very own.

I would practically run off the bus every day, stopping long enough to buy something from the store if I had money, or go into the post office in case my mother had left mail in the box for me. Jim would always come out whenever any of the neighborhood children came in, smiling kindly and asking how our day had been, or what we were learning in school. I enjoyed talking to him for a few minutes, before skipping happily down the road.

"Well Miss Daleen, how are you today?" Jim asked.

"I'm fine, but I don't see any mail in my box." I was disappointed.

Jim grinned. "Then you'll be happy to know that's because it's too big to fit into the box." He turned and picked up a big bundle and opened the small door between his work area and the customer service area.

"I think this is yours," he said, handing it to me.

"It's my weekly delivery of *Grit* newspapers!" I practically danced out of the building, yelling as I went. "Thank you, Jim!"

The papers were too heavy to dally, but on other days I would stop to gaze at the specks of bright orange hidden among the tall bushes alongside the road. My hand would be poised to touch one of the small, delicate flowers when it would suddenly pop without warning, exposing a tiny curled green vine and a few white seeds. One of the things I really enjoyed during late spring and early summer was to try to pop as many of the little buds as I could. Sometimes, I would pluck them very carefully from their stems, place them in my open palm, and make a game out of trying to reach home with the buds still intact, because even stepping too hard could cause them to pop. Then I would sit down and with barely a touch, I would watch the remaining ones burst open, revealing the amazing coiled green tendrils inside.

From the general store to my home, it was a short walk down a small hill and past the touch-me-nots, over three sets of railroad tracks, and across a bridge under which ran a small creek. Each day was an adventure, and I often stopped just to watch a groundhog or a rabbit run by.

Our home sat at the end of the bridge. Sometimes in summer, I would stand and look over the railing to the water far below, dreaming about how nice it would be to take off my socks and shoes and climb over the rocks. I knew they would feel good, because for several years while growing up, that's how Carla and me, and all the neighbor kids, stayed cool on the hottest of days.

My girlhood dreams came alive and found fruition in the tiny town. I was an entrepreneur, so by age eight I spent countless hours dreaming about what I would do if I could earn my own money. Not long after, I got the job delivering more than fifty newspapers on my bike, covering a two-mile route each week.

Dad had convinced me to get the route selling the quarter-a-copy papers. Having grown up during the Depression with a single mother and four other siblings, he had once had a *Grit* route himself.

One ordinary house near the middle of my route, though, created within me a fear that threatened to eat me up. That's because "Lurch," as I named him, lived there. He was tall and towered above me, and he scared many neighborhood children. He was also a stranger and because he looked mean and had a deep voice, I was terrified he would kidnap me. Fortunately, his parents usually answered the door, smiling and trading coins for the *Grit* I held out, eager to leave before Lurch could appear. Each time, I talked inside my head, telling myself, just like my mother had chided me, that Lurch only looked mean. That he was just different, and that he did, in fact, actually have a problem: he was a boy trapped in a man's body.

So one day when I nervously knocked at his door, praying his parents would answer, I was hardly able to speak when Lurch looked down at me. I swallowed hard and managed to squeak, "Here's your paper."

"Hold on," he said, turning away.

I wanted to bolt. Instead, I tried to tell myself that he wouldn't hurt me, that my parents had asked Jim, who told them Lurch was harmless.

But it seemed to be taking Lurch more time than it should just to get the money to pay me. My mind began racing: could he be getting a knife?

The door opened in the middle of my fanciful fears, and Lurch reached out, coins in his palm. "Here you go," he said, smiling as he emptied them into my hand.

"Thank you," I said, handing him the paper and turning to leave. I forced myself to walk slowly when my feet wanted only to flee, because I knew he was standing in the doorway watching. But as I got on my bike and glanced back, I saw him wave.

I gave a shy wave back.

I hated to spend the money I collected from my customers each week, knowing I was my only reliable source for getting more. But even beyond carefully counting and stashing it away in a dresser drawer, was the joy of sitting down at the end of the long route and reading the weekly serial story within each issue. I would lay on my stomach across my bed, head in hands, and read furiously, trying to race to the final few words to see how it ended. Most of the time, I was forced to wait until the next week, and the week after, until the story finally ended weeks later.

I got lost in other reading adventures, especially Nancy Drew mysteries. I read every book I could get my hands on, and when it was time for our family vacation, I always took along a tall stack of books I had gotten at the library, or borrowed from classmates. About four hours into the first day of our trip, I could count on hearing one of my father's favorite expressions. A geography and history buff who taught us all the names of the states and their capitals, Dad loved to relate tidbits of information about the places we passed, and it irked him that his eldest child wasn't as interested in our travels as he was.

We were driving through St. Louis, Missouri, when he spoke up. "There's Scott Joplin's house," Dad said to no one in particular. Or so I thought.

"Remember Daleen? He's the famous jazz pianist."

My ears barely caught the sound of my name being spoken, and by the time I looked up, I saw my father glaring at me from the rearview mirror. "For crying out loud, Daleen, get your nose out of that book! You're missing all the famous sites and some beautiful scenery."

Groaning in protest, I laid the book across my lap, careful not to lose my place. I rolled down my window. "Moo, moo," I said, talking to the cows grazing along the fences.

It didn't take too long to pacify Dad, who soon lost interest in me and instead tried to debate some political issue or another with my mother.

"I'm telling you, Eileen, there is no way Tricky Dick wasn't behind the break-in. Gordon Liddy's crew isn't smart enough to have done it on their own," he said, thumping the steering wheel in earnest.

Knowing his tirade could take awhile, I grinned and quietly turned my book over—eager to find out what mystery my hero or heroine would take on next!

It wasn't just the loosely structured history lessons or following the trials of my main characters that made the trips memorable. By day two, Dad would pop the top on a beer can, leading to Mom's dismay, expressed by the thinning of her lips.

"Don't worry, Honey. I'm just having this one," Dad told her stony profile.

The rest of the trip became a battle of wills between them, with Mom growing silent every time Dad opened another can of beer, and Dad growing annoyed every time she tried to ask him to stop drinking.

"If you wreck, one of the girls could be hurt."

"I'm a good driver, and I'm not going to wreck."

"Well what if the police stop us, and realize you're drinking?"

"They won't. Now can we please talk about something else?"

We were fortunate, because in spite of Dad's drinking, he always held a steady job. He wasn't usually a mean drunk, but Dad wasn't home much, either, and most of the money he earned went to buy beer.

With or without the beer, survival is something that seems to come natural to Appalachian people. I learned this after Dad, who hadn't even had a drop to drink at the time, almost died because he wanted to watch the World Series. It happened early one morning after he climbed a tall ladder to install a TV antenna on our roof.

"I tried to tell him to wait until the dew was gone, because it was a slate roof and I was afraid he would fall," my mother cried afterward.

Dad would have none of it. He was going to put the antennae up there, "by God or else!" Mom is fond of adding when she tells the story.

Turns out, it was "or else." I was in the kitchen when I heard a noise and turned to look. I saw something go flying by the window at the same time I heard my mother scream. By the time I ran out the back door and around the corner, Dad was laying on the ground at her feet.

Mom was right there when it happened, standing on the same spot where he landed. First the tools came falling off, and she somehow managed to move the ladder and then leap out of the way, seconds before Daddy's body came hurtling to the earth like a falling meteor.

"I knew he'd kill me if I didn't move," she said. "And he would have, because when he hit the ground, he bounced three feet back into the air." The only thing that saved his life, the doctors said, was the deep layer of peat moss that covered the earth where he landed.

He broke his pelvis in three places, and his back in two. Dad spent the next five weeks in traction in the hospital, where we would drive to visit him each day. Because children weren't allowed to visit, Mom would open the window to his hospital room so Carla and I could climb through. Then she would pull out the six-pack of beer Dad had asked her to bring, pop a top, and hand it to him.

CHAPTER FOUR

Dad transferred to Martinsburg, leaving us behind, but later he convinced Mom to join him there. We lived in a spacious trailer park with yards so big we couldn't hear our neighbors talking to each other. Tall trees were scattered throughout the park, giving us lots of shade. Second only to swimming in the neighbor's pool across the street, my favorite pastime occurred when winter came and the ground froze, allowing us to skate on the pond behind our trailer.

Mom bought used ice skates from a secondhand shop for Carla and me, and we would walk down the hill to the pond below, where we would tie the laces over the worn, white leather. Then we carefully tested the water before skating onto the frozen pond. Mom made sure the ice was thick enough it wouldn't break, but she was afraid of water, so she wouldn't skate with us. Once I learned to skate, I went around and around on the ice, pretending to be Peggy Fleming. I was pulled from my childish reverie only after I tripped over a small branch that had frozen into the water's rough surface.

I missed my *Grit* route, but my parents allowed me to babysit two neighbor boys on the weekends. And I mowed lawns, so I could add to my growing savings account. Because we were close enough to tour the nation's capitol, I spent some of my money while visiting the Smithsonian Institute and other sites there. We visited the Lincoln Memorial, the

Washington Monument, and Ulysses S. Grant's Memorial, but most often we toured the National Air and Space Museum, where Dad proudly showed us "The Spirit of St. Louis" and the Apollo 11 command module. He used those times to teach us the history of flight, from the Wright Brothers to Neil Armstrong and the NASA space program.

Aviation was the greatest part about living in Martinsburg with Dad. Since I was just a little girl, I had known about my father's love of flying, because he would regale us with stories about famous aviators. I learned not only about such famous flights flown by Chuck Yeager, Charles Lindbergh and "Lady Lindy," as my father called Amelia Earhart, but also about every space mission the American astronauts or Russians cosmonauts ever made.

Dad got his flight instructor's certification, so he worked part-time as an instructor in the evenings and weekends—which was good because it seemed to keep him from drinking. He had also talked my mom into running the tiny airport café. The daughter of a chef, friends and neighbors had always praised her home-cooked meals. Each day Carla and I would get off the bus, don aprons, and help wait on the customers who called her "Crystal," while Mom served them coffee for ten cents a cup.

Mom's little café soon became quite a popular place for pilots, who would often fly there just for her delicious lunch specials—especially on Wednesdays: that was spaghetti day. Several times, well-known politicians or celebrities would land at the little airport and eat there. Once, after Ray Charles' jet landed there, the crew invited her inside.

"You should have seen it—even though he's blind, he has bright colors all over the interior," Mom told us.

But it was Paul Newman, who raced cars at the nearby Charles Town Racetrack, that Mom always dreamed of meeting. But she never saw him. "I waited for him, though" she laughed when telling the story.

When we weren't busy helping Mom, Carla and I would ride our bikes all around the property, or tease and torment the airport employees. Sometimes we even went flying with Dad or Mom, who was taking flight lessons herself.

Aside from the impression being an "airport brat" left on my mind, two major news events were molding both the nation and my young mind: newspaper heiress Patty Hearst was kidnapped by the Symbionese Liberation Army and the nation learned that Nixon had been involved in the break-in at the Watergate Hotel. At home, my parents closely followed the twists and turns of both stories. They had discussed the Watergate scandal at length, and kept abreast of Hearst's subsequent criminal activity, talking about the incidents after the evening news. At age eleven I soaked it all in, keenly interested in the outcomes. It was summer before the climactic end occurred and President Richard Nixon resigned. After having watched Walter Cronkite talk about Watergate and Patty Hearst every day on the six o'clock evening news for what felt like years, I recognized the role the media played in the world. And by then, I knew I wanted to be an observer who wrote about that world.

Our move to the Eastern Panhandle was bittersweet because Dad's drinking began to grow worse, causing more and more friction at home. That's because Dad started spending every weekend and even some weeknights out drinking with Bruce, his best friend and coworker. When we finally met Bruce one night at a pizza parlor, I realized it wasn't his fault, for Bruce drank far less than Dad did.

We soon grew to love Bruce during those evenings together. He also became a cheerleader of sorts, for when I turned into a gawky teenager, Bruce would offer praise and encouragement whenever he saw me practicing the piano, reading my lines for a school play, or working on a writing assignment.

One day while Bruce was visiting us, I walked around the trailer with a book balanced on my head, trying to perfect my posture and dreaming of the day when I would model for some famous magazine.

"Why, how elegant you look. You're going to end up modeling for sure, as tall and slender as you are. They won't be able to resist you, with your great posture and poise!" he said, making me blush and yet feel graceful at the same time.

Because West Virginia is a rural state, by his or her twelfth birthday every child knows how to drive and shoot—not at the same time, though. People either need to put food on the table or they're avid hunters, or perhaps both, so many children learn to use a shotgun or rifle. That's why, when I was nine, Dad and my Great-Uncle Paul took me out for target practice—and much to their amusement and pride, I kept hitting the bull's eye. The next thing I knew, Dad had gone to Heck's Department Store to buy me my own 30-30 rifle, which I proudly carried while I tromped along with Dad through the woods behind our house during deer season. Knowing how jealous the boys in my class would be if they saw me, I was never more proud.

Driving a vehicle was equally common for preteens. A heavily agricultural state, much of the land is used for farming, and everyone in the family pitches in. Many of my friends also began driving as young as I did, but most of them learned in a cornfield on a tractor, not in a Pinto station wagon on a four-lane highway because their father was drunk.

At the airport, teaching flight students, Dad was sober as could be, but any other time he had an open can of beer in his hand. One Saturday, he talked me into going with him to a

Navy surplus sale at the Baltimore harbor. We were there all day and not long after we left, he steered the car into the parking lot of a beer joint.

My heart sank, as I recalled the words he and Mom had exchanged that morning. "All right Dale, she can go, but only if you promise not to drink and drive."

He gave my mother a patronizing smile. "Eileen, I won't drink while Daleen's with me. I promise."

So in the parking lot, with my father turning to me, I wondered what I should do to keep him from drinking. "Would you like to go inside and get something to eat?" Dad asked.

I shook my head. "Can't we eat when we get home?"

"Aren't you thirsty? I'm thirsty. Come on, let's get a drink before we head home." He was already opening his door.

"But Mom said—"

"I know what your mother said," he said sternly, "and I'm saying we're stopping here to eat. Now come on. You can't stay in the car by yourself."

I had never defied my father, but as I followed him inside, it was with crossed arms and a sullen expression. A few minutes later, as I sat on the tall bar stool sipping a soda, the door opened and Bruce entered.

I ran over, hugging him. "Uncle Bruce! What are you doing here?" He smiled and returned my hug, before shaking hands with Dad. "Hi there, Dale. How was the sale?" It dawned on me then they had arranged to meet in advance. I picked up the stack of quarters my father had left on the counter and walked over to the skee ball machine.

"Dad, why don't you play a game with me?" I asked, thinking maybe I could get him interested in something else, so he wouldn't be tempted to drink as much.

"In a few minutes, Honey," he said. "Let me talk to Bruce first."

I played alone, until Bruce came over and put his hands on my shoulders. "Hey there, it looks like you're having fun. Can I join you?" he asked.

I beamed, and couldn't help but notice my father, his back to us, ordering another beer. "Yeah," I said, handing him a quarter for the machine. "Mom's going to really be mad at him," I muttered.

He raised his eyebrows, and then smiled conspiratorially. "She sure is."

It was hours later when we finally told Bruce goodbye and left. I made sure I fastened my seatbelt, because Dad was really drunk. I was terrified we would wreck, and had visions of dying in some horrible accident. But we hadn't been on the highway for long when my father pulled off the road.

"Daleen, do you think you could drive? I'm having trouble seeing."

"What?" I had never driven before, but it suddenly made up for all the hours I'd been forced to spend in the bar.

I get to drive! The idea was so exciting my anger evaporated.

He was already out the door and staggering around the car when I scrambled over into his empty seat, which I slid forward until my feet rested against the gas pedal and brake. Then I put on my seatbelt and after a few minutes of instruction from him, I hesitantly pulled onto the highway. The drive home usually took about an hour, but with me at the wheel, it took much longer. Nervous exhilaration combined with an odd sense of being older than I really was, but I was also terrified I'd do something wrong. When we were two miles from home, I felt exhilaration: we're still alive! Dad had somehow managed to navigate me from the Beltway to a two-lane road, to the narrow country lane we took to reach our house. Together we managed to escape any major mishaps. But then he yelled at me.

"Daleen, slow down!" Dad yelled. "You're going to miss the bridge."

The bridge. A large, rusty, metal bridge. I braked too quickly, jerking us both, and the Pinto spun to a stop near the middle of the narrow road, just inches from the edge of the bridge and the steep embankment next to it. My heart was pounding so hard I thought it would burst and my palms were almost wet from sweat.

"Okay, now back up a little," he said, not quite as loud.

If you think you can do a better job, then you get behind the wheel, I wanted so badly to tell him. But after we got home and Mom found out—she always did—she told Dad unequivocally that if he ever pulled such a stunt again, she would return to Preston County. Like a child caught doing something wrong, Dad looked suitably remorseful and made her yet another promise I knew he couldn't keep.

Some of my best Martinsburg memories came from my monthly flights to the orthodontist with my flight-instructor father. Pastel-blue skies punctuated by soft, cotton candy clouds made for a fairytale experience. To a twelve-year-old, climbing into a two-seat Cessna 152 and flying into the wild blue yonder was the most exciting thing ever.

Dad taught me how to scan for other air traffic, and while I watched him skillfully handle the controls of an airplane, I found I actually enjoyed being with Dad because he was completely sober. Each flight, I pestered him to teach me to fly, much like I had years earlier about taking dance or piano lessons.

One bright cloudless day during takeoff, adrenaline rushed through me as the little plane gathered speed on the tarmac. But fear joined the adrenaline's coursing, too, so I prayed silently. *We aren't going to crash. Dad's a great pilot and he's always careful while flying. We aren't going to crash.*

It worked—just like it did every time, allowing me to forget my fear while I learned to believe the mantra inside my mind.

"Dad, when are you going to teach me to fly?" I asked him, excited.

"When you're older," he said, smiling at me before returning his attention to the instrument panel.

"But that's what you said last year," I whined.

"How about when you're fourteen? That's not too much longer."

I groaned. Fourteen was more than a year away. "Please Dad, I want to learn to fly."

"I'll teach you when you're older. The FAA won't even issue you a pilot's license until you're sixteen," Dad said.

It was a major promise, another of the many my father could never keep, leading me to bottle up my feelings tightly inside, so no one would know how their words or failings hurt me.

By the time the Martinsburg chapter of my life closed, I had not only succeeded in that effort—I was beginning to believe men couldn't be trusted. That they didn't keep their word. While my trust was tainted, though, somewhere within me, I kept hoping for better—for more from them. It seemed I was destined to be an eternal optimist, someone who, despite seeing the flaws in others, refused to give up on them. Maybe that's because my mother never completely gave up on my father. Ever.

But I did. I gave up on him forever, the first time I was raped. That's because when I turned thirteen and all hell broke loose in my life, my father—the one person who could have protected me—was gone.

One month later Dad didn't come home from work. I wasn't sure what happened, and Mom didn't tell us. When she arrived late that night to pick us up from the friend's house where we'd gone after school, nothing was said about why we went somewhere other than home on a school night. When I got off the bus the next day, Mom was packing our things.

"Why do we have to move? I like it here." I slammed my textbooks onto the table.

"Because I said so, that's why," Mom sighed.

"Whenever Dad says that, you tell him that's not a real reason." I glared at her.

"Well it's going to have to be reason enough this time."

"But I have a candy route now, and someone else will take it if I'm gone," I moaned.

By then I was a seventh grader at Musselman High School, and had begun making and selling old-fashioned stained glass candy the previous fall. It began as a fluke, after a family friend who knew how much I loved to bake gave me a book full of candy recipes. I made a batch of cinnamon candy and shared it with my classmates, and it was an immediate success. They began asking for more and before long, I had my own business venture. Suddenly, upper classmen I didn't even know would stop me in the hallway, asking if I was "the blond chick who makes that hot candy." I took their orders and spent every weekend making large quantities of peppermint and cinnamon candy. Sometimes, I would carry twenty bags or more to school. Students began to recognize me, and I had never been so popular.

I hated to leave, since I was feeling less shy than I usually did. "Please Mom, I don't want to go back to Independence. I have new friends here now," I told her.

"I'm sorry Daleen, we just can't stay here anymore. You'll get used to being home again with your friends there. Besides, you can take up your *Grit* route, too. I'm sure your customers will love having you back."

I ran into my bedroom and plopped down on my bed, staring up at the ceiling. *Why can't I just stay with Dad?*

But I knew that wouldn't work. Living with Mom made more sense because I was the oldest.

She'll need my help with the girls, I thought.

It was several months before I learned the real reason we left: Dad had called Mom from jail that night he hadn't come home, whining about being arrested for driving drunk. We only saw Dad on weekends after that, and by the time I turned thirteen, my parents lived in separate houses, in towns 200 miles apart.

Over the next few years our visits became less frequent, and Dad never did teach me to fly. When he went to work overseas, the visits stopped all together, leaving me vulnerable and destined to become a pawn in someone else's plans.

CHAPTER FIVE

Back then, I understood nothing—and thought I knew everything. From thirteen to sixteen, when most girls experience shopping trips and teenage angst through broken relationships, I experienced a combination of forcible rapes, and rapes without force when I was silently compliant, which only enhanced my feelings of guilt and shame.

Eddie was always taking Kim and me places, and in plain sight, he was a gentleman. The kissing and fondling began when no one was looking.

"Knock it off!" I scowled at him. In return, he smiled and tousled my hair like a big brother.

I had fallen asleep on the Leigh's sofa one night, when I awoke to find Eddie standing over me. "Can I have a good-night kiss?"

"No," I murmured, half asleep.

He reached under the covers but I grabbed his hand and smacked it. "Don't ever do that again!" I hissed.

"All right, if that's what you want." He stood up slowly and turned away. Only when I heard his bedroom door close did I allow myself to exhale. Though relieved he had gone, I was also sad. For what, I didn't know.

In spite of my resolve and his promises, it kept happening. I longed for someone to show me attention. Eddie did that, talking to me as if I was his own age. I told myself I trusted and loved him, and convinced myself he wouldn't do anything to break my trust. But he always did.

My shame cut long and deep on the first day of high school, as I wondered if anyone noticed the change in me. I felt like the scarlet letter "A" was branded onto my chest.

I was excited to be a freshman, but I also felt different.

You are different.

Living among the mountains, the coal mines, and the cornfields, I knew most girls my age were still virgins. They might have experienced petting, but that was about it. Living in God-fearing homes, they knew sex was only for married people. Otherwise, they risked the wrath of their father's belt.

But the sexually active girls made no bones about it. Labeled "loose," their actions were chalked up to having a bad home life. It explained—but didn't excuse—their promiscuity, and they talked openly about sex.

In gym class all I could do was listen silently. "We were just necking in his truck and before you knew it," a big-bosomed girl named Cathy said, "He unfastened my bra!"

Cathy's cohort Paula joined her friend's raucous laughter. They snickered loudly until the physical education teacher, Mrs. Niles, glared at them.

"You two want to do laps, or do you think you can finish warming up like everyone else?" she demanded.

"No ma'am," they replied.

I looked far above the bleachers to a window where light had somehow found its way through the grime, and wondered how Mrs. Niles had missed it. Concentrating on tiny details inside the gymnasium kept me from hearing things I longed to know about, but which simultaneously repelled me, as I tried to figure out why their experiences were so different from mine.

Whereas they even seemed to enjoy sex, every time Eddie touched me, I wanted to die.

Maybe it's me. There's something wrong with me, or else I would like it, too.

But they couldn't know I really was one of them, that I wasn't a virgin. I didn't want anyone to know. My friends would think I was a slut—like the girls who had sex with every guy they dated.

After gym, we filed past Mrs. Niles toward the showers. For all her gruffness, she had a heart of gold. She treated her students with respect and expected excellence in return. I admired her and sometimes envied the close relationship she had with her basketball players, girls whose athleticism—unlike my own— wasn't confined to volleyball and swimming. I knew they confided in her, for after class they often lingered at her office door.

Maybe I could talk to her. She'll know what to do. Or, I could talk to Mom.

Always reserved, Mom wasn't easy to talk to, especially about sex. The very topic seemed to make her uncomfortable. Besides, it took all the time she had to care for my sisters, along with cooking for the two boarders we had taken in. I longed to confide in her, yet I knew I never would. I was too ashamed. I hated myself for allowing the sex to continue, feeling totally responsible.

Instead, I buried myself in my books so I wouldn't think about it. If I wasn't studying, I was reading. But where I once read mystery novels or dime store romances, I now read harder, grittier pieces like *Helter Skelter*, which led to terrifying nightmares. And quite often, I woke up thinking I was the pregnant Sharon Tate, about to be murdered.

Winter arrived with a vengeance when a heavy snow began falling in January, and didn't stop until the mountains were buried beneath a twenty-inch blanket. During the month-long school closure, Neal, an older boy who drove the kind of van most fathers feared their daughters going anywhere near, began flirting with me.

Not long before, Eddie had lost his job and went to Tennessee to find work. He didn't even tell me goodbye. In defiance, I responded to Neal's flirtation. He invited me to a sled-riding party not far from my house, but when Mom said I couldn't go, I climbed out my bedroom window and jumped into the deep snow below.

Walking up the hill, I knew my mother might find out, but I didn't care. As I drew closer, I could see a bright glow and I heard the sound of muffled chatter. Rounding a corner, I saw a rough-looking crowd gathered around the big bonfire.

"Hey Daleen," Neal grinned.

"Hey," I waved, feeling awkward beside his friends.

Someone offered me a bottle of beer, which I turned down, and what I thought was a cigarette. I didn't want them to think I thought I was too good for them, so I took a drag. The nicotine from the cigarette seemed to open my brain, causing everything around me to become exaggerated, as I realized it was marijuana.

"So you wanna ride?" Neal moved beside me, and I suddenly felt very liberated from my restrictive mother.

"Sure," I shrugged nonchalantly.

"You can sit here," Neal motioned to the empty spot on the wooden flyer in front of him. As I sat between his legs and wedged my feet against the metal steering bar, he pulled me even closer.

"How's that? You ready?" Neal's beer breath warmed my ear.

I nodded, acutely aware my derriere was smack up against him. Pushing off, we went flying down the hill. Part of me hoped he would kiss me; another part feared he might. Neal stood up when the runners ground to a stop.

"Here you go," he extended his arm. I let him pull me up, until our faces were just inches apart, when a loud voice intruded.

"That was some ride, huh?" Neal's friend Jackson and a few other teens pulled up next to our sled. "Makes me want another beer."

The moment was lost, and Neal grabbed our sled. We headed back up the hill as the runners from other sleds cut through the snow, swishing by in a blur. Back at the top, I warmed my hands before the fire, and tried to figure out how or where I fit in. I knew Neal's friends lived to party, which was why the booze flowed freely; Jackson had even had a brush with the law. No doubt, before the evening was over, the alcohol would be ditched for something stronger. What that was, I didn't know.

And I didn't want to find out. Try as I might, I couldn't sustain my initial excitement, for it wasn't my type of fun. If I chose to become one of them, all I could see was a future with nothing in it. That wasn't what I wanted for myself.

I rode down the hill several times until everyone began pairing off, but when Neal brushed a strand of hair from my eyes and asked me to stay, I was no longer the rebel, happy to have broken out of her jail cell bedroom. The last ounce of defiance had drained away, and I headed home. I knew my irate mother was waiting, but I could handle that. Because I would also find those things I was most comfortable with, which had always sustained me and given me purpose.

I had so much free time during Eddie's absence I started hanging out with the girlfriends I had neglected. Looking back, I wasn't sure how it happened. Somehow Eddie gradually took more and more, until there was none left for anyone else. But soon, I was having slumber parties where we stayed up half the night eating popcorn and watching movies, or having rowdy pillow fights.

During the big snowfall, Dad returned from Martinsburg for a weekend visit, and taught me how to operate the snowmobile he used at remote job sites. Roaring through the white fields gave me a sense of control and power I craved. Little in my life was within my control, so those hours spent on the snowmobile, my hand on the throttle as the big machine went faster and faster, gave me that. Not only did I have complete control sitting astride it, I was the only teen in the neighborhood with a snowmobile, so I achieved immediate popularity, as neighbor kids waited for an invitation to join me. Which I gladly extended, happy to have friends join me for the night rides I loved, when the silver moonbeams bounced off the ice-encrusted snow, casting reflections in every direction.

When school resumed that fall I was a sophomore—who was free of a boyfriend. Boys suddenly went out of their way to get my attention, and I instinctively raised my guard until they lost interest. But I didn't give the cold shoulder to a new transfer student who began teasing me. The day I looked up to see Jay Alexander striding down the school bus aisle, a mischievous twinkle in those robin egg eyes told me exactly what he had in mind.

"Is this seat taken?" Jay's smile was blinding, his teeth even and white.

I gave him a nervous smile and a half-nod, and he sat down.

"I didn't think so," Jay grinned. I couldn't help but notice the way his blond hair waved and curled over the edge of his shirt collar.

We began sitting together every day. If he had football

practice after school I missed the way he made me laugh, so I began making excuses to stay after myself—just to watch him practice. When friends teased us about being a couple, we both denied it was anything other than platonic, but I knew Jay enjoyed seeing me squirm whenever someone said it. I began wondering if it was his way of hoping our relationship might become romantic.

After I met Jay, I began wishing I had never known Eddie, and found myself hoping he never returned. Jay wasn't just nice; he was sincerely interested in what I said, and teased me about being "a brain." The best part, though, was the physical contact: it only occurred during those daily bus rides, when our shoulders or maybe our legs would lightly touch.

Jay could never know that after the first time in Eddie's bed, I had secretly promised myself to him. But with Eddie gone, I began having second thoughts. He never called or wrote, and any news I heard came from Kim or his mom. The day after I told myself we were through, Eddie returned. I came home from school to find his truck in our driveway. I was so disappointed, and found myself thinking about Jay.

I slammed the heavy front door as I went inside, yelling for Mom.

"I'm in here," she said.

In the kitchen, Mom was scraping her famous butter cream icing from a bowl. A chocolate cake sat near her elbow, and Mom placed the last dollop on top.

"What's Eddie doing here?"

Mom covered the cake with plastic wrap. "He's out back, unloading firewood."

"Jerk," I muttered under my breath.

"He got a new job, in the coal mines. Isn't that great?"

I stayed silent.

"Look, I know you're still mad at him for leaving, but he

even offered to bring us coal from where he works. He's really eager to help."

I bet he is! I thought. *But what else is he eager for?*

"As long as you don't expect me to entertain him. I'm too busy to spend time listening to those tall tales he tells." I turned away, but not before I caught her quizzical expression.

"What happened to make you so crabby?"

I shrugged. "Nothing. I just think, sometimes, he isn't exactly honest."

"Well, he's always been prone to exaggeration, but if he's here helping, what difference does it make?"

I headed for my bedroom, needing some privacy. "None, I guess," I grumbled.

But as Eddie became a regular visitor, it grew hard to ignore his efforts to gain my forgiveness. It wasn't long until his playfulness caused me to talk to him again. I convinced myself he was a good guy because he always wanted to help, and I learned he was really proud of being a union coal miner. He talked of little else and I could tell he felt less like an outsider, and more like he had joined the ranks of his closest friends, whose families had been in the mines for generations. He seemed to believe being a coal miner gave him a special status.

After he brought us coal when Mom was worried about being able to afford it, took us places when her car broke down, and fixed our leaky water faucets, I slowly dropped my guard. Gradually, I began to think he really did care about me. Maybe he was trying to make up for everything that had gone wrong between us.

Without even realizing it, we began "dating." Mom usually insisted we take along a chaperone, but a few times Eddie arranged things so we were alone. Then time fell away and I was thirteen all over again, as helpless as a cornered mouse, waiting for a menacing cat to pounce.

We were alone the night we went to see "Gone With the Wind." When Eddie suggested we sit in the very back row of the theatre, I groaned. I wanted to say "no," but didn't know how.

He did drive me here, and paid for my ticket. Plus, he took me shopping and bought me new clothes.

But I struggled throughout the movie to keep his hands off of me, and when it was over, I swore I would never go anywhere with him again. Darkness had fallen during the drive home. Eddie patted the seat beside him. "I won't bite you," he grinned.

I moved just enough to make him happy, but not so much we would be touching. One arm went around me, as he steered with his other arm.

I froze. "I'm fine where I am."

His fingers brushed against my breast, and I tensed up immediately. "Eddie, please," I began.

"Oh come on. It won't hurt anything, and besides, it feels good, doesn't it?"

I clenched my teeth together, as I tried to remove his hand. He held it there tightly and I finally sat there, staring stonily ahead. Suddenly he turned into an abandoned lane beside the main road.

"What are you doing?" I demanded.

He turned off the lights and pulled the emergency brake. The noise it made could have been my own jarred nerves. "I want to go home," I told him quietly.

But he wasn't listening. Instead, he wrapped his arms around me and began kissing my neck and my face. "I need you. Please don't tell me 'no.' I took you to the movies, didn't I?" Eddie asked.

"But this is wrong. I already told you—" His mouth cut off my words and the next thing I knew I was laying on my back on the seat, my blouse and bra around my neck.

"Please. I want to be married before we do this," I pleaded with him.

"We're going to get married someday, so it's all right." He had my jeans unzipped and was tugging at them while I held on tightly with both hands. But he was stronger than I was, and I soon found myself staring up at the ceiling.

Somewhere, Scarlett and Rhett were in a carriage, riding furiously past burning buildings, desperate to escape from Atlanta.

Over and over the scene replayed itself in my mind until Eddie sat up and pulled up his pants, leaving me to fix my shirt and jeans.

He reached out and tried to touch me. "I'm sorry. I don't know what came over me, I won't do it again, I promise."

I was silent, leaning against the door as far as I could.

He sounded close to tears as he mumbled, "I'm really sorry."

I was too tired to speak. I tried to convince myself what we had done wasn't wrong. Besides, it had already happened so many times it didn't matter. I knew God would never forgive me. But it didn't stop me from asking him to.

My relationship with Jay was doomed after that night. Jay knew Eddie had returned, and one day he told me he was going to find a way to make Eddie jealous. Jay's words were light and off-handed, but I sensed he wanted more than just friendship. Eddie was working late one Friday night when I went to a school football game, telling myself what Eddie didn't know wouldn't hurt him. After the game, I was waiting for him to leave the locker room when I saw him walking toward me. Jay had changed from his football uniform into blue jeans and when he patted my back, I noticed how his hand seemed to linger where it fell against my hair. My cheeks grew warm as I looked at him.

His eyes looked like puppy dog eyes, and my heart fell. What I'd suspected all along was true. He did want more than just friendship. I felt sick with shame.

So do I, Jay. But I can't. I'm used, and if you knew that, you wouldn't want anything to do with me.

We rode home with one of Jay's friends, but after walking me to my front door, Jay hesitated.

"See you Monday," I smiled.

"Can I call you tomorrow? There's something I want to ask you," Jay sounded nervous as he turned to leave. I could only nod my head and try to smile.

Inside, I leaned against the door and sighed deeply, knowing he wouldn't get the chance, because I was going to break his heart. A sense of sadness settled upon me, for something that could never be.

I can't ever be with anyone else. Eddie took care of that.

When Jay called, I told Mom I didn't feel well.

"I'm sorry, Jay, can I take a message?" I heard her say.

"No, nothing serious," Mom said, scribbling something on a scrap of paper. "I'll be sure to tell her," she said.

"Jay said he hopes you feel better, and asked if you'll call him when you do."

The paper had a phone number I already knew by heart, and I stuck it inside the book. I didn't return his calls, and by Monday I knew Jay sensed the change in me. I had crawled back into my shell, knowing there could never be anything between us.

I'm not worthy of you, Jay. If only you knew the truth, you'd hate me.

We spoke less and less, until we eventually stopped sitting together. I hated losing Jay's friendship, because I knew he truly cared for me. By the end of my sophomore year, I heard he was going steady with someone else.

The following spring Dad told Mom he was going to work in Amman, Jordan, and she promised to join him there. They agreed I could stay behind, attend summer school and stay with a family friend so I could graduate a year early.

Dad was home preparing for his overseas trip when Eddie stopped by one weekend. But his demeanor clearly implied he didn't like Eddie being around his daughter. Deep down, I knew Dad was right, when he said he wouldn't sign the papers so we could get married.

That wasn't all, though. "Your dad thinks you could do better," Mom whispered.

But I have to get married, to pay for my sins.

I knew my father was hurt, because his ultimate dream was for me to obtain a master's degree in music or the arts at some prestigious college. Dad refused to say anything else, except he would not allow us to get married.

"But Mom married you when she was sixteen," I complained, thinking about the girls my age who were already married. It seemed to be a trend in our community. Granted, most of them had gotten pregnant first. But once in awhile, you saw a couple where a baby hadn't been the defining factor in their decision.

Eddie stood silently aside, while I did all the talking. "I said 'no' and that's final." Dad's jaw was set.

Eddie finally spoke. "We should probably listen to him, Daleen."

I glared at him. He was so mealy-mouthed, afraid to say how he really felt. Or was he? Standing there looking at him, I realized I didn't even know.

In June, Mom—who was six-weeks-pregnant—took my sisters and joined Dad in the Middle East. I stayed in Martinsburg with family friends until summer school ended. The Baylors were so close-knit and happy. I loved being with them. Although close to Kelby, their oldest son, I got along well with his younger brother, Brian, and even enjoyed playing with Tommy, who was a little older than Jackie. During the week, the two older boys would walk me to school, and when I returned in the afternoon, after chores and dinner, we would spend time listening to music or running around town.

Every weekend I rode an Amtrak train back to Preston County, where someone would meet me at the train station. On the Martinsburg end, Kelby and Brian walked me down to the depot, carrying my suitcase. We stood and talked, trying to pass the time until the train came. Kelby never said it, but I knew he didn't want me to leave. Or rather, he didn't like that I would see Eddie during the weekend. For some reason, Kelby had taken an immediate dislike to Eddie.

I tried not to think about Kelby or Eddie during those rides across the lush, green countryside. They gave me a chance to dream, to read or to simply enjoy my time alone. It made me feel grown up. Still, I was a little nervous at the sight of all the strange men who boarded it each weekend. Most of them wore business suits, and just sat there reading the newspaper or playing chess, making them look harmless. But I had to force myself to stop thinking about how they might try to hurt me. Closing my eyes, I gave myself a pep talk, reasoning that the chances of them trying to rape me were pretty slim. Each time, after I overpowered the fear in my brain, I could calm down and enjoy the ride.

But that didn't stop me from watching my fellow passengers during the six-hour journey, trying to guess by their manners and grooming what their lives must be like, off the train.

I looked at the other women and wondered if they had all had experiences like me. Or if their smiles, like mine, hid secrets deeply buried under layers of shame and worthlessness.

Then came the weekend I missed the train. I was upset because it would be another week before I could go home again. Kim and I had a big weekend planned, and she was supposed to meet me at the station. When I called to tell her what happened, Mrs. Leigh answered, and offered to send Eddie to get me. That was the last thing I wanted. I tried to say 'no,' but in the end I said I guessed it would be all right.

Kelby confronted me afterward.

"I'm sorry if you think you love him. You aren't ready for marriage. I'm a year older than you and I'm nowhere near ready. Besides, he gives me the creeps. What business does a man his age have with a girl who's only fifteen?"

Kelby's words annoyed me.

"He loves me, that's what. Besides, I'll be sixteen in August!"

Kelby scoffed.

I told him Eddie had good qualities, and he was just like family. That didn't matter to Kelby, who had his mind made up. *You're just jealous,* I thought. *If you really get to know Eddie, you would see how nice he is.* But something kept me from saying it and a little voice deep within me said Kelby was just concerned. It also said something else.

You're lying. Eddie doesn't love you. If he did, he wouldn't touch you the way he does. He wouldn't keep breaking his promises to you.

Kelby and his family were going away that weekend, so they were gone by the time Eddie arrived. When I went upstairs to get my suitcase, he followed me. I usually slept in the lower twin bunk in Tommy's bedroom, and as I started to move toward it, Eddie grabbed me and tried to push me down onto it.

"Eddie, quit it. Not here. It isn't right!" I pushed him away and for once he meekly listened, laughing as he patted my bottom.

I locked up and we got into Eddie's truck. When he had been on the road for a couple of hours, I woke up from where I was laying on the seat to find us pulling into a roadside stop. I wasn't quite awake. "What? What's wrong?" I asked.

"It's all right. I just stopped to get some sleep. I'm really tired and can hardly keep my eyes open. I only got two hours' sleep last night." He was spreading out a sleeping bag behind the seat, where there was a large space for storage. "Come on, you can lay back here with me," he said, climbing over the seat.

"That's all right. I'll stay up here. There's not enough room back there for both of us."

No, please Dear God. Not again. Please help me not to let him touch me.

I could feel the shivering begin.

He grabbed me, playfully pulling me down on top of him. "Look, there's enough room if we sleep like this," he said, beginning to kiss me. I felt his hands slide down my back, across my buttocks, where they stayed. "See, now, isn't that nice?"

In my mind I saw a patrol car stop, and a police officer come over to the truck, finding us undressed. I saw him take me away, and throw Eddie in jail. The thought terrified me.

"I want to sleep up front. I'm not really tired anyway. I already slept." I tried to argue. His hands were inside my jeans, and as I began to struggle, he laughed like it was a game, and wrestled me around until I was beneath him.

"Please, Eddie, no, not here." I begged, hearing the desperation in my voice.

He didn't even seem to hear, and was unfastening my jeans, as one hand reached between my legs.

"You make me so hot! If only you weren't so sexy, and didn't make me so hot!" He leaned closer and began nibbling at my ear.

I kept seeing the policeman, over and over again, as he took possession of my body. I didn't move, didn't even try to get away, when he was through and climbed off.

I don't care. It doesn't matter anymore.

It had happened so often already. What was one more time?

As he slept, I tried to tell myself how much I loved him, that he loved me in return. I felt guilty for being pretty, for tempting him so much, and then and there, I wished I had been born ugly.

Maybe that would have saved me from him.

Sitting there parked at the rest stop, I felt a sense of profound shame, because every time he touched me, I became aroused. I had tried to keep from feeling anything, steeling myself against what I knew would happen, but it never worked. If anything, his touch caused a burning sensation within me, so I knew Eddie must be right. I must have wanted it—waited for it to happen.

I couldn't sleep at all, so after awhile, I turned on the radio, slammed the glove box open and closed, and made all kinds of noise, deliberately waking him up. I wanted to get home, so I could take a bath and forget everything.

I don't know how I faced everyone the next morning as if nothing had happened, since his mother asked why we didn't get there until long after they had gone to bed. Eddie lied and told her he couldn't stay awake, so he pulled over to sleep. I didn't say anything, and my silence served to corroborate his story. By then I had been doing it for so long, it had become easy.

I wished then I could tell someone. Then we could get married and everything would be okay. Secretly I wondered, perhaps even hoped, that if Mom ever found out she would yell and scream at Eddie. But I knew, deep within, that it was my fault, because I let him have what he wanted all the time. Mom would know that, too, and hate me. So I remained silent.

CHAPTER SIX

Because Dad arranged for me to fly from Washington, D.C., to Jordan to visit for a month, Bruce was taking me to the airport. "Can I drive your car? I've been practicing with Kim," I told Bruce.

"I don't know if that's a good idea. It's a four-lane highway and the cars just fly." He sounded worried.

"I promise I won't wreck. I'm a good driver. You'll see. Please let me," I begged him, as excited as a child with a lollipop.

Smiling, he said, "Well, I guess I'll let you drive part of the way, at least. That way I can see how you do." He handed me the keys with a smile.

I jumped up and down, hugging him. "Oh thank you!" I could hardly wait to get behind the steering wheel.

On the way, we stopped for dinner and Bruce teased me about the Arabic men I would meet. "I wouldn't be surprised if some sheik didn't kidnap you and take you to his harem," he joked.

"Bruce, you're silly. That won't happen," I laughed.

After dinner he let me drive all the way to the airport, about forty-five minutes away. Bruce kept saying how well I was doing, and seemed impressed, so my ego received a healthy dose of self-esteem along the way. At the terminal, we stood in line together as I checked my luggage, walked easily and quickly through the metal detector at the security checkpoint, and then sat down to wait together until it was time to leave. My hair was in a chignon, I had on mascara and lipstick, and I wore a cream-colored cotton dress and strappy high-heeled sandals. I bought the outfit especially to wear on the trip, with money my parents had given me. I felt quite grown up.

By the time I boarded the jet, I was so excited I couldn't contain myself. I was going to be flying for twelve hours, from North America to the Middle East, over the Atlantic Ocean and the Mediterranean Sea, to a continent and a country I had never been to—my very first transatlantic flight.

We taxied along the tarmac and I silently prayed for a safe journey. Then it was time for take-off. The huge jet lined up with the dashed white line on the runway and began rolling swiftly, picking up more and more speed. The momentum pushed me back against my seat and, looking out the window, I saw the plane's wheels lift off from the ground. I watched as everything below us began shrinking. I couldn't believe we were actually airborne!

For the next hour I just sat there, mesmerized by the white, billowy clouds that floated by. I had a bird's eye view as we flew right through, and often above, them. It looked like we were floating on dozens of soft, fluffy balls of cotton.

Eventually I dozed off, waking a few hours later to watch the in-flight movie. After it ended and darkness surrounded us, I pulled out the novel I brought along to read. Two meals and another nap later, I heard the pilot announce we would reach our destination in an hour. I thought about my family, who had been living in Amman for two months.

I wondered about the city I would soon be in, and imagined meeting Queen Noor, the American beauty who had become Jordan's queen just a year earlier. I recalled my father's voice when he told the story of Carla Halaby, the young Arab-American woman who had agreed to marry King al-Hussein. Fifteen years and an entire culture separated them.

"King al-Hussein gave Carla Halaby her Arabic name, Queen Noor al-Hussein, which meant "light of the king," he said.

I saw the look that passed between my parents, a certain sparkle in their eyes, and I noticed something in their faces as they smiled at each other. I didn't understand my parents, or how their lives had ended up as they had, but I sensed that their own age difference made them feel a connection to the royal couple.

It was light again when the plane began its descent. I peered out the window to see hilly, sand-covered terrain peppered with military vehicles that looked like Matchbox cars. Neighboring Iraq was in the midst of a civil war, so the local militia was always alert for possible terrorist activity. All too soon, I found myself shuffling toward the exit ramp.

The sun's scorching rays hit me as soon as I stepped into the sunshine. My fair-skinned father stood out from the dark Arabs, sandwiched like a piece of Swiss cheese between two slices of pumpernickel bread.

"Dad!" I yelled, hugging him. Not known for being physically demonstrative unless he was drunk, Dad tried to hug me but was obviously embarrassed.

"You look older. I almost didn't recognize you," he teased. "Your mother's waiting outside."

Dad stowed my suitcases in the trunk as Mom and the girls took turns hugging me. Then we headed through what looked like desert into Amman. Dad said the city was laid out on seven "jabals," the Arabic word for mountains. Each one was named Jabal—like Jabal Amman or Jabal al-Hussein.

"We'll bring you to see the ruins next week," Mom promised.

I was mesmerized as Dad drove through the city, passing old buildings decorated with bold-colored tiles and ornate Arabic script. Floral gardens bloomed everywhere, and the people seemed to come from all walks of life, from every corner of the world. I couldn't wait to return and explore everything.

Everyone tried to talk at once as Dad wound the car through busy city streets. Mom described their luxurious rental home, while Carla told me about the cute neighbor boys, and little Jackie jabbered away. I looked at my suntanned family, amazed and exicited we were actually together.

I felt like I had just stepped into the pages of a storybook where there really was a happy ending. When I entered my parent's house, I believed it might just happen. I walked around, finding something more beautiful in each room. Exotic Arabic rugs covered the chipped marble floors. Ornate brass chandeliers hung suspended from the ceilings, while hundreds of pieces of cut crystal caught and held the sunbeams. There was even a bidet in the bathroom. I only knew what it was because our friend Shirley had one in her house. "They're in all the Jordanian homes," Mom laughed.

Near daybreak I woke to the sound of ringing bells, and thought the sound came through my open bedroom window. My eyes didn't open again until late that morning, when I traipsed into the kitchen and found Mom making breakfast.

"Did I hear bells ringing?" I asked, leafing through a newspaper.

"Yes, the Muslims stop whatever they're doing and pray five times a day. You'll get used to it. We don't even notice them anymore."

"Like the trains?" I asked.

"Yes," Mom said.

I walked onto the balcony and stood looking at the large city sprawled below us and far into the distance. Even the air felt foreign. It was hot and dry and had an unusual fragrance. Neutral-toned stone structures with flat roofs filled the city, their plain beige or brown exteriors no doubt belying the same elegant interior our own home had.

"I promised our landlord I would bring you over for coffee this morning," Mom said. "The people here are very hospitable and love to entertain. They live next door and their daughter Aminah is a little older than you."

After breakfast, I showered and went with Mom, who made introductions as an older woman cheerfully waved us inside.

"I make coffee," Mrs. Dabdoub said, bustling into the kitchen. "Have you ever had Turkish coffee?"

"No."

"Then I make you some. Come and sit down." She took a small, long-handled ceramic pot and scooped a scented, fine powder into it, before adding a mound of sugar. Then Mrs. Daubdoub asked me about life in America. "You meet my Aminah tonight at dinner," she said.

We chatted until she turned to remove the steaming liquid, pouring the beverage into tiny porcelain cups with even tinier handles, before placing them on matching saucers.

"They're beautiful," I said, tracing the etched gold.

"Thank you," she beamed proudly. "Let grounds settle to bottom before you drink. I hope you like."

I was soon sipping a rich, sugary coffee unlike anything at home. "It's delicious," I said.

Mom took me to the local market later, and I watched her buy foodstuffs and pay with Arabic currency, laughing as she tried to understand the man behind the cash register.

That night we went to the Dabdoubs for a small dinner party and I fell in love with Middle Eastern food after eating a delicious chicken and rice dish called mensef. It was made with pine nuts and yogurt. I also met Aminah, whose lovely full figure captivated us when she put on a colorful traditional costume and belly danced for us. As I watched her, the music captivated me. Before I knew it, Aminah was reaching for me, leading me onto the floor. Everyone clapped, encouraging me to join her.

I blushed and grew embarrassed. "I don't know how," I said, trying to pull away.

"You see, you dance," Aminah smiled, "like me." I tried to imitate her graceful gestures, but she had to stop and show me how to move my hips. In my blue jeans and cropped top, I felt out of place among my new neighbors, but they encouraged me as I tried to learn their native dance.

The next day Aminah took me by taxi into downtown Amman. "Stay close," she said, as she warned me about the throngs of people.

We were just emerging from the taxi and Aminah was paying our driver, when I felt a pinch on my backside. I quickly turned and saw an elderly man swathed in black hurrying away.

"He pinched me," I stammered, pointing. Immediately Aminah began yelling in Arabic, a long string of what I could only assume was obscenities.

"You have to be careful. Some men here are just bad," she said.

I found the open air markets amazing, and stared at row after row of dried meats, clothing and other items that hung from the ceilings and the walls. The odors combined, reminding me of a cross between the time Dad had butchered our two hogs and the fabric I used to make some of my clothes.

For the next few hours, we walked throughout downtown Amman, and Aminah pointed out the best shops for bargains, showing me how to barter with the shopkeepers.

"I don't know if I could do that," I said.

"They expect it," she said.

What surprised me most was seeing that many women were not covered from head to toe in fabric, especially the younger ones. Like Aminah and me, they opted for a more Western style of dress, and wore no head covering, or hijab. But every time I passed a woman wearing a niqab, or face covering, I tried to look at her eyes. I wondered how she felt about being covered in such a way. I didn't know if I could do it, although I did have to admit it had an exotic appeal to it.

The days evaporated as I met Dad's colleagues, the teenage sons of an ambassador who lived next door, and Mom's new friends. We visited several places in the city and beyond and it was almost time for me to leave when Dad took us on the Dead Sea outing he had promised us. I peered out the car window at miles of rocky pastures. There were camels and other livestock, and far in the distance I saw a group of people walking together.

"What are they doing?" I asked.

Dad looked in the direction I was pointing. "They're Bedouins, wanderers. They travel from place to place on foot."

As we descended the narrow road leading to a huge body of water below, Dad gave us a short geography lesson. "The Dead Sea has four times the amount of salt as other oceans, with a high mineral content. It sits below sea level and all of the rocks look white because of the salt," Dad said.

As soon as the car came to a stop, Carla and I jumped out, running to the warm water. Mom played with Jackie at the water's edge, and we laughed as the salt-saturated sea caused our bodies to float to the top. I tried repeatedly to dive beneath the water, but the buoyancy kept pushing me back up.

"Here," Dad handed me a newspaper. "Try reading it while you're floating."

I took the folded newspaper and leaned back, opening it with both hands. "It's amazing!" I cried. Hours after we left I could still taste the salt on my tongue, and remembered how wonderful it felt to read while floating.

Dad's drinking had begun much earlier, and once we were back on the road, we ended up getting lost. Dad tried to find his way back home but after several beers, his normally good sense of direction had disappeared. After what seemed like hours of aimless driving, the car screeched to a halt and Dad turned around in the middle of the road. As he pointed the car in the opposite direction, Carla and Jackie began to whine.

"Shut the hell up," Dad yelled.

Dad only swore when he was really drunk or aggravated, and he rarely swore at us, so the girls immediately grew silent. Before long we stopped in front of an official looking sign written in Arabic.

"Dale, I don't think this is a good idea," Mom said.

"It's fine," Dad said, driving through the open gate.

But in the next instant, loud shots rang out. My parents looked at each other and Dad spun the car around so fast a large cloud of dust appeared. Everyone else was terrified, but Dad acted like being shot at happened every day.

"They're just warning shots, probably from some Jordanian military compound," he said calmly.

Still, it sobered him up, and Dad said we had one more site to see. "Do you know where we are?" He asked me when we finally stopped.

I thought the old building sitting there was a religious structure, but it wasn't as nice as the others I had seen in Jordan.

"We're in what's considered the most revered part of the Holy Land. This is Mount Nebo. I thought you might enjoy seeing it," Dad said.

I looked around, remembering something about Mount Nebo from my Bible studies. "Isn't that where Moses was?" I asked Mom.

"Some people believe this is where he was buried," she said. "The church would have been built later."

We wound our way up a walkway made from mosaics, many of which were loose and falling away. The church was closed for the day, but we toured the exterior. The view included the entire Jordan Valley and rooftops from faraway houses. It was spectacular. I thought of Moses' 40-year trek through the wilderness, and the decree denying him entry into the Promised Land.

For a man who whose only claim to spirituality was the agnosticism he sometimes expressed, it was a thoughtful gift to a daughter whose life would be forever changed by the time he would see her again.

A few days later I told my family goodbye and excitedly boarded a jet that would take me to London. I was going to see the stage play *Annie* and then stay overnight before returning home. Dad had surprised me a week earlier, when he told me his British friend, Alan, whom I had met in Amman, would meet me in London with my ticket.

"I can't believe it!" I threw myself at Dad and hugged him when he told me.

"Since you enjoy the theatre, I thought you should see it," he grunted with a small smile.

But just after take-off, the pilot's voice came over the intercom. "We're having engine trouble and need to return to the airport. But don't worry, we'll get you back in the air in no time," he said.

I sighed and tried to relax, and prayed for a safe landing.

We landed without incident, but the airport was packed with wall-to-wall people. I tried calling my parents from a pay phone, but they weren't home. So I dug out my novel and began reading until we boarded a plane headed for Greece. We would get off in Athens and wait for another plane to take us to London. As I left Amman for the second time, I felt torn: I wanted to stay with my parents where I would be safe, but I longed to see Eddie again. As the bustling city of seven hills became a speck among a sea of beige, I pulled out my journal and began writing. I never wanted to forget my trip.

The airline promised the Athens layover would be brief, but it wasn't. And we weren't allowed to leave the airport. The only good thing about landing there was seeing the beautiful city from the air, where much of its ancient architecture still stood. I held my breath when we circled the island and I glimpsed the Greek Parthenon perched below us.

The layover lasted all day. At first my curiosity got the best of me, and I walked through the airport, watching the sparkling blue sea from a window. Then I spent too much money in the gift shop. Finally, when I realized I was going to miss *Annie*, I grew frustrated. I wasn't alone; everyone was frustrated. By the time we decided we were stranded, our flight was announced. Long since tired and bored, we boarded yet another big jet, which flew us nonstop to London.

I went from Heathrow International Airport to the hotel room Dad had reserved for me, fell into bed and woke with a start just a few hours later, returning to the airport. I slept during most of the flight home and was happy to see Bruce when the plane landed. He took me to the Amtrak station, so I could head home to Preston County. I had already called Eddie's parents and Mrs. Leigh told me how much they had missed me. "You be careful now, Honey. We want you back in one piece," she said warmly.

Jet-lagged and exhausted, I boarded a train and slept most of the way there, where Kim met me.

It felt so good to be home, and I was secretly happy that Eddie was working.

Two hours later, after telling them about my trip and handing out the gifts I had brought, I slid between the crisp sheets Eddie's mom had put on his bed, insistent I sleep there.

I was still asleep the next morning when I felt something moving on my breast. Bolting upright, I saw Eddie in bed beside me. A split second later I realized he was naked.

"What are you doing here?" I thought I must be dreaming, but his roving hands told me otherwise.

"Get out, now!" I spat at him. "Do you want your folks to come up here? They'll kill us both!" I tried to pull the covers up as I pushed him away.

He stopped long enough to wrap his arms around me and look at me wickedly. "They would if they were here."

I stared at him. "I don't believe you. They wouldn't leave us alone together. If you don't leave this minute, I'll scream!" I tried pushing at him, but he just laughed.

"Go ahead. They can't hear you because they're not here. Mom needed something from town, and made Dad take her," his shrug was blasé.

Then his eyes darkened. "I couldn't stand it without you. I've had to wait so long, and I can't wait anymore." He began kissing my neck and, taking my nightgown strap between his teeth, he pulled it off my shoulder, exposing the white skin beneath. "Oh God, you are so dark." He buried his face in my neck.

"Please, I, I—" I couldn't finish. I was already on fire. I couldn't help it, but I didn't want to feel that way. My body turned traitor as I felt the pressure build and a return of the tenseness I had tried to forget. I stiffened, willing myself not to give in, but within minutes I had. I lay there, feeling disgusted and dirty.

Eddie stared at me, a victorious look in his eyes. I tried to move as far away from him as I could, but he just pulled me closer. "Oh man, do you ever make love good. I worship you. I would do anything for you," he said.

Yes, anything except not touch me.

I turned away, clenching my teeth to keep them from chattering. I squeezed my eyes shut so I wouldn't be able to see him.

Please God, forgive me for sinning against you. Please, please help me to be stronger next time. Help me to not do anything to tease him, and help me to make Eddie behave himself.

But I knew God wouldn't help me. He hadn't helped me before, so why should he now? God knew I was a hypocrite.

Later that morning, after I bathed and tried to block out what had happened, Eddie's parents came home. Suddenly I found myself questioning Eddie's intentions—and his honesty. Chatting over tea, his mom told me that while I was gone, Vonna, a very pretty neighbor girl of thirteen, had visited them.

"I don't know why she came over; she just kind of invited herself, but I'll tell you, she won't come again!" Mrs. Leigh said.

"Why not?"

"Well, because she propositioned Eddie, and left a note under his pillow." Before leaving for work, Eddie apparently had torn it to shreds, tossing it into the trash. But Mrs. Leigh was putting some clean laundry on Eddie's bed when she saw the shredded paper. Out of curiosity, she picked up one piece and then another, until she had taped them all back together, like a jigsaw puzzle.

Mrs. Leigh assured me that Vonna's parents had been informed about their daughter's conduct.

But something didn't sound right. I kept quiet, but at the back of my mind was a very nagging, persistent voice that questioned just how faultless Eddie could have been. I remembered when he promised he would never touch me again, but then he did. Or the times I saw him look at other women, an odd expression on his face. I never said anything about it, but if he noticed my gaze, he seemed to change completely, almost as if he'd donned a mask. Each time, I chocked it up to my overactive imagination. Still unsettled about the whole matter, I went to see Kim.

"How did you find out?" she asked, looking surprised. "I was going to tell you, but I would have broken it a little easier. Look, all I know is what Eddie said, but I did see the note. It just said, 'Maybe next time we can go a little farther,' or something like that."

"That little brat! I'd like to slap her!" I began. Then I stopped. "But what about Eddie, do you think he . . ." I left the question unfinished.

Kim looked uneasy. "Do I think he started it? I don't know. He wouldn't tell me anything, except what Mom already told you. But if he did, well if I was you, I wouldn't have anything else to do with him," she said indignantly. "He's my brother, but you're my friend, and I don't want to see him hurt you."

I was upset and confused. I didn't know what to think. Part of me wanted to believe Vonna had instigated everything, yet another part held back. That part of me knew Eddie was capable of having been the one who got the ball rolling, so to speak. By that night, I had mustered up enough courage to ask him directly.

"I don't know. Nothing," he said.

"You do know. After all, you're the one Vonna wrote the note to," I said angrily.

His face went blank when he heard my words. "Nothing happened. It wasn't my fault, really. She just . . . " he laughed self-consciously and avoided my gaze, looking embarrassed. "Well, she threw herself at me. And I told her that I wasn't interested in her. That's all."

"Are you sure Eddie?" I wanted desperately to believe him.

He shook his head like he thought I was crazy. "Now look, I told you, nothing happened. If you don't believe me, ask her and she'll tell you."

Disgusted by my distrust, he turned and walked away. "This is crazy!" he muttered.

I was so confused after talking to him I didn't know what to believe. I was hurt and bitter for a long time afterward, and treated Eddie coolly whenever we were together. It was only a matter of time, though, before I began to come around, and eventually convinced myself it didn't matter.

Whatever happened, it didn't mean anything to Eddie. He still loves me. I told myself that at least a dozen times a day. But I never, ever forgot it, and stashed it away in a compartment of my mind where, as the years went by, where many similar memories would be stored for safekeeping.

Attending summer school permitted me to skip an entire grade, so in September I returned to West Preston High School as a senior. But it wasn't the same. Where I had once earned straight As, taking great pride in my work and carefully doing my assignments, I no longer studied as much, nor researched like I had before. Instead, I threw my papers together at the last possible minute, and when report cards were handed out, I took home Bs and Cs. Because learning came naturally, though, my grades were okay. I knew my attitude had gradually changed, but I just didn't care anymore.

The only exception came in my journalism and English classes: in the first, students wrote and edited the school newspaper, and I was assigned to be the school correspondent for two local newspapers; in the second, my teachers praised me for something they called my "lovely use of alliteration." I didn't really care what that was or how I did it, I just loved to write. Somehow I stayed focused enough to do so.

Then everything changed when Mom called in December, saying she and the girls were returning home. Because she was six months pregnant, I wondered if something was wrong, but she insisted it wasn't. I enjoyed living with Kathryn, who had become more like a beloved aunt than a family friend. She believed any girl younger than eighteen was too young to date, which had effectively kept Eddie almost entirely away from me—something that, deep down, I found I really liked—so I had mixed feelings about Mom's return. Kathryn said it was for the best, since a teenager needs her mother. I knew she was right, because I needed to tell Mom the truth.

I'm going to tell her, I thought. *Even if she thinks I'm a terrible human being. But maybe, just maybe, she'll understand.*

The minute I saw her at the airport, I nearly blurted it out. But during dinner she said Dad's drinking was worse, so I kept quiet. After hearing he had thrown a beer can at her, I couldn't burden Mom with my problem—she had too many of her own.

It was easier that way, since Eddie's words kept running through my brain. "Don't tell anyone. You know what will happen if you do," he had said anxiously. "My parents will kill me and you'll get in trouble, too."

So it became far easier to keep our secret, than to ever try and tell anyone. By then I knew several girls who were doing the same thing. There was Susie, who was having sex with a guy in his late twenties, and Patty, whose older brother's friends would invariably end up in her bedroom after the lights went out. They were just two girls among many others.

As I thought about those girls—other girls like me, I believed—I wondered why so many of them were being picked up by much older boys, men even, when school let out. The guys would hang out in their big, fancy trucks at the pizza parlor, parking next door to the school. And every day, girls would cross the invisible barrier that prevented their adult boyfriends from coming onto school property, but which never seemed to keep the girls from leaving it. Little did I know that by the time spring arrived, Eddie would join them in his big Ford. It all left me with even more questions about them, and myself, than I had before.

Once Mom returned, there was plenty of work to do. Leaky faucets or water pipes that had frozen and burst needed fixed; the house needed a thorough cleaning, and we were again without wood and coal. Eddie made sure he was right there, doing anything we couldn't do for ourselves.

Soon he began coming to the house straight from the coal mines, after his shift ended late at night. My bedroom was next door to Mom's, but the small creek below our windows virtually cut off any sound between the two rooms. Just on the other side of the creek, the shrill whistles from the hourly trains would blow when they went roaring by, cutting through the black night.

When we first moved to Independence in the early 1970s, coal was king and trains ran constantly on the three sets of train tracks beside our house. Every morning I would jump out of bed and run downstairs to find Dad already dressed in dungarees, his morning coffee in one hand and an ink pen in the other, poised above the daily crossword puzzle. Because Dad was having a hard time sleeping, they became his early morning gripe sessions. There at the kitchen table, he told Mom that because of "those blasted trains making all that noise," he wasn't sure the house had been a good investment after all.

Not only would the trains blow their whistles long and hard, but the tracks were so close to our house that its large, old windows would rattle all the while. Then just eight-years-old, the huge masses of steel were like toys to me, and I couldn't understand my father's anger. I would stand outside on the blackened railroad bridge that bordered our property and watch the fully-loaded locomotives lumber by, as car after car of coal passed by.

But we had long since gotten used to the large locomotives and slept peacefully through the commotion, making them a perfect accomplice for Eddie. He had to walk through my room to reach the spare bedroom. He might wake me with a kiss, quietly pleading with me to come to his room. Or some sixth sense awoke me, as he stood over my bed watching. Sometimes, I had no warning until his skin touched mine, and I refused his request. But that only resulted in him returning to my bed later.

No matter how hard I tried to stay awake, so I could plead and beg, just when I thought he really wasn't coming back, I fell asleep. And then he would return, as a train came roaring by. I would feel a touch somewhere on my body, and before I knew what was happening, he was on top of me. I tried to writhe out of his grasp silently, scared to death my mother would wake and find us. It was a thought I couldn't bear so most of the time, I just laid there and prayed for it to end.

Sometimes when Eddie was laying on me, I thought I heard the sound of metal squeaking; the bedsprings on my bed were quite old, and sounded as loud to me as if someone had broken a plate glass window. My heart began racing and I told him to stop. All the while he was with me, he whispered in my ear continually, saying things I could never imagine myself hearing about. I wondered where his vast knowledge of sex came from, and I hated what I heard.

To block out the squeaking and what was causing it, I returned to my childhood days, where I could breathe deeply of both the train's diesel fumes and the creosote from the bridge, which turned warm and gooey when the sun's rays touched it. I climbed onto the lowest rail, while leaning over the top one, looking into the creek bed below. Then I took my fingernail and scraped the soft stuff that had turned to oozing black tar, and which bubbled up between the boards. I squeezed it into shapes between my fingers until it left dark stains against my pale flesh.

Or I tried to count the empty cars that flew furiously by, and when one with an open door neared, I began running alongside it, grabbing the edge and flinging myself up into the car, so the train would carry me far, far away.

After Eddie left my bed, I tried to cry tears that refused to come. I thought I loved him, but wondered how I could, when I felt so dirty. I wanted to get up and shower, to turn the water on as hot as it would go and scald every touch and kiss away, but that would only wake Mom. All I could do was lay there, hating myself and loving him, as the aftermath of his antics mocked me.

One night after everyone had gone to bed and I was free of Eddie's torture, I laid down on the floor beside the heat register. I hoped it would warm the coldness deep within me while I peered into my mother's well-worn poetry book, searching for an answer to the lies and hypocrisy I was living.

What's wrong with me? Why do I feel so alone? I hate myself. I hate you, Eddie! Please God help me! I prayed.

I think it was the rebel—that part of me still needing to be exorcised, and which had lain dormant for too long—that made me do it. In the kitchen, I reached into the cabinet for Dad's homemade wine and poured myself a glass, drinking it in one long gulp. Then a second, and a third, glass.

I knew better, but I didn't care. I returned to my little corner and tried to figure out what I should do about my life, which I felt powerless to change. By the time I was becoming drowsy, I remembered I still had to bring in the coal.

To reach the coal bin, we had to cross the length of the yard behind the house. The wood was stacked right against the house, making it closer, but also requiring several trips outside.

Since the roof leaked, the black stuff inside the coal bin was wet, shiny and frozen solid. Using the pick, I finally broke it apart and found some dry coal below, which I shoveled into two five-gallon buckets. I felt lethargic by the time they were full, so when I tried to pick them up, I only made it a few feet across the yard. I stood there, dizzy, before dropping the buckets and collapsing onto my back in a bed of snow. The sky overhead was filled with tiny, sparkling gems that winked at me. I didn't want to move, but the dampness from the snow began seeping through my clothes, and I vaguely recognized that I should get up.

I could just lay here and go to sleep, I thought. *It would be so peaceful and painless. They'll find me tomorrow, when it's too late.*

I don't remember making it back inside. Nor do I recall dropping my coat, boots and gloves to form a path that led Mom straight to me. All I remember is someone holding my hair back from my face while I threw up in the toilet, asking the same question over and over again, "Daleen, what's wrong with you?"

Even without the alcohol numbing my brain, I couldn't answer her question.

Winter soon left and spring arrived, and on a warm day near the end of March, Mom went into labor. I stayed at her bedside, feeding her ice chips and rubbing her back when the contractions grew strong. I had gone to all her Lamaze childbirth classes, so I basically knew how it happened, but nothing prepared me for the raw, natural beauty of childbirth, or the intensity with which it can engulf a woman. After several hours, my brother Michael was born, letting out a lusty yell as he entered the world.

A nurse gave him to Mom to hold, and after taking him and cooing softly at him, she placed him at her breast to nurse. I watched, amazed, and then went to call my father overseas, leaving a message for him to call Mom at the hospital. I made sure she was all right, and after holding my baby brother myself, I went to school, like it was just another day.

One morning not long after Michael was born, I woke up and ran to the bathroom, where I threw up in the toilet. The virus lasted for days—until a terrible thought came to me. I stared into the toilet bowl, gripping the rim tightly with both hands as waves of nausea hit me: *I haven't had my period.*

My head began spinning, making me feel even worse. Getting up, I wrung out a washcloth and wiped my face, staring at the mirror. Looking at the dark circles hanging like half moons under my pale eyes, I didn't see myself but my mother, while pregnant with Jackie and more recently, Michael. I stood and stared into my reflection, barely able to comprehend it.

You can't. Absolutely can't. Be pregnant.

Overnight I had changed, going from a budding journalist to a scared girl whose dreams were evaporating right in front of her eyes.

I'm just another sad statistic: a teenager trapped by a pregnancy I don't want and a future I didn't ask for. Now I really am like all those other girls.

As if in a trance, I told Eddie.

"You're what? What did you say?" He stared at me.

"You heard me." I kept thinking about what it would mean, and how, when I grew fat, everyone would know what had happened—the terrible thing we had done together. I hated it, and I hated Eddie for doing it to me.

"When was your period?"

"I'm not really sure." My soft voice was quieter than usual. We never used birth control, because I never planned to have sex. But when we did, Eddie always promised it was "the last time."

I heard Eddie say we would just have to get married. "Does your mom know?"

I shook my head. I knew it was going to be such a big disappointment to her, considering how she tried so hard to raise me to live by Bible principles.

"I don't even think I can face her." I stared out the window.

I couldn't, so I took the coward's way out, writing a letter telling her I was pregnant. I told her how sorry I was and I wanted her to know it wasn't her fault. It was mine.

After I left it on my bed and went to school, I could hardly concentrate the entire day. When the bus dropped us off again that afternoon, I walked as slow as possible, wanting to delay the inevitable. The minute I saw her, I wanted to cry. Mom mustered a smile, and even asked me how classes had gone. I gave some vague answer and then, after Carla left the room, she began talking. She didn't raise her voice or yell, just kept speaking in that mild, flat tone of hers. I wondered how she could be so calm, when I was in agony over what I had done, and what was going to happen.

"You need to see an obstetrician, just to make sure. If you are, then since you and Eddie want to get married, you should do that right away. I'll deal with your father," she finished.

I nodded, unable to speak. We lived in the Bible Belt, that part of Appalachia filled with God-fearing church folk; where the Ten Commandments were still revered, and parents weren't afraid to use the "rod" so they wouldn't "spoil the child." Due to her own deep religious beliefs, I suspected Mom felt she had somehow failed me—failed to teach me right from wrong. But she would never say so out loud. She didn't need to, because the words lay there unspoken, for a long time to come.

What happened next made me wish I had died that night in the snow. More than a few girls bore the fruit of a big belly, waddling down the hallway. Some of them had already gotten married, wearing a wedding band as well as a new last name. But when we were placed in the national spotlight, after our school was featured on an episode of *20/20*. I think everyone was stigmatized. According to that segment, West Preston High had the highest number of pregnant teens of any school in the country; overnight we became the topic of conversation for everyone in our county, if not the nation.

Mrs. Niles shook her head when she heard the locker room buzzing. "It's pretty sad when a school gets national attention, not for academics or even sports, but for this. We'll be the laughingstock of the country," she frowned.

I wasn't counted in that study, but knew I should have been. If anyone else had known I was pregnant, I would have been responsible for the number climbing even higher. If anything, the news only made me feel more ashamed, like an outcast, and I guarded my secret even tighter, determined no one would know what I had done.

The next few weeks were a complete blur. Eddie broke the news to his parents and though they seemed to be disappointed, his mom was also excited at the idea of getting a grandchild from the deal. It was agreed his father, a minister, would perform the ceremony.

Mom and I went shopping and found a simply styled wedding gown with an empire waist and a short train. "I feel guilty about wearing white." I grimaced while standing before the floor-length mirror. "White is for virgins."

"I'm sure it'll be all right this once," Mom said absently, paying for the dress the only way she could—with the same credit card she had to use to buy us our new school clothes every year.

Seeing her pay for it added to my guilt. I knew she had stretched our thin finances to the limit already, by buying me a senior class ring, a yearbook and my senior photos. Now, she was paying for my wedding gown. Because I was pregnant and had to get married, I knew I could never repay her for everything she had given me.

Soon afterward, Eddie drove a shiny new sports car to our house. I knew it was his peace offering to me, paid for with guilt money. Then suddenly it was graduation night and I was wearing my cap and gown while marching across the football field. Mom was there, but Dad was still overseas. Upset and disappointed in me, he refused to come home.

While I nervously marched to "Pomp and Circumstance" beside a friend I had known since childhood, I wrestled with myself. I was so mixed up—I was leaving school, forever— and in seven days I would again be walking down another aisle, but a very sacred one. I felt like all the people in the audience could tell I was pregnant, but I knew the flowing graduation gown covered my waist, which hadn't even begun to expand. I still felt like everyone knew—as if something about the way I held myself, or the expression on my face, would give away my secret.

I was also annoyed with Eddie. He said he had to work, so he couldn't come to my graduation or the party afterwards. I was hurt and disappointed, and had no idea how that same excuse would soon become a constant in our life.

We were married the following Saturday in a state park under a canopy of spruce trees in front of a small group of family and close friends, just two months before I turned seventeen. While I was getting ready, I thought about the upcoming ceremony—how important it was, and how everything had led me to Eddie.

On that day I knew we were meant to be together. I was always looking for connections in my life and in the lives of others, so when I learned Eddie's parents had both been in San Francisco not far from where I was born and later, that they, too, had returned to West Virginia to be near family, I truly believed it was meant to be.

The romantic story Mrs. Leigh told was made more so because she had sworn off men—and love—forever, and there Mr. Leigh was, tearing down all the barriers she had built. After her divorce, she had gone to California to visit her brother's family and when she later returned to West Virginia, she met Mr. Leigh while working in a little Morgantown café. Fresh out of the Army, Robert immediately asked her out.

A petite woman with chiseled features and thick, dark hair worn in an elegant coiffure, she was the perfect foil for his own movie star looks. Because she'd become bitter, she turned him down cold, and was annoyed to find him waiting for her, after her shift ended. He insisted on walking her home. Those walks quickly became a ritual, which was how she learned they had been in San Francisco at the same time.

I pulled myself away from the past and looked out a window, seeing the tall green branches that scraped against the blue sky. It was lovely weather, and as I changed into my wedding gown, I couldn't help but feel ashamed. As though she sensed what I was thinking, Kathryn hugged me.

"It doesn't matter, white is for brides—all brides," she smiled.

I hugged her and felt tears well up behind my eyes. She was so kind and understanding.

Then it was time to walk down the aisle, a green, grassy path beneath the tall trees. I passed our guests, and then stood nervously beside Eddie. I loved him with all my heart, and just knew we would be happy. He looked down at me and smiled, and then Mr. Leigh began the sermon. We took our vows, and my finger shook ever so slightly as Eddie placed the slender gold band upon it. Then it was my turn, and I wondered if he was nervous. Mr. Leigh told us we could kiss then and Eddie lifted my veil.

He lowered his head and I felt his lips meet mine, very gently, but then, more passionately. I had my arms around him, but didn't feel comfortable kissing in front of so many people. I tried to pull back, but he wouldn't stop so I just turned my head some, hoping that would keep everyone from seeing so much. The next thing I knew we were walking back down the aisle, hand in hand, amid joyful shouts from our guests. We posed with the bridal party while cameras flashed from every direction.

We cut the cake and fed a small piece to each other. We talked to our guests, accepted their congratulations, and opened our gifts. Then it was over, and we were in our car, pulling away from the curb. A timid look at my new husband told me he was equally immersed in his own thoughts. As if sensing my gaze, Eddie grinned. "Boy they really did up the car good, didn't they?"

Several relatives had decorated it with crepe paper steamers and tissue paper flowers. They wrote "Just Married," on the rear window and tied pop cans to the bumper of our little black sports car.

"I'm going to pull over before we get on the highway and take those things off. I don't want them dinging the new paint job," he said. Eddie took particular pride in making sure all his vehicles were clean and well-maintained. That sense of responsibility was one quality that had endeared him to me, and I was certain it would make him a good husband.

So what if he had never said those three words: "I love you"? I knew he did and, more important, that he would be an excellent provider.

The overhanging branches in the dense forest created an umbrella over us as we left the waving crowd behind. It darkened the car's interior, immediately making it more intimate. I glanced into the visor mirror: my cheeks were flushed and my eyes sparkled, reinforcing my belief that new brides are supposed to glow from happiness. I certainly felt happier than I had in a long time, which reinforced my belief that I had done the right thing for our baby, our families and most of all, for God. I didn't know where life would lead us, but I knew with enough faith, we could accomplish anything together.

That's when the full force of what I had done hit me: I was honoring God's family arrangement by marrying my unborn baby's father, trying to give that child the best life possible. Saving my family the embarrassment of having an unwed daughter—something that seemed to happen in every other house in the county—was just a bonus. Most important, from that day forward, never again would sex be wrong or leave me feeling dirty and ashamed. So in a way, I was saving myself, too.

By the time I realized that wasn't even possible, it was too late.

CHAPTER SEVEN

I mused on the past three years and a twinge of conscience caused me some concern, as I again remembered no one but us—and God—knew what we had done. With a mental shrug, I pushed my guilt out of the way.

We're married now, so everything is going to be all right. Nothing will ever make me feel bad again, I thought.

That's when I realized sex would come without shame, and felt a blush creep up my neck.

Nothing can make it wrong now, I thought.

As we drove Eddie broke the silence, interrupting my attempts to talk to God, and reassure myself. "I can't wait to get to the hotel. Are you hungry? I'm not."

I felt the blush return, but ignored my embarrassment. "I'm getting there. Remember, I'm eating for two now, so by the time we arrive, I'll probably be famished."

"That's too bad, but oh well. If you must eat, you must eat," he sighed.

Thirty minutes later we walked through the hotel lobby in our wedding finery, making me wish I had changed clothes after the ceremony. Everyone we passed gave us a big smile and all I could think was: *they know we're going to have sex. They know what we're going to do.*

I tried to banish the thoughts from my mind, acknowledging that making love was something every couple did.

Since we were married, there was no reason to worry that other people would know we were intimate. And it worked—until Eddie picked me up without a word, sweeping through the bedroom doorway. The fears and feelings returned just as he lowered me onto the bed and began kissing me gently.

I tried to kiss him, wanting to regain the sense of pride I felt when his dad pronounced us husband and wife. But within seconds the intensity of his kisses changed and I found myself just staring at the ceiling, my eyes chasing the pattern there. I gave myself a mental shake, while wondering if he expected me to make love right away.

I knew I needed to tell him I had to get something to eat, or I would be sick.

"Eddie, can we go get dinner? I'm so hungry I feel sick."

His eyes looked sorrowful. "Are you going to make me wait some more? I already hurt bad, can't you take care of me first? You don't know how good it feels to hold you again, to touch you." He ran his hands over my breasts. "It's been so hard, going without you these last few weeks. I thought I would die." He groaned into my ear, as he began caressing me.

"But Eddie, if I don't eat now, I'll get sick," I protested.

"Oh all right." He was pouting, but showed no sign of stopping. The more he kissed me the worse I felt, and as the seconds slowly ticked by, I knew with a certain amount of anguish that we wouldn't leave the hotel until he had gotten what he wanted.

It's not that he doesn't care about my feelings; he just can't stand his own anguish. That's all, I told myself.

"Oh Daleen, I have to have you now. I can't wait anymore."

I believed the consummation of our marriage was something that should be savored, but by then I was so ill I could barely respond.

I felt like an observer watching the stage, as Eddie unbuttoned my gown, trailing kisses down my back as he did so. The dress fell in a crumpled heap. Eddie got undressed too, but without clothes on, he frightened me. It was still difficult for me to touch his naked skin and not feel odd: getting married hadn't changed that. But he was in such a hurry that it was over in a matter of minutes. When he was done, I felt awful. I forced myself to get up and go in the bathroom. I begged Eddie, who was nearly asleep, to get up and get dressed. I felt anger building within me.

We went to dinner but I was so nauseous I pushed my half-eaten meal away and drank my soda. It seemed to calm my stomach and by the time Eddie finished eating, I was feeling better.

Back at the hotel, I showered and came out of the bathroom wearing a new negligee. I had no sooner gotten under the covers than Eddie was all over me, as if the pre-dinner sex hadn't happened. As the night wore on, my body became the basis for some kinky sexual experiments. I drank two glasses of champagne—more than enough to dull my senses—so I wasn't always conscious. Or at least, not enough to try to get him to stop. When I opened my eyes the next morning, I realized I was imprisoned within Eddie's embrace. I came awake more fully after smelling the alcohol, and suddenly had the sensation of swimming in a wine vat. With a jolt, memories of the previous night came flooding back.

I lifted Eddie's arm from where it lay across me and stumbled into the bathroom to take a hot shower. My head felt heavy and I was dizzy. I leaned against the shower stall to keep from falling when it hit me: *I don't feel any different now than I have during the past three years. No wonder I drank so much champagne.*

I wondered if all new brides felt that way—dirty and ashamed—or if all new husbands behaved in a seemingly sex-crazed manner. It wasn't the hot water that made my cheeks burn, as some of the more daring things he had tried came floating back into my consciousness.

I'm just his toy, to be used for his own sexual gratification.

Stepping from the bathroom, I saw he was still asleep. As I watched him, I didn't know what to think.

But he does love me. And I love him. Maybe if we just work on it, maybe if I try to tell him how I feel, that's all it will take.

Less than twenty-four hours after our wedding, I began to wonder if I really knew the man sleeping beside me.

By August, I was plagued with so many questions and doubts I had trouble concentrating. Our nightlife was filled with what seemed to me to be scripts taken from a porn magazine. Except for one thing: I wasn't a willing partner to Eddie's outrageous sexual desires. Still, that did nothing to stop him from trying to convince me to take part—or coercing me, if nothing else worked. Force was used as a last resort, but frequently enough to keep me from erasing the wedding night memories branded into my consciousness.

Maybe that's why I suddenly remembered Eddie's furious rages before our marriage, and all the times he would jump in his truck and squeal the tires, speeding away from whatever had angered him. After only eight weeks of marriage, the full impact of that behavior struck me literally and figuratively.

Eddie worked day and night. If I said anything about his penchant for spending more time in the coal mines than at home, he exploded, calling me a nag. The first huge argument came one balmy summer evening as he tailgated another car crawling along at a snail's pace. Eddie grew angrier and edged closer. Nervous and frightened, I finally asked him to slow down. When he ignored me, I repeated my question. Suddenly he jerked the steering wheel and the car veered sharply. I could smell hot rubber as the tires squealed to a stop and only my seatbelt kept me from hitting the windshield.

Nausea gnawed at my stomach and my fingers clenched and unclenched nervously as he hurtled a string of obscenities at me. Throwing the keys down, Eddie jumped out and slammed the door so hard my ears hurt.

"Since you're such an expert you can just drive the damned thing yourself!" He kept screaming as he walked away.

"Where are you going?" I yelled frantically, climbing halfway across his seat. But the desire to go after him died with his next words.

"I don't know. But I'm sure as hell not going with you! Get out of here and enjoy your movie!"

"Come back. Please don't leave!" I yelled again. But he didn't turn around.

I sat there for a few seconds, trying to decide what to do. I knew I could go to the movie, but I no longer wanted to. It felt like I sat there forever, wondering what I had done wrong.

Obviously, it must be my fault, since he's furious with me, I thought.

But he was doing the tailgating—not me, another voice cried out.

That doesn't matter, though. I never should have criticized his driving habits. I know he's sensitive, but I didn't pay any attention to that. I was just concerned about myself, the ping-pong ball bounced back and forth inside my head: *I was in the wrong. No, he was. No, I was.*

I heard vague sounds of music coming from the console and suddenly realized I was sitting inside a car that was parked in the middle of a dangerous curve.

I could be killed!

I finished crawling into the driver's seat and turned the car around, hoping to reason with him. When I saw him walking along the road I slowed down, begging him to come with me.

"I'm not going to, so forget it. Just get out of here and leave me alone!" he shouted.

"Eddie, come on. You can't walk home." I pleaded with him, inching the car alongside him.

"Why not?" He demanded, looking like a pouting school-boy.

"Because it's too far. Come on, get in and we'll go home."

He said nothing and kept walking, giving me no choice but to drive home without him. Back at the trailer, I went inside, knowing it would be hours before he got home. I tried to sit down and read, but the words on the page kept blurring and my eyes burned with unshed tears. I couldn't concentrate. I looked outside at the darkening sky, and felt a return of the familiar fear I felt whenever I was alone at night. I felt like such a failure.

My husband had run away from home, and it was my fault.

Hours later, I finally picked up the telephone and began dialing. But when Mrs. Leigh answered the phone, I wasn't sure what to say.

"Mrs. Leigh, is Eddie down there?"

"No, should he be?" she asked.

"Well, I thought he might be . . . " I stopped, unsure of what else to say. It was hard enough just to tell her that much. "We had a fight, and I just thought maybe he had come down there," I heard a stranger's voice say.

"Well, he'll be back when he's not mad," she laughed. "I'm sorry; I didn't mean to laugh. But you know what a hothead he is."

That much I did know. After all, she had warned me about his temper enough times, hadn't she?

July arrived before we knew it and we began preparing for our belated honeymoon. I longed for the beach and an entire week together. Our trip coincided with Mom's visit to see Bruce, so Eddie and I planned to stop there on our way to the beach. We pulled in late at night and went right to bed, knowing the next day was going to be full of activities Uncle Bruce had planned for us.

After a full day of sightseeing, we went out for pizza and then returned to Bruce's apartment. I told Eddie I was really exhausted, and after telling everyone goodnight, I went to bed. But it was too warm and I kicked the covers off, trying to sleep. I could hear laughter and talking from the living room, and I knew everyone was busy playing Gin Rummy. I had almost dozed off when I heard someone yell. I realized it was Carla. She was screaming, and I heard her voice through the bedroom door.

"Stop it, you pain in the butt! Don't ever touch me again or I'll have my boyfriend take care of you. He knows what you've been doing and he's just waiting for a chance to beat you up!" Then I heard her crying, and other voices joined in.

I quickly threw my robe on and when I opened the bedroom door, I could see Eddie, looking surprised from where he sat on the couch. Seeing me, Carla began yelling again, "I mean it, Daleen! So help me God, if he ever lays a hand on me again, I'll kill him!"

"What's going on?" I was dumbfounded.

I looked back and forth between the adults. I felt a sick feeling begin in the bottom of my stomach because I already knew what had caused Carla's outburst. Eddie just sat there, not saying a word. Mom was trying to calm Carla down, and Bruce was at the table, his cards still in his hands, his face a mask of something similar to shock. The two little kids had stopped playing on the floor, and looked confused and frightened.

"He's had his hands all over me for months and he won't stop it. I wasn't going to tell you, Daleen, but he won't stop. I just can't take it anymore!"

I turned to Eddie, the anxious feeling growing stronger. "Eddie, what did you do?" My quietly spoken words hid the anger and fear I felt. He shrugged, and seemed to be trying to figure out what to say, when Carla spoke up.

"He kept rubbing his foot against my bottom, that's what he did! I was sitting on the floor watching television, and I told him to stop, but he just kept right on doing it!" She looked daggers at him, and I knew she was telling the truth.

"I was just trying to play, that's all. I didn't mean to upset you, Carla." Eddie finally found his voice.

"I don't think that's how you play with a thirteen-year-old, Eddie," my mother said quietly.

He said he was sorry, and everyone tried to push the incident aside. I told Eddie I wanted to see him in the bedroom and turned away, hating that my family had witnessed it, knowing they would surely feel sorry for me, his new bride.

I don't need their pity!

I was silent as he followed me, but once the door was shut I confronted him. I unleashed the anger on him in full force. "How dare you touch her like that? Why did you do it Eddie? Why?" I demanded.

He wouldn't look at me, though, instead running his fingers through his hair, as if he was as distressed as I was. "I don't know, Daleen. I told you, I was just trying to have fun with her. I didn't mean anything by it. Besides, she's always going around teasing me. You didn't know that, did you?"

That silenced me for a minute, but then I decided it didn't matter, even if there was any truth in it, because he was twenty-two and she was only thirteen.

Just like me. Just like me.

Somehow I forced the thought from my mind.

Besides, he was married and had no right to touch another woman like that, especially one who was underage. All of a sudden, all my energy ebbed away. I was exhausted and when I spoke my voice was strangely flat. "I don't believe you Eddie. From what Carla says, this isn't the first time. Is that right?"

I waited for his answer, but he tried to skirt the issue, saying she must not have minded it. I realized he wanted to convince me it was Carla's fault for flirting with him. "She just has to run around wearing those skin-tight blue jeans," Eddie continued, trying to pin the blame on her.

Too tired to argue, I laid down on the bed. Eddie curled up beside me and tried to comfort me, but I ignored him, refusing to listen. I was deaf to his words, and kept reliving the entire scene, over and over, in my head. I could see him touching her, see her try to tell him in a way that no one would notice, and then, when he didn't stop, see her turn on him, screaming and swearing. It hurt terribly, to think my husband of only one month would do that to me—and my little sister.

It also hurt because I knew it was true. I knew it because that's exactly what he had done to me. And that's exactly what I had tried to do—keep the secret, keep silent, be the good little girl and not get him into trouble.

Thank God Carla had the sense to speak up, to break the silence.

Eddie kept pleading with me to listen. "I'm sorry, Daleen. I really am. I didn't mean to hurt you, really. I thought—I don't know what I thought. Please forgive me. I love you so much!" He whispered against my ear, stroking my hair back from my face. I kept my back to him and when he began to run his hand over my stomach, I smacked it away.

"Don't dare touch me! I don't want you to touch me, do you understand?" I was still furious, but at the same time, I could feel his body against mine, and smell the clean scent of him. I desperately wanted to believe him. But I couldn't. It just wasn't possible.

Not now. Maybe not ever again.

"Daleen, I won't let you go. I won't. I don't care if you won't make love to me, I'll just lay right here beside you, all night, and hold you." His voice was that of a little child whining in anguish, trying to get what he wanted. But I was beyond caring, and buried my face in the pillow, trying to forget everything I had just seen and heard.

The next morning, it was like the night before hadn't even happened. Everyone except Carla smiled and laughed when we parted company—she was nowhere to be seen. I knew Mom and the kids would spend the rest of the weekend there, while Eddie and I headed to our honeymoon.

They all wore masks. I saw their blank faces, devoid of any emotion from the previous night, and I wanted to shake them and scream: "This isn't normal. You know it's not normal. Why are you ignoring it like it's nothing?"

But I wouldn't. I couldn't. That would be unacceptable, and it would mortify both my mother and my uncle.

A polite young lady doesn't do things like that. I could just hear my mom's response.

So instead, I waved goodbye as we pulled away and began the four-hour drive. I don't know how I managed to keep up a conversation, since I was still in shock over Carla's outburst.

In the end, I think I just filed it away with all the other things that had happened which I couldn't or wouldn't face— questions for which I had no answers—afraid of what they would really mean, should I peer too close. Instead, I was subdued. Eddie tried to make me laugh, putting his arm around me, and by the time we arrived at Virginia Beach, I had mellowed a little. I was still uncertain of him—and myself—since

I didn't know how I really felt. I wanted to believe if I loved him more, he would quit acting like that with my sister.

And Vonna, the voice inside my head reminded me.

The tiny cottage had a kitchenette barely big enough for two people. We went to buy groceries and when we returned, I put everything away while Eddie made the bed. After dinner, we climbed into it. As we made love, Eddie told me how much he loved me. I told myself I would make him so happy he would never want anyone else again. I knew I could do it and as I clung to him tightly, I was determined to make my marriage work, and to never let him go.

The next morning we went sightseeing, before returning to the cottage for lunch. "We'll have to try both beds out before we go home." Eddie was grinning, but I caught the hidden meaning behind his words as he slipped his arms around me. "What do you think?"

I just smiled. But I was really wondering how long his unquenchable desire for sex could last.

Surely after a few months, sex will grow old, I thought.

We walked down to the beach, and I felt self-conscious in my swimsuit. It was a one-piece, and hid the pregnancy well, but I still knew I wasn't as slender as usual. My swollen belly had left me with misgivings about my body. It served to accentuate my crime, and was something I was starting to struggle with.

As we spread out our blanket on the sand, I wondered if I would ever look as good as the other women who were stretched out sunbathing all around us. I hoped so, because I couldn't stand being fat. More important, I knew Eddie wouldn't like it.

Holding hands, we entered the water and began romping around in the waves. We played for hours, splashing each other and swimming and collecting shells, before returning to the blanket. The sun was directly overhead, burning into our skin, but the ocean breeze kept us from noticing. Eddie just sat there, so I tugged on his arm, asking him to lie down beside me. He said he wanted to watch the water, so I closed my eyes and felt the delicious warmth of the sun melt into me.

I don't know what it was that finally caused me to glance up, but that's when I saw him staring at some girl in a tiny bikini. She walked in front of our blanket, as I watched his eyes follow her hungrily.

I was afraid he would catch me, and quickly closed my eyes. I felt weird, like I was looking into someone else's window while they undressed. Now and again Eddie would rub lotion on my back, making polite conversation, but I sensed his mind was elsewhere. So every so often, I peeked up at him. He was either gawking at a girl whose figure looked like an hourglass, or practically leering at another whose bathing suit resembled strings of spaghetti.

"What're you doing?" My calmness belied the seething feeling beneath my skin.

"Oh, just watching some kids play, that's all." He quickly turned his gaze from a woman who was laying with her bikini top unfastened, to some children who were busy building a sand castle.

You're lying. I wanted to say it, but couldn't. So I began to sulk, refusing to talk except for one-word answers, when no answer would have been rude. I couldn't do that.

Eddie quickly realized I was upset. He turned to me, asking what was wrong.

"I just don't understand why you have to look at every woman on the beach and then deny doing it," I said angrily.

He looked at me like I was crazy. "I wasn't! I was just watching those kids over there." He pointed in their direction.

"What makes you think I was watching the women? You know, I have my own woman to watch." His voice was silky smooth.

I was fed up. It was bad enough to do it: but to do it and then lie about it? "Look Eddie, I've been watching you. Every time you get quiet, I look up and see you staring at some gorgeous blond with a big bust."

For an instant, he looked guilty. Then he smiled. "All right, so I like women with big chests. I admit it. But I have not been staring at every woman here. Why should I, when I can stare at you?" His dark brown eyes bored into my own, and he sounded sincere. I stared at him.

Maybe I was mistaken, I thought.

Deep inside though, I knew I hadn't imagined it. At the same time, I wanted to believe him. I thought he loved me, so why would he need to look at other women? I finally convinced myself I had been mistaken, that Eddie hadn't really been staring like I thought. But by then the day was spoiled.

"If you can't trust me, let's just go." I knew Eddie was cross with me, and it made me feel guilty for not trusting him—for spoiling our day together at the beach.

We spent the rest of our honeymoon lounging around, seeing the sights and relaxing on the seashore. Our nights were filled with passionate sex and once, Eddie even asked me if I would go skinny dipping in the ocean.

"No, I don't think so." I was busy cooking at the stove.

"But it'll be fun. Wouldn't you like to swim naked in the ocean?" He pleaded.

I shook my head. "I don't want to go skinny dipping. That's just not me. You know that." But I was terrified someone would find us—see us—and know what we were doing. Just the thought of anyone seeing me naked made me feel guilty, like I was doing something bad. I couldn't do it.

Two days later, we made the long drive home. It was dark when we pulled into the driveway many hours later and Eddie began packing his lunch for work the next day. I went to bed, utterly exhausted, full of questions and doubts.

CHAPTER EIGHT

But my doubts never lasted long because at other times Eddie was the perfect husband. He worked at a coal mine where they had rotating shifts, so one week he would be on days, the next he would be on afternoons. During day shift, I got up early to fix him breakfast. But if I was too ill, he would kiss me tenderly as he got up.

"You stay in bed. I'll fix it," he said.

"Remember to kiss me goodbye before you leave." I was already falling back to sleep.

Whenever I did get up to cook his breakfast, I was usually half asleep and Eddie would kiss me as he went out the door, gently pushing me back toward the bedroom. "Go back to bed."

This was the Eddie I knew and loved, the man who took such good care of me.

But then the long hours at work took their toll. I tried waiting up for Eddie so I could see him, but after realizing he was pulling yet another overtime shift, I went to bed. I was sound asleep, until a loud commotion outside woke me. It took me a few minutes to realize the noise was men's voices. I lay there quietly for a few more minutes. I thought Eddie's truck must have broken down, since he had been having some problems with the carburetor.

After what seemed like hours, the front door opened and I heard Eddie's metal dinner pail and Thermos crash to the floor. Either he was angry, or something was wrong. I was out of bed then, quickly crossing the room to meet Eddie in the hallway.

"Hey there. What's going on?" I followed him into the bathroom. "Did your truck break down again?"

"No, my truck didn't break down again. I wrecked it. I had to have it towed it home." His voice was tired but hostile, and directed at me.

"Are you all right? You didn't get hurt, did you?" I was suddenly frightened.

He stood at the sink wetting a washcloth, and as I looked at him closely, I saw a streak of blood on his forehead. My hand flew to my mouth. "Eddie!"

"I hit my head. Can you find the cut and tell me how big it is?"

I quickly found a large, wet spot on his head, matted with blood. "Eddie, you need a doctor!"

With trembling fingers I parted his hair, until I could see the large gash better. It looked deep, and I was afraid he could have a head injury. "How bad is it?" His voice was grumpy. "I'm not going to a doctor, at least not tonight, anyway."

"It looks like it went deeper than it should have, and yes, you are going to the doctor. I'll drive you there. You need stitches."

But his refusal was adamant. "Maybe in the morning. Not now. Just clean it up, will you, and then bandage it for me." I stared at my husband's reflection in the mirror. He was still covered with black soot, and only the whites of his eyes showed against the darkness of his skin.

I pursed my lips together tightly, knowing it would be fruitless to argue. I carefully washed the cut, afraid of hurting him. I wished he would go to the doctor. I thought it might be dangerous to wait until the morning, but I knew he wouldn't change his mind. Instead, I prayed he would be all right.

"What happened, Eddie?" I had been so concerned about his injury I forgot to ask about the accident.

"I fell asleep and ran into a telephone pole and some guy's garage." He told me how he began dozing off, only to wake up enough to continue driving. The next thing he knew, he heard a terrible noise, and then was tossed around the truck cab. When he came to, a man was leaning over him, trying to talk to him. Eddie said he told the man not to call an ambulance. When he got out, he realized he had sheared off a telephone pole just before the truck had plowed through a garage, less than five miles from home.

"Do you realize how fortunate you are? You could have been killed. I'm so glad you're all right." I gave him a hug and clung to Eddie, afraid if I let go, it would actually turn out to be worse than it was. "Please, please, stop working so much overtime. You're killing yourself. Tonight is proof enough of that. What good is all the money in the world if you're not alive to enjoy it?" I looked into his eyes, pleading with him, hoping the pain and worry in my own eyes would convince him. He looked awful, and any adrenalin from the accident had worn off, because he was clearly exhausted.

"I just want to go to bed, Daleen. My head is killing me." Eddie moved slowly toward the bed, and as I helped him undress, I thanked God he was still alive.

The next morning came much too soon, but I called Eddie's parents, telling them about the accident and reassuring them he was all right. Mrs. Leigh was upset, though, because I hadn't called her sooner. I told her it wouldn't have done any good, and would have only gotten them out of bed.

"Besides, Eddie wouldn't go to the doctor, because he said it's just a cut."

"I'll be right up to see him," Mrs. Leigh said.

Within a few minutes she was there, and after seeing

the gash, she grew agitated, telling Eddie he better go to the doctor. He finally gave in, saying he would go—just to make her happy. I drove him there but after an exam, the doctor said the cut wasn't as bad as it looked, and just bandaged it up.

Eddie didn't seem to suffer any side effects of his head injury, but after that things just snowballed out of control. I was defrosting the fridge one day when I heard someone screaming. Rushing toward the front door, I saw my next-door neighbor. "Daleen, get out! Your trailer's on fire!" Ruby screamed.

I froze. It took a fraction of a second for her words to sink in. Finally able to move, I ran outside and looked in the direction she was pointing. "Down there. Look!" she yelled.

I saw them then: bright yellow and red flames crawling out from under the back of the trailer. "Oh no!" I cried. "Call the fire department, quick!"

"I already called! They're on their way," Ruby said.

"They'll never make it!" I knew the fire department was only a few miles away, but it was also staffed with volunteers who had nine-to-five jobs and families to feed. "It'll burn down before they arrive!" I ran toward the trailer then, knowing it would be fully engulfed any second.

All our belongings—childhood mementos, wedding gifts, Eddie's new stereo, my new sewing machine, the newly purchased drapes and carpeting, and everything else that was in there—were going up in flames.

But the smoke was already building up inside, and I knew I couldn't endanger my unborn child: we could replace the material goods, but not the baby. I didn't realize I was crying until Judy yelled for me again, asking if I wanted to use her phone.

With shaking hands, I dialed Eddie's work number. "Arkwright Number 2," a voice answered.

"My husband, Eddie Leigh. Can you get a message to him? Tell him our trailer's on fire!"

Then I went outside, to stand with the crowd of gathering neighbors and the volunteer firefighters who had just arrived. I looked at the trailer, which was covered with red-hot flames. Their tendrils reached toward the surrounding trees and smoke poured out, blanketing everything it touched. I looked around and watched as our home went up in flames.

We had escaped with our lives, and I knew that was what was most important, but I still felt like I should have done something. I had let everything burn. My favorite childhood belongings were gone: old school papers, saved from first grade through graduation; the fabric I brought home from Jordan a year earlier; all kinds of books I had read or planned to read, and my journals.

I was devastated by the loss of my journals, which I'd kept since I was twelve, writing reflections about life on their pages. They contained my hopes and my dreams, and my insight into the people, places and things around me. They drew a line of the life I had lived, almost like a roadmap. Sometimes, when I meditated on something from the past, I went back and read the passage where I had poured words onto paper. Reading what I had written there helped me to sort out my thoughts and put everything in perspective. It wasn't a loss to anyone else, and of no monetary value, but those written words were part of me. They helped me understand myself. As I stood there watching them burn, I wondered how I would ever make sense of my world without them.

We moved in with Eddie's parents after the fire, so we were in his old bedroom when I went into labor in early December. For the last few months, the baby had been determined to let me know it was there. It would begin to move around, kicking me in the ribs and causing mini camel humps all over my balloon belly.

At Lamaze classes, I felt self-conscious because I knew several other couples from high school. One girl had gotten pregnant during the school year, and got married about the same time I did. The first time I saw her, I felt vaguely uncomfortable. It was impossible for me to keep my due date a secret, since they were all posted on a blackboard. I was horrified when I realized she would know I had gotten pregnant before I was married. I was ashamed about my secret relationship with Eddie, and for getting pregnant. I was afraid she would think I was a slut. Somehow I forced myself to remain cool, as if getting pregnant was something every sixteen-year-old girl did.

Eddie had gotten off work just a few hours before I went into labor, and we were in bed making love. I had begun having back pain during intercourse, and often just the act itself was enough to make me wish we could forego sex. If I experienced pain, I usually grew tense and Eddie, sensing the change, would ask if I was all right. When I confessed how painful it was, he said we could stop if I needed to. But he made no effort to do so, so I just gritted my teeth and went through with it.

So that night was the same as the others: he was soon satisfied and sound asleep. I looked at him, torn between love and loathing, but not knowing why. I rolled over so I could be alone with my thoughts.

But later that night, the pain became unbearable. Intense pressure in my lower back woke me up. It hurt so much I couldn't lay still, so I got out of bed to make some hot tea. The cramps started right away, but I thought it was false labor.

The baby isn't even due for another month, I thought.

But instead of decreasing, as I knew false contractions should, the pain increased until I could no longer stand it.

Clutching my stomach, I kneeled over Eddie, trying to wake him up. "Eddie, I think I'm in labor." I was nearly in tears.

"But you're not due for another month," he protested sleepily.

"I know, but I think the baby's coming," I moaned.

He bolted upright in bed. "Do you think? I mean, could I have done it, when we made love?

I shrugged, but said nothing. Deep down, I thought the lovemaking was a factor. "I can't think about that right now," I snapped.

Or about him. The baby within me needs all my attention.

It took almost an hour to reach the hospital, and I kept thinking about the baby.

If it's premature, will it be all right? Will they have to put it in an incubator? What if it isn't developed completely? What will its chances of survival be? Oh please, dear God, let it be all right.

"It's a girl! You've got a beautiful baby girl, folks." My obstetrician held her up for me to see, after many hours of hard labor.

I took the tiny baby girl the nurse handed to me, marveling at how beautiful she was, and held her against me. A thousand emotions swept through me, from amazement to ferociousness, as she lay there nursing from my breast. When she fell asleep her tiny arms were crossed in front of her, and her little legs were pulled up next to her stomach. I rubbed her head, which had the softest blond fuzz on it. Not much, but enough to know it was there. The baby we later named Mileah looked like she would fit into a breadbox. I loved her the minute I saw her.

Over the course of the next two days, a few high school friends stopped by. Their response was the same: "I didn't know you were pregnant!" "I didn't know you were married." "Why didn't you tell me?"

Carla had broken the news for me, calling them after Mileah was born, because I couldn't bear to tell anyone. The shame was still too strong. I didn't want them to know I was a hypocrite, pretending to be a "good" girl, while secretly doing bad things.

When the questions came, I donned my brightest smile and pretended like nothing was wrong. "She's premature." I tried to be vague about how many weeks early Mileah had arrived. If their math was good, they could have figured it out, but if not then maybe—just maybe—they wouldn't.

But some questions were more difficult than others. "I didn't think you were going to have any kids," or, "I thought you were going away to study music."

I found myself torn between guilt and a strong maternal desire to show my beautiful newborn to the world. I let them think I had changed my mind about a lot of things in life, including the decision to get married and have children. If they went away confused about my answers, they were no more confused than I was.

I only knew I had accepted what life had given me. No, I didn't want children, at least not for several years, after I had accomplished some things in life I wanted for myself. And yes, I was going to study music, but my father's drinking made sure that didn't happen. Besides, my life course had been mapped out from age thirteen: I was going to marry the only man I had slept with, for that's what good girls did. I couldn't do anything else.

That was something my friends would never know.

When Mileah was two-months-old, I became so sick I could barely get out of bed. My head and stomach hurt, my throat was raw and swollen, and I had a fever when I awoke to the sound of angry voices coming from the living room. I heard a man's voice, and what sounded like a woman screaming. I staggered into the living room and saw Eddie leaning forward on the edge of his chair. No one noticed me, as I watched the scene on television, where the bad guy was getting ready to rape a woman. My stomach began turning somersaults.

"Eddie." He didn't hear me. "Eddie?" Entranced by the drama, he was oblivious to anything else.

"Eddie." I called once more and he came over and put his arm around me.

"What are you doing up? You should be sleeping."

As he helped me back to bed, I looked at him. "Do you think that's something you should watch?"

"You know how those shows are." He tried to brush it off, making me feel even worse.

I tried to block out the sounds coming from the TV by covering my head with the blankets, but I still heard enough to know that when it was over, the bad guy had actually succeeded. When Eddie came to me, I feigned sleep. I didn't want him near me.

Within a week, we began house-hunting. I wanted to have a say in what went on in our home, which wasn't possible while living with Eddie's parents. Eventually we found a small garage apartment just across from my old high school. After some fresh paint and wallpaper, it looked nothing like the dingy old apartment it once was. The ivory wallpaper had a flocked design that complimented the plush hunter green carpet. Simple white sheers hung over the window blinds, and the entire effect was peaceful and soothing. Just a week or two there and we settled into our new routine. Eddie slept late in the mornings, while I got up and did housework. When he woke up we loaded Mileah into the car and ran errands, or stayed home together. Mostly, Eddie worked on his truck, adding a new stereo or putting on bigger tires. I often teased him, saying he loved it more than he did me.

After he left for work, I played with Mileah and puttered around the apartment. I loved to clean and organize, or spend my time baking and planning our weekly dinner menus. Since Eddie didn't get home until after midnight, I went to bed alone during the week. I had long ago learned to dread the nighttime, and was often anxious about Mileah's safety. I worried someone would break in and rape or murder me, and take her. Our bedroom was just big enough to squeeze in the crib. Having Mileah there made me feel better, since I was close enough to protect her. But I still tried to stay awake until Eddie came home.

He had changed jobs, supposedly to cut back his hours, but before long he began working later and later. I was growing more tired than usual, trying to care for a newborn and a household. Eventually, I was so tired I started to doze off waiting for Eddie, while reading in the rocking chair, or sewing at the kitchen table. I had to swallow my fear just to get a decent night's sleep. If he wasn't home by midnight, I turned in, so exhausted I fell asleep right away.

Then came the beginning of a succession of nights that felt like a recurring nightmare. As if in a dream Eddie came to me, kissing me down there. It took me awhile to wake up and realize what was happening, and I begged him to stop. He did, but only after he was finished. By then I had kicked like a wild animal, to try to get away from him. I quickly learned it was fruitless, because I was no match for Eddie's size and strength. Besides, that tactic seemed to only heighten his pleasure as he grabbed my legs and held me so I had no chance of escape. Like I had for so many years, I just laid there and hated myself for being such a traitor and giving in to him.

Then he slid up and over me, pinning me beneath him as I asked in a voice devoid of all emotion if he would please let me get my diaphragm. I didn't want to get pregnant. Most of the time he said nothing, or he said "no," and I began to struggle against him. It was no good, and any fight on my part only fed his hunger. I simply learned to accept the fact that he was going to do what he wanted anyway.

One hot night when he was finished, I stumbled to the bathroom. When I turned on the light, a stranger stared back at me. I peered dumbly at the marks on the woman there. Bruises covered her neck and breasts and her arms were red and splotchy from where he had held her down. Her lips were puffy and there was an ugly mark on her shoulder.

You are so ugly. I hate you! I thought.

Her neck looked terrible. It reminded me of the girls from school, the ones everyone knew by reputation. They would come to school every Monday with those dark, telltale rings on their necks. Sucker bites, they called them.

I hate sucker bites.

I ran cold water on a washcloth and wet my swollen face, averting my eyes so I couldn't see the mirror. My entire body felt bruised and battered.

Why? Why won't he listen to me?

I ran the hottest water I could in the bathtub, hoping it would wash away the filth. Then I scrubbed and scrubbed until my skin was almost raw. An hour later, I painfully and slowly climbed out of the tub and put on a clean nightgown, leaving the room bathed in darkness as I returned to bed.

To him.

I turned toward the wall and moved to the very edge of the bed, as far away from him as I could get without falling out. I needn't have worried. As usual, once his greedy passion was satisfied, he was already fast asleep.

My last waking thoughts were of my baby. Since Mileah was only seven-months-old, I knew if I got pregnant, she wouldn't even be two when that baby came. I didn't want that. I desperately wanted to give Mileah all of my love.

The next morning I awoke to bright sunshine pouring into the room, but I was greeted with the memory of a horrible nightmare. Eddie was still asleep, his back to me. I felt sore all over. I knew then it hadn't been a dream. What had happened had been as real as the new day before me.

Oh God, please don't let me get pregnant.

I thought about my life, and what was happening within my marriage. I knew I didn't want another baby in the near future, if ever. I still couldn't face the fact we had some serious problems, but somewhere in my subconscious something told me that bringing another child into our family would be a serious mistake. Besides, Mileah needed all of my time and attention, something I repeatedly tried to tell Eddie. It was useless. He pretended to agree and to respect my feelings. Then he would just do the same thing. Again and again. It had become a cycle.

That morning, I grew distant and silent, and was barely able to make myself talk to him. Sensing my unspoken anger he did his best to appease me all week, trying to humor me with pretty words and expensive trinkets.

But as that week and those after it passed, if anything, Eddie's bedroom behavior grew worse instead of better, and if I didn't insert my diaphragm before he got home, then he wouldn't let me use birth control. Sometimes during sex, he told me he would gladly get me pregnant again. I thought it must give him some sort of satisfaction, or make him feel more like a man.

Then came the day when I knew without a doubt I was pregnant. After confirming my worst suspicions with a home pregnancy test, I sat down at the kitchen table, my head in my hands, praying to God for answers.

Why won't he listen to me? It's all his fault. He won't let me use birth control, and he refuses to take responsibility for it himself.

When Eddie came home that evening, I told him I was pregnant. My words were devoid of emotion, laying like the cold steel of a knife blade between us. When he leaned close to hug me, I couldn't return his enthusiasm. By then, it was all I could do just to lay beside him in bed without acting on an intense desire to strike him.

"I guess you're not very happy about it, are you?" Eddie propped himself up on one elbow.

I gave him a stony stare. "What do you think? It's not your body. You don't have to get fat and be sick and then give birth. Babies are a lot of work and you're never here to help. You're always working overtime. Besides, Mileah's still a baby. She needs more than I can give now, and when this baby comes she'll have to share it!" I turned away, feeling repulsed by the sight of him.

You did this to me.

"Well, I guess saying 'I'm sorry' won't change things now, but if it helps any, I am sorry." He sat there, waiting to see if that did the trick.

He didn't have long to wait.

"You're sorry? You're sorry! Now's a fine time to be sorry, don't you think?" I hissed through clenched teeth. I was angrier than I had ever been in my life. "Don't you think the time to be sorry was when I asked you to let me get my diaphragm and you wouldn't let me? It's too late now." I rolled over and closed my eyes. I couldn't stand the sight of him.

I knew he was gone when I felt the mattress move as his weight shifted. What I said was mean and hateful, but I didn't care. His selfishness and carelessness had gotten me pregnant.

Just like the first time, a voice within me said.

The next few weeks were so strained Eddie and I barely spoke, and for once he didn't try to touch me after work. Sometimes he would make a bed on the floor in the living room and sleep there. I no longer cared.

I had no patience with him, because my morning sickness lasted all day long and sapped my energy. Sometimes I drove to Mom's house, just so she could help me with Mileah.

But something else was happening, something I just couldn't put my finger on. Eddie's angry outbursts were becoming more and more frequent, and he began complaining about money. We didn't have a shortage, but it was tighter than ever before, because of the cut in pay he had taken by changing jobs and going to a non-union coal mine.

I tried to tell you, but you wouldn't listen. I don't know anything, do I, so why should you listen to me? I thought it, but didn't say it.

I had long ago learned that telling him "I told you so" never produced positive results. Besides, we still had enough money to eat out a couple of times a week, and occasionally I went shopping for new clothes. We were by no means living close to poverty level, as he tried to say in the middle of one tirade.

Because he was a poor money manager, Eddie let me handle our finances. After the bills were paid each month, I put the rest aside. If I was shopping and saw something reasonably priced that I liked, I bought it. Often Eddie and I would see furniture or some other big item we wanted, and he would always decide to buy it. I told him we could afford the purchase, but it wouldn't leave us any extra to put aside for an emergency. He didn't seem to mind, though, until the day he realized there wasn't anything left for his precious truck.

That's when he hit the roof. I tried to account for the money, explaining that we had just bought an antique love seat and matching chair. I reminded him that we had also shelled out money for new appliances, because the apartment wasn't furnished when we moved in, but he wasn't listening. He kept yelling at me while I was making his lunch.

"It's all your fault. If you didn't spend so much, we would have more money and I could get that new CB radio for my truck. I don't know why you have to buy everything you see!"

"That's not fair. I always ask your permission before I buy anything that costs very much. You know that."

He shook his head, an ugly scowl on his face. "Oh yeah, go ahead, say it's all my fault. It always is, isn't it? It's never your fault, is it?"

"That's not what I meant—" But he cut me off.

"Well you listen up little girl, you aren't any better than I am. You hear me?"

I fought to stay calm. "I hate it when you call me a little girl. I know I'm only seventeen, but I am not a little girl."

"Yeah, sure. But you're not the woman you think you are, the one who's so much better than her husband." He lashed out at me sarcastically. Then he walked away. I wanted to cry, but couldn't find the tears. I looked at the mess before me. There were slices of bread with mustard on them, lunchmeat was scattered all over the countertop, and an open Thermos sat waiting for hot tea. What I did next was pure instinct.

White grains looking deceptively like sugar poured noiselessly into the container and steam rose into the air as I struggled with shaking fingers to pour the unusual tea mixture into his Thermos. I hurried, afraid he would come into the room and catch me. When I saw I was still alone, I quickly screwed on the stopper.

Suddenly I was seized by a fit of laughter, which I smothered by biting the back of my hand. But a small grin still threatened to pull up one corner of my mouth. I tried to keep a straight face as I thought of his reaction when he went to take a drink of the hot liquid later that night.

How dearly I would love to be a little bird watching from some quiet corner! I refused to allow myself to think beyond that. I couldn't, or else I would have turned coward and stopped. The grey metal lunch bucket sat silently beside the front door just as it did every day, waiting for Eddie to grab it and go to work. Every muscle in my body was tense and I prayed he wouldn't open the Thermos before he left the house.

But I needn't have worried. He paid no more attention than he usually did. It was the home-cooked lunch he complained about. I took it in stride, having long ago grown used to him saying how much better my mother cooked than I did. But when the sarcastic remarks continued as Eddie tugged on his steel-toe mining boots, I felt like I was going to explode.

I stood at the sink washing dishes and almost instinctively, the small paring knife in my soapy hands seemed to fly of its own accord across the room. The blade stuck in the door facing just a foot away from him, and he turned with a look of surprise on his face. Any anger was yet to break out—or else he was dumbfounded that his meek and mild wife had thrown a knife at him.

The minute it left my hands, I knew I shouldn't have. I couldn't even understand what made me do it. It was so out of character for me. Eddie looked at the knife and turned to me without saying a word, disbelief written all over his face. I was terrified he was going to hit me. Instead, he just laughed.

I was so ashamed of myself.

What has gotten into me?

"Just leave me alone and go to work!" I said angrily.

"My, my, aren't we testy?" Eddie taunted as his tongue came unglued.

"Yes I am, thanks to you." I retorted. Eddie stared back

at me before shaking his head as in disbelief. The knife fell to the floor as the door closed behind him and I looked at it, wishing I hadn't missed. Then I went into the bedroom and looked down at my Mileah, amazed she had slept through the noise. Stretching out on the bed, I fell into a deep, dark sleep.

Later that night when Eddie came home from the mines, he didn't bother me. I didn't even know he was there until I woke to Mileah's cries of hunger. Walking over to her crib, I picked her up and held her against me.

"There, there, Little One, Mommy's got you now. I'll feed you and you can go back to sleep." I whispered to her softly, knowing she was the one person who needed me, who loved me. My eyes had adjusted enough in the dark to make out the outline of Eddie sleeping in the bed. I wondered why he had come to bed without trying to wake me.

That's unusual.

I crawled back into the bed, hoping against hope that Mileah's whimpering wouldn't wake him. I pulled my daughter beside me, opened my gown, and let her eat. Her tiny mouth was warm and I lay there watching for a long time, until her trusting eyes slowly closed.

The next morning I awoke to find Mileah nestled up against me in the middle of the bed. Eddie was still sound asleep, and I thanked God for a night of peace. I still wasn't sure how he would react to the knife incident or the salt in his tea, but since he hadn't harassed me during the night, I felt relatively safe. Maybe proof of my newfound courage had caused him to reconsider his own behavior.

I was mixing up some cookie dough when I heard movement behind me. Turning, I saw Eddie; he gave me a curious, unsettled glance in return. Quelling the pangs of nervousness I felt, I put on a brave front. "Morning. How was work yesterday?"

"It would have been a lot better if I'd had something decent to drink." He leaned against the countertop and stared at me, and I had to fight to keep from smiling.

"Why, was something wrong with your tea?" I asked innocently.

"You know damn well there was. You put salt in it, didn't you? I drank about half of it in one gulp, before I realized something was wrong."

I couldn't help it when the corners of my mouth turned up.

"You probably think it's real funny, don't you? It wouldn't have been so bad but I was a couple of miles underground, so I didn't have anything else to drink the rest of the night," he grouched. Getting the orange juice from the fridge, he took a big swig.

"Eddie! You don't drink from the container. Get a glass."

He ignored me. "And, as if that wasn't bad enough, when I bit into my sandwich, the cheese still had the plastic wrapper on it, and the peeling hadn't been taken off the bologna." He seemed to be getting less angry as he talked, and I was no longer afraid he might start screaming.

But I was surprised to find I felt sorry for him. I felt guilty, too, because he had gone without anything to drink for more than eight hours. "I'm sorry, but you made me so mad! You had no right to talk to me like that, and then walk off without even saying you were sorry!" I said.

He leaned down and kissed my cheek. "You're right."

We looked at each other, neither of us speaking. "But I am sorry, and I do love you. I don't mean to give you a hard time about the money; I know you're doing the best you can."

"I love you, too." The whisper was barely spoken before he reached over and pulled me to him, pressing me against the warmth of his flannel shirt.

"I'm sorry, Eddie." I looked at him, hoping he believed me. We kissed then, a kiss that spoke of heartaches and mistakes, and a desire to make things better.

For a short time, I imagined a miracle had occurred, thanks in part to my small act of defiance. It felt like our home was becoming a place of peace, and Eddie even bought me a white gold necklace. It was a small rose-shaped pendant, with a diamond in the middle. He said he hoped it helped me to forgive him.

And it did.

I was seven months pregnant when we found an old two-story house just a mile from my childhood home. It was big and needed a lot of work, but only cost $16,000. I fell in love with it, but Eddie was less enthusiastic. I could see all of its possibilities; he could only see all the work. Finally, he agreed we could do the work ourselves. By the time we finished remodeling, he said it would still be a bargain. So in late March, we moved in. One month later, the coal industry took a nosedive and Eddie came home with a pink slip.

I spent the better part of April cleaning and sprucing up the place, since it had been vacant and had layers of dirt and grime everywhere. Instead of moving into one of the upstairs bedrooms, we turned the dining room into a bedroom so I wouldn't have to climb the stairs after the baby arrived. I had found a midwife, and we were going to have a home birth. I wouldn't even have to leave the house.

At times like those Eddie seemed like a good husband, one who thought about the needs of his increasingly pregnant wife. That was when I questioned my own nagging doubts about his angry outbursts and controlling behavior. During early April, we worked together hanging drywall, painting and papering the walls, and plumbing the bathroom. We got along fine, even though he was a hard taskmaster. I think he pushed himself so he wouldn't have to think about being out of work; I pushed myself, too, driven by the desire to get everything done before I went into labor.

Eddie said he was glad to have some time off, but after three weeks, it took its toll and stress soon became my constant companion. While being together all day every day had at first seemed a good thing, we were running out of patience with each other. We depleted our savings and our finances grew tight, since unemployment compensation was one-fourth of Eddie's regular wages. The previous summer we had bought a top-of-the-line Toyota station wagon, which was as much as our monthly mortgage payment. I thought the car was more than we needed or could afford at the time, but Eddie insisted we had to have it.

Trista was born in early 1982, entering the world after a long and strenuous labor. I was frightened because she wouldn't cry at first, but soon she began yelling and my midwife said she had good lungs. I gathered the small bundle up and held her tightly against me. Trista had dark hair and petite features and I thought she was perfect. Just as I had with Mileah, I fell in love with her the moment I saw her.

It wasn't long before my joy turned to fear, though. It happened about the same time Eddie realized the layoff was going to last longer than predicted, making the tension between us even thicker.

That's when I saw myself picking Trista up, and simply letting her fall out the window. I had that same sensation with Mileah, but only once. After Trista was born, though, I found myself staring out the window, caught up in the reverie before I even knew what I was doing. All it would take was a few short steps from the bed to the window. It took a huge amount of willpower just to pull my mind's eye away from what I was seeing, but it felt so real—as if I was really going to do it—that I forced myself to walk as far away from the windows as I could, whenever Trista was in my arms. I couldn't even bear to stand nearby and try to look outside, for fear I would act on what I was sure was an evil impulse that lived somewhere deep within me.

As if that wasn't enough, the chaos, as well as caring for two small children, left me too tired for sex. But I would often wake up in the middle of the night to find Eddie fondling me. Asking him to stop never worked: He simply continued doing whatever he wanted until he had used my body to reach a climax. The times when Trista was in the bed with us were the most unbearable. She would fall asleep while nursing and then he would want to have sex.

"Not with the baby here. We can make love in the morning, before she wakes up," I said, praying my logic would make a difference. It never did. "Just let me put her back in her crib first," I pleaded. Unhearing and uncaring, he selfishly went ahead, while I lie as still as possible so my baby wouldn't wake up.

The daytime stress was different. I told Eddie we would be better off selling the station wagon and buying a used one, so our monthly payments wouldn't be so high. But he stubbornly refused to let it go back to the bank or to sell it and buy something more affordable. I finally applied for food stamps since there wasn't enough money at the end of his unemployment check. Because I refused to lie and told the social worker we had a plush new car, our food stamp application was denied.

We had no choice but to join our friends and neighbors, and the many other mining families who stood in line at the local senior center to get cheese, rice, and other commodities. Using the little cookbook pamphlet that came with the free food, I became quite adept at making meals that cost next to nothing.

But then October arrived—and with it another conception. I knew I was pregnant when I began throwing up in the mornings. No sooner had I gotten out of bed, than a wave of nausea would attack me.

Just like when I got pregnant with Mileah and Trista.

I couldn't bear the thought of another baby. Trista was only six-months-old, and Mileah wasn't quite two. I was exhausted from the demands of motherhood. That's why, a few mornings later, I sat down on the cold bathroom floor and asked God to let me die.

CHAPTER NINE

Sitting on the cold bathroom floor I realized something: I wasn't yet twenty, and wouldn't be for another year, but I was going to have a third baby.

My God, I'm still a teenager and I already have two children, I thought. *But I feel many, many years older.*

In that moment I hated my life. Most of all, I hated Eddie for not putting a leash on his passion. I wondered if I was doomed to spend the rest of my life barefoot and pregnant.

I told Eddie I was pregnant with the same lack of emotion and excitement I had with Trista. It seemed to make him happy and his attitude improved, reminding me that, in a weird way, it helped Eddie's ego to be able to say he had gotten me pregnant. After all, he didn't have a job and evidently couldn't get one. But here: this was proof that he was a real man, or so he seemed to think.

I worked hard to not let my resentment show, keeping my feelings to myself. I had already learned the more I said, the less good it did. Besides, he never understood, anyway. I tried to make it easier, by staying away from the house. When I returned from visiting Mom or my friends, I knew I would have to deal with his anger, but I didn't care. It was the only way I could keep from going insane.

Within a month, I began selling cosmetics, scheduling

appointments for facials in women's homes. It forced me to be outgoing, as I taught them how to care for their skin and apply make-up. I quickly excelled, holding several appointments a week. Eddie's initial response had been hesitant. But because we were desperate for any extra money to help pay our bills, he accepted it. I knew he also felt guilty because I had to work. That was something he had promised would never happen.

But after Eddie learned it meant he would be left caring for our two young daughters, he grew resentful. I would be almost out the door when his verbal attack began. "When you come home, the house is going to look the same as when you left, because I ain't gonna do your work. I've got stuff of my own to do, so you may as well know that ahead of time," he snarled.

Another time while we were eating dinner, he complained again. "At least you get to leave the house. I can't do anything other than watch TV with the kids, while you run around."

I sighed and put down my fork, rested my elbows on the table, and laced my fingers together. His attitude was interfering with my digestion. "Fine, then, would you please just take care of the girls? Make sure their diapers are changed and they're bathed before bedtime?" He said he would, but countless times I arrived home to find them sound asleep, filthy from playing, with dried food on their faces. I would just stand there and want to cry. How could he not bathe our babies and let them go to bed looking like little urchins?

The confrontation that followed was never pretty.

"What did you do tonight, Eddie?" We were in the kitchen and I tried to keep my tone neutral, so he couldn't read any criticism into my question.

"While you were gone, having fun, I was here taking care of everything. We watched TV and then the girls went to bed," he shrugged.

I continued speaking in a low, calm tone. "Did you read them a bedtime story?"

"Yes, Your Highness," he said. "I did just as you asked. I didn't get to the dinner dishes, though. I'll do them tomorrow."

That was what he always said, but rarely did, so resigned, I went to the kitchen and started them myself. By the time I was finished, I had made up my mind that I couldn't leave the house a disaster, so I did housework until one or two in the morning. Eddie had gone to bed hours earlier, angry that I wouldn't join him. If he did wake up when I crawled into bed, exhausted from a day that began eighteen hours earlier, he insisted on his marital due. Depending on how I felt at the time, I would either try to reason with him, asking if he would just let me get a few hours sleep first, or I would be compliant and do nothing. I had long ago learned that, either way, it was "damned if you do, damned if you don't." He always got what he wanted in the bedroom—even if he had to take it.

My prayers were answered the day Eddie returned to work, and I knew I could have some solitude without fearing his next outburst. It also gave me a chance to devote more time and attention to Mileah and Trista.

I held them and felt a deep sense of frustration and despair, knowing they were the ones who would suffer because of the unborn child I was carrying. Just as I had less time to give Mileah after Trista was born, so it would be once this baby was born—only more so. It was so unfair, and I hated it. At times I think I even hated their father. Then I reminded myself I shouldn't hate him—just his selfishness. After all, wasn't a woman supposed to love and respect her husband? Those were the Bible values I had been raised with, and I didn't want to break God's laws.

It was hard, though. Part of my time was spent trying to patiently reason with Eddie, helping him see that when I was too tired to have sex, I wasn't rejecting him. Other times I ignored him and tried not to think about it. Then I was cold and distant, because I couldn't trust myself to say anything. I locked myself away in a shell, refusing to let him penetrate it.

One late night after the girls were asleep, we were sitting at the kitchen table together, eating a piece of my blackberry cobbler. Eddie was telling me how another miner almost got killed on the previous shift. "That mine certainly has its share of accidents, doesn't it?" I asked.

"It's nothing but a dog hole." He shook his head. "Most of them are though, anymore."

I looked down at my bowl. "Well, at least you don't have to worry about running across any porn there." I looked directly at him.

Okay Eddie, now you say, 'That's right, Daleen, there's no pornography at this mine,' I thought.

Instead, he said nothing. I waited, but Eddie continued eating his cobbler.

"I think this is probably the worst place I've worked, as far as safety violations go. I tell you, we're lucky someone hasn't gotten killed yet." Eddie was so anxious to ignore my comment, I knew my suspicions were correct.

That mine has porn, too. No wonder Eddie had been in such a foul mood lately, and prone to not coming home when he was supposed to.

As in the past, whenever Eddie started acting out sexually, he would harass me first and when he grew tired of that, he would become distant. It was as if he knew what he was doing was wrong, that it was only going to create more problems for our family. And by doing those things, because they interfered with our relationship, he felt more guilty—and angry. I knew it answered several recent questions about his behavior. But I wasn't going to jeopardize his good mood.

"Why don't they do something about it? I thought the inspectors came and fined them for things like that," I asked.

"They do, but only if they find out first. If, say, an inspector gets delayed at the face, and the men inside have advance warning he's coming in, they can hide some of the violations before he ever makes it inside the mine."

"Well, it's always the same old story, isn't it? Coal first, safety second." I took a sip of my milk. Without any conscious thought, the next words out of my mouth flowed freely of their own accord. "They don't, do they?"

"Don't what?"

"Don't have *Playboy* or *Penthouse* laying around? You didn't say anything earlier when I mentioned it." I looked right at him, and his expression told me he was lying.

"Well, I don't know. I'm always too busy running my butt off to notice."

Uh huh, I'll bet you are.

He was trying to sidetrack my question. "Eddie, I only mentioned the pornography because I know it's a problem for you, because when it's a problem for you, it's a problem for us."

"Well, since we haven't had sex for about a month now, that should tell you it's not a problem, shouldn't it?" His words dripped with sarcasm.

"That's only because you want me to do things I don't feel comfortable doing. Plus, I'm pregnant and working, too. Besides, that's not the point—pornography is. Do you still read it?"

"Why do you continually badger me about this? Didn't I tell you they don't have any of that garbage at the mines?" he fumed.

"No, you didn't. You merely said you were so busy you wouldn't notice if they did." I looked directly into his eyes. "So, do they?"

"Yes! Are you happy now? Yes they do!" he screamed.

I refused to back down. He could give me a straight answer, because I deserved that much.

After several minutes of silence I gathered enough courage to ask my next question. "And do you read it?"

"I haven't read any for awhile now. There, does that satisfy you?"

I was silent. To Eddie, that might mean a week or a year, and I would never know. But I was finished pressing the issue, and exhausted from the mind game we had just played.

During those early years I had several friends—but none close enough to confide in. Mom was my closest friend. By thirty-seven, she still had four children at home between the ages of fifteen and two. But I never told her what was happening inside my home, especially anything sexual. I knew she'd be mortified if I even tried. Wanting to protect her, I couldn't let her know how hard it was to live with someone whose moods changed like the wind. Besides, she adored her son-in-law. Continuing the pattern he began years earlier, Eddie still went out of his way to cut her firewood, haul her coal and do household repairs.

I only talked to God. And he kept me going, so I could get up each morning and care for my children, my house, my job and my husband. Eddie was last on the list because I was the only person who could or would take time to care for the other three. There was no choice, and Eddie contributed to that by not caring whether I became pregnant, by refusing to help with either the children or the housework, and by spending most of his time at work. I put the household chores first because someone had to do them; my family's physical health depended upon it. And my daughters came first because I was all they had, and it was my responsibility to care for their emotional, mental and spiritual health. They had no one else.

Unfortunately, Eddie's return to the mines didn't last more than a few months, until the day he came home with another pink slip. His employment cycles seemed to coincide with my pregnancies, making the rollercoaster ride we were already on even bumpier. As time slipped by, and with it, any chances of available employment, he became more and more depressed. Little by little, Eddie's depression began reaching out to those around him. Especially me—I just didn't know it yet.

Gabriella was born in the middle of a hot, humid summer in 1983. She came into the world wrapped in the same burst of energy and excitement that would mark her own, exuberant personality. From the minute she was born, "Gabby" was different. She wasn't quiet and content like her sisters; she was loud and vocal and let everyone know she was there.

The day after her birth I was lying in bed sorting through my clients' cosmetic files, when my manager called. "Daleen, you're crazy, do you know that? Don't you think you should be resting?"

"I feel great. Besides, I need to figure out how to reschedule the appointments I had for this week. I hope you don't mind, but I think I'll wait a couple of weeks before I get back into the swing of things."

She laughed so loud I had to hold the receiver away from my ear. I knew that would tickle her. "Only a couple of weeks? Don't worry about the appointments you already booked; I'll see that someone takes them for you. You just get some rest and take care of that little angel. I want to see her the first chance I get, so don't forget to let me know when you're up for visitors."

We hung up and I finished jotting notes on the remaining files, before laying everything aside and closing my eyes.

I should just let everything go until I actually feel like doing it—after I've spent lots of time with Gabby. Why can't I? I wondered. *Why am I so driven? Why does my every minute have to be filled?*

I couldn't see that I was frantically searching for anything that would keep me so preoccupied I wouldn't be able to think, or feel, anything. I had no idea it would take another seven years and countless more acts of abuse before I found my answers. If I had known then how the violence would spill over onto my children—even the newborn daughter who lay sleeping just a few feet away from me—I would have taken my babies and run into the night.

Two weeks later, I returned to work and Eddie played babysitter. Only this time, it was three children, not two. For a while, I was pleasantly surprised when I returned home and found the house neat and clean, with dinner waiting. It was a relief to sit down and just relax while I ate. But even that wasn't as pleasant as it could have been, because Eddie made subtle comments that implied he resented me working at a paying job while he was "stuck" at home caring for the girls.

I bit my tongue, knowing he felt threatened because I was earning a paycheck while he was being forced to play nanny and housekeeper. But inside, I kept wishing that he appreciated the golden opportunity he had, of being able to stay home and enjoy the time with our beautiful, intelligent daughters.

I hadn't been back to work a month when I returned home one night and found the downstairs looking like a hurricane had struck. In that minute, the tiredness that tugged at every muscle threatened to overwhelm me. I went into the kitchen, which was even worse. Dirty dishes were piled everywhere. The kids had spilled some sticky substance on the floor, and it was in a big puddle. Crumbs of food were scattered around and under the table, and there wasn't a clean spot in sight.

I cautiously yelled for Eddie. When he didn't answer, I went upstairs. My steps were heavy and I sensed my resentment building. I didn't feel like cleaning house any more than I did climbing the Empire State Building. When I reached the girls' room, I saw him stretched out at the end of the big bed they shared. I stood just inside the doorway, watching them sleep as the pale light of the moon sneaked in through the window. I tiptoed over and kissed each girl softly. They smelled so nice and clean and had their nightclothes on. At least he bathed them. That was nothing short of a miracle.

I shook Eddie's shoulder, trying to wake him. I was upset and I didn't care if he knew it. His eyes opened and I turned and went out, going into our bedroom to put on some old clothes so I could clean. He followed me and lay down on our bed, half-asleep. I slammed a dresser drawer and his eyes opened.

"Are you upset or something?"

"Not at all," I answered tersely.

"Yes you are. You're mad at me because I didn't clean the house, aren't you?"

We had had the same discussion so many times before, but I never could make him see how I felt. Why try to get it through his thick head now?

I sighed and swallowed my anger. The last thing I wanted was an argument.

"No, Eddie, I'm just tired. That's all."

"So come to bed with me. We can get up and clean the house in the morning."

"That won't work. I have an afternoon appointment and there are other things I have to get done in the morning. I'll just have to clean tonight. Just go to sleep." I started to leave, but his voice followed me.

"Yeah, yeah, all I am is a stinking babysitter. No good for anything but changing dirty diapers and taking care of kids."

I was just pasing the door to the kids' bedroom when he flew toward me in a rage and grabbed me. "I've had about enough from you! I may not have a job, but that's no reason for you to think I'm lazy. I'm not, do you understand? I'm not lazy!" His eyes were wild, and I was afraid he was going to wake up the kids.

"Let go of me!" my voice was a low hiss.

"No, you're coming downstairs with me and I'm gonna' show you what a good worker I am." He tried to pull me down the stairs and I clutched at one of the dowels in the staircase. I didn't know what had set him off, but at that moment it didn't matter. He jerked at me until I slipped on the stairs, falling as he pulled on my arm. I felt pain run through the upper length of my leg at the same time I heard the sound of my pants rip.

"Darn you, let me go! You've hurt my leg."

He let go of my arm and watched as I twisted the pant leg around, exposing a long, ragged tear. Under the tear was a pencil-thin red cut on my leg, and it was starting to burn. He saw the cut and tried to touch my leg.

"Don't you lay one finger on me," I glared at him with hatred. He looked like he might try to anyway, and the fear and anger gripped me tighter. Then he turned and slowly went down the steps.

"All right Daleen, if that's the way you want it." His voice became deadly calm, as he turned from Jekyll to Hyde in a heartbeat.

I heard the girls tossing and turning but somehow they slept right through the commotion. I sat and stared into the distance, seeing nothing. I wondered why Eddie had to get so angry.

Is it me? Do I do that to him?

He often accused me of provoking him, and sometimes I believed him, but deep down I knew I wasn't to blame. I got angry, too, but I always controlled my temper. I knew he could do the same, if he would try.

The next few days were cool and tense. I tried to tell Eddie how hard it was for me to return from work, only to find the house a disaster. Besides, I was still nursing two babies. Pleading, I tried to reason with him, telling him I needed his help. But he didn't want to hear what I had to say, and would only reply that "everything" was his fault.

"That's all right; my shoulders are broad. I can take the blame." His sarcasm wasn't lost on me, and I knew he really thought I was the problem.

He took to sleeping in the girls' bedroom, near the foot of their bed. I was torn between longing to have him near me in case I needed protection, and relief, knowing I would be free from his sexual antics. My mind wandered to some of the nights when I had been too tired to have sex, when he had insisted anyway.

That's why I already have three children. Thanks, but no thanks. That I can do without, I thought.

Despite my best intentions, the depression that had begun to creep over me like purple phlox caught and held me fast. It seemed to come and go, and many times I sat and stared out a window, letting my mind fill with peaceful nothingness. To a place without any problems, where everything was calm and tranquil and I was happy, and life was good. During those times, my relationship with Eddie was different. We were friends, not enemies, and our love was good.

But it was a happiness I could only dream of, one which lasted for brief snatches of stolen time here and there. As soon as one of the babies tugged on my shirt, or I heard the teakettle whistle, I came out of my faraway trance. Then I realized it had only been an elusive fantasy.

I didn't give up, though. I tried to be a better wife, a better mother. When the urge to complain was right on the tip of my tongue, I bit it, numerous times. If Eddie yelled at me because I forgot something, or simply for no reason at all, I calmly answered him, refusing to rise to the bait and yell in return—especially when the children were around. I wouldn't place them in a position where they saw the two most important people in their lives fight and argue. Instead, I quietly told him I would gladly discuss it later, but not in front of the children.

I had the strongest desire to keep peace for my children's sake, so they could grow up happy and healthy. Sadly, whatever I did to avoid conflict wasn't enough. Eddie didn't listen to me when I asked him not to argue in front of them anymore than he listened to me about anything else. It took years before I learned how the harsh and painful consequences of his selfishness had affected my precious offspring.

My self-imposed improvement program was strenuous, but I hoped it would make a difference. Armed with nothing but the hope that the love I thought we once had would somehow return, I developed a schedule so I could cram everything into twenty-four hours. Cooking, cleaning, caring for three babies, plus working a part-time job, had an allotted time slot. Many days I didn't go to bed until two or three in the morning, only to get up four or five hours later and begin again. Things were a little better between us, and I thought my efforts might just pay off.

It made me believe anything was possible.

Anything but not be pregnant. Within weeks it became all too apparent I was pregnant. Again. It was difficult to the point of unbelievable, and I kept it to myself as long as I could, thinking that if I ignored it enough, it wouldn't be true. I was so angry: angry at having to carry, sustain and give birth to another human life. And that life would take precious time and attention away from my three daughters. The fact that it could turn out to be a boy didn't make it any easier.

If it is, he'll grow up to be a replica of his father, someone who uses and looks down on women, I thought.

I was surprised at how clearly I could see the truth, even if only momentarily.

I think being so angry helped me remove my blinders. Anger at the man who continued to treat me as his plaything, as a toy for him to do with as he pleased. More and more, my three other pregnancies kept returning to my thoughts, and the more I thought about them, and how they came to be, the angrier I became.

And when my secret finally got out, and people learned I was pregnant with my fourth child, that didn't make it any easier. Our families and friends teased me, asking questions I couldn't answer truthfully.

"Don't you know how those babies keep happening?" They winked at me while I slowly died inside.

Of course I know. But do you think you could please explain it to my husband? I wondered. *He's the one who doesn't seem to understand. Or care.*

I wanted to scream and tell them I knew exactly how and where babies come from, but I couldn't seem to do anything to prevent it. Instead, I mustered a smile and made some flippant reply.

The day came when I realized I had to tear my thoughts away from the past: it was gone and nothing could change that. Although it seemed to work, I was still upset because another life was growing within me.

I perked up when Eddie went back to work, since it meant we wouldn't have to scrape by, living on fried mush and macaroni and cheese; only going to the doctor in an emergency; and avoiding the malls and department stores because we didn't have a spare nickel. Even Eddie's anger abated, providing some well-deserved peace and quiet. As always when mining coal, his hours were those of a madman: twelve, fourteen, even sixteen hours a day.

Still comfortable in my role of a woman who denied the impact of the violence within her own home, I resented him for forcing me to single-handedly do everything. I failed to see those long absences from home for what they really were: a blessing in disguise. I should have though, because whenever Eddie was there with us, he would spend all his time either yelling at the girls to be quiet, or at me to keep them that way.

CHAPTER TEN

The day I decided to kill my children and myself was just like any other: Eddie went to work, the mail came, neighbors chatted and trains rumbled by. Only I had changed, so that day my world stood still, and my thoughts suddenly coalesced into one singular, cohesive plan.

For years, I had seen a vision of myself dropping my babies from an open window. But more often now, while driving near a steep embankment or over a bridge, I had other thoughts: *if only I close my eyes, and take my hands off the steering wheel, it will all be over.*

I never could do it, of course. But the pattern persisted, plaguing me for many years.

And that day I found myself swimming in a sea of desperation, not knowing how to tread the water that swirled around me, as a silent undertow threatened to drown me and one day bled into another. And another. And another. It didn't make any difference what I did or how I spent my time—I just couldn't stop being sad.

I love my children dearly, and wouldn't trade them for anything, I thought. *But I didn't want any babies, and I wanted to be able to choose when I did. I've had no say at all, in any of their births—all because of him. And now, I can't even make my marriage work. How on earth will I ever escape from this war zone: the one inside my home, the other one inside my mind?*

Still in my nightgown, I sank onto the couch, and watched as the room went fuzzy. The tears were right behind my eyes, trying to get out. I wanted to stop them, tried to ignore the utter despair I felt, and to hide my pain from my children. But slowly they escaped, forming little trails down my cheeks, and another fear occurred: a fear of scaring the daughters who played in a corner, oblivious to everything but each other.

Like a drunken robot, I stumbled into the bathroom and out of their sight, turning the lock behind me. Unseeing, I reached for the spigot and heard the water splash against the tub. Somewhere in a coherent corner of my mind, I hoped it would drown out my pain. Sinking slowly down the wall to the cold vinyl floor, I began sobbing, feeling nothing but the pain. Quietly at first, until I managed to lift my arm and pull a towel down from the shower rod, burying my face in it. Sobs wracked my body, and I heard a guttural cry like a wild animal come from somewhere deep within me. With the raw sound came freedom from days, months and years of silent anguish, as the bottled-up feelings that had waited for so long to explode flowed freely down my cheeks.

I knew then what I had to do. I was going to take my children, get into my car and drive over a cliff. I watched it happen. I knew just where to do it. I saw the car speeding up, going faster and faster as it gained momentum, flying down Bird's Creek Road. But instead of making the deadly curve halfway down the mountain, I took my hands off the steering wheel and we simply sailed over the edge of a tall cliff, coming to rest several hundred feet below, in the forested valley that became our tomb.

The explosion happened just as we hit hard rocks and earth, and I felt my throat begin to close, as a mixture of fear and smoke began to overtake me.

But my children were still alive—and howling in pain. Their mangled and broken bodies had somehow survived the crash, but their shrieks tore through me, just as flames of fire began creeping toward us, ready to do what the car crash had not.

A crying sound just outside the bathroom door startled me, waking me from my reverie: *No! I don't want them to suffer. It will have to be something else.*

"I can't do it, I don't know what to do," I choked into the fabric pressed against my mouth. "I don't know what to do to fix things. Oh God, help me, please!" The desperate plea was torn from me, as I struggled to keep my children from hearing my torment.

Then, almost of its own accord, I saw something else. Unlike any of the other thoughts that had played out in my mind during the past few years, an unfamiliar one came to me and like the frames of a movie reel, I watched myself get into the car and sit down beside my daughters. As I turned the key in the ignition, the car began filling with fumes. The long rubber hose I had hooked up to the exhaust wound around the car and into a tiny window. The hose had rags stuffed around it. As the air started feeling warm and heavy, I began to feel at peace. There was no pain, as a slow drowsiness settled upon me. My glazed expression saw their father finding us hours later, much too late to save us.

After all, I couldn't leave my children behind, for their life would be a continuation of the hell my own had been. At the hands of their father, who knew what would happen to them?

That final thought tore through me, and I looked down at my swollen stomach, external evidence of another impending birth. My hands wrapped around my belly, as if instinctively trying to shelter the unborn baby from the part of my brain that was thinking about harming it.

How can I even think of doing something so terrible? I sat there, my arms wrapped tightly around my torso, rocking back and forth and trying to make sense of my life.

I recalled the day I knew I was again pregnant: it was August and I had just turned twenty-one. My three daughters were already a handful and I didn't want another child—so I prayed that something would happen. Anything to make it go away.

But that was in the beginning, when I was so distraught I wondered if there would ever be a time I wasn't pregnant. When I was not at the mercy of a man who did whatever he wanted, with me and to me, without a second's hesitation.

Just as I had done with its sisters, I started telling the baby I was carrying, "It isn't your fault. You didn't ask to be born, and you have no control over what happens. It isn't your fault, and you deserve to live." I kept repeating that until finally, miraculously, the negative feelings vanished. Even though I wasn't thrilled about giving birth to a fourth child, I had grown to accept it. It took me almost the entire nine months, but I did it.

My tears slowing, I thought of my unborn child—all he or she might become—and how snuffing out that tiny life would be much more wrong than trying to endure the abuse. I thought of Mileah's stubborn pout, the way her chin jutted out defiantly whenever she couldn't have something she wanted. I pictured Gabby, thumb in mouth, curled up like a kitten, sound asleep on the stairwell. And Trista, toddling down the street in a diaper, a bright blue Cookie Monster doll tucked under one tiny arm.

Then I tried to conjure up an image of this unborn child. With blond hair and blue eyes, it would no doubt have the same features as its siblings. But what of its personality? Would it be helpful and older than its years, like Mileah? Or quiet and solemn, like Trista? Or perhaps rambunctious and ornery, like Gabby? Would it be another girl? What if it was a boy? Would he follow in the steps of his coal miner father?

Please no, not that!

There was no way to know. But I wanted to find out.

"No!"

I screamed the word, as the sight and sound and thought of my children—all dead—threatened to drive me mad.

I want to live, and give the child within me a chance to live—no matter what!

Besides, I'm too stubborn to die.

I had found a stronghold to cling to, knowing I had to be there to take care of them, to raise them into responsible adults—because no one else was going to do it. The hope was so tangible I could almost reach out and touch it.

I can't leave them, and I can't kill them. Or us. Nothing—no one—is worth that!

I stood up slowly, wet a washcloth with cool water, and then patted my face with it. The woman in the mirror stared at me, and I realized I was a mess.

What could have caused you so much pain that you're ready to give up? How did you get to this place? You have your whole life ahead of you!

As I placed the neatly folded washcloth on the sink, I turned away from the reflection there. I couldn't bear to look into the mirror, for it had always mocked me. Today was no different.

Turning the doorknob, I took a deep, ragged breath and went to tend my children. My smile was fixed back in place by the time they came running over to me.

I had no idea how I came to be on the bathroom floor that day, for I was still blind to the truth: I was psychologically and physically abused, battered by the man who claimed to love me, yet who seized every opportunity to prove otherwise. I just wasn't ready to see it. But the feeling of being a cornered animal, with nowhere to go, did something to me—it made me fight that much harder to keep living.

That was when I forced myself to face the situation squarely. If things weren't going to get better, then fine. But I was going to do the best I could with whatever I had at the time. Each day was a struggle, and there were times when my thoughts returned to that day in the bathroom, and I wished I had just gone through with it. But they were coming with less and less frequency and instead, I was learning acceptance. Whenever I felt like throwing up my hands and giving up, I remembered my children—and how dependent they were on me. Their father certainly wouldn't, indeed, wasn't capable, of caring for their needs. So it was up to me. That was my outlook on life.

It gave me a sense of renewed strength, but it really was no different than the same outlook I had adopted since I was old enough to realize I couldn't trust the adults in my life. I was the only person I could trust.

The fourth and final pregnancy was the hardest on my body. I gained more weight than I had with the others, causing my back to feel like I had carried cinderblocks around all day long. By evening I was exhausted, miserable, and at times I even hoped I would miscarry. I felt like a horrible person for even thinking it, but I had so little time and energy I didn't see how I could possibly have enough left for a fourth baby. Someone, maybe even more than one of them, was going to be short-changed in the process—but I also knew there was nothing I could do about it.

The night we called the doctor was a moist spring one, with the evening dew just starting to dampen the grass. My contractions were hard and close together, and I prayed the baby would wait for the doctor before making an appearance. I tried to rest between contractions while Eddie puttered around downstairs.

We had found Dr. Roper several months earlier: he was the only doctor within the tri-state area who still did home births. The doctor and his nurse, Norma, had only been in the house a few minutes when the pains began getting stronger. He told me my cervix was dilated three centimeters.

"It might be awhile," he smiled kindly. "Why don't you try to get some rest, while I go into the next room and take a nap myself?"

I tried but as soon as I shut my eyes, the pains began again. I finally eased my swollen body downstairs, trying to look more graceful than I felt. Eddie was in the kitchen entertaining Norma, who was probably ten years his senior. He was laughing as he made popcorn and I was struck by the irony of it all: he was flirting with another woman while I was giving birth to his child. It was so surreal I couldn't even comment on it. I simply retrieved a snack and returned upstairs, hearing his laughter echo as I climbed back into bed.

Somewhere along the way I managed to doze but as night turned to early morning, the pains returned with a burning intensity. Dr. Roper said I was completely dilated, and the baby would make an appearance any second.

Everything happened rapidly after that. Suddenly, Dr. Roper was supporting two reddish shoulders, just as the baby slipped out into the waiting world. "It's a girl—No, it's a boy!" the doctor sounded incredulous.

"It is a boy!" Eddie was amazed as he watched Dr. Roper lay the squirming, crying infant on my stomach.

No, they must be wrong, it's another girl, I thought.

But when I looked, there was no mistaking him for a girl; he was definitely a boy. Who weighed almost 11-pounds, Dr. Roper said. I was amazed. To have a son—well maybe the pregnancy had been worth it after all. I was just stunned he was mine.

As with his sisters, the baby boy remained nameless for a few days, when we agreed on "Slade." He never stopped smiling, which earned him a favored position with everyone in the household. He never cried, either, and would just whimper, but after eating or getting a diaper change, he was as happy as ever. I grew to love him more each day, and soon wondered how the girls and I had survived without him.

But I had to make sure he was my last baby: Dr. Roper had spoken with me about future birth control, since he was concerned because I had given birth to four children in five years. After thinking long and hard and praying fervently, I made the agonizing decision. I told Dr. Roper I wanted to have my tubes tied. I knew my procreative powers were a gift from God, and under normal circumstances, I would never even consider the procedure.

I know Eddie will never leave me alone, and it will only be a matter of time before I'm pregnant again. You know I can't give these four children all the time and attention they need, so please forgive me for doing this. I have no other choice, I told God.

Dr. Roper referred me to a colleague and the day of my consultation appointment, I couldn't stop thinking about the impending surgery.

It's his fault I have to do this. If only he would have listened some of those times when I asked him to wait. If only he wasn't so selfish. If only . . .

I pulled into a parking space outside of the health department, stopped the car, and chastised myself.

That's not going to get you anywhere. It won't turn back the clock, nor will it change Eddie.

But I also knew he could at least have had the decency to do something himself, instead of forcing me to do this.

As I entered the building, I began running my four pregnancies through my head. *It's been a constant since age thirteen*, I wasn't sure where that thought came from, but suddenly it came to me, a long-forgotten high school memory from years earlier.

Running a comb through my damp hair after gym class, I realized I was going to be late for English. Again. Mrs. Tallman would mark me tardy, but I didn't care. Coming out of the locker room, I nearly collided with Mrs. Niles. "Berry, you're going to be tardy." Her head seemed to shake perpetually, as if she never quite knew what to make of her awkward, adolescent freshmen.

"I know." I rushed past her and then stopped.

"What's the matter? Don't know the way to class?" She couldn't hide the laughter in her voice.

"Um, well, yes, I mean—," I floundered. "Do you have a minute?"

I saw a faint furrow appear between her brows, before it vanished. "Sure thing. This is my planning period, so I've got plenty of time," I saw white, even teeth as she smiled.

"I just have a quick question." I swallowed hard and studied the floor, where a tiny piece of gravel had sneaked in behind the gym teacher's back, daring to defy her spotless wooden planks. Looking up, I spit it out. "Do you know what I can do? I mean, where I should go—" my voice trailed off entirely.

"You're pregnant?" her tone wasn't judgmental, but I sensed her surprise as she played with the pencil above her right ear.

"No!" I said quickly. "It's just that, well ... I think I may have something." My cheeks flamed as I choked on the words.

"Piece of cake," she said, and the small room seemed to fill with air again. "Let's go see the guidance counselor, and she'll give you a pass for your next class, so your tardy will be excused."

I managed to suck in some much needed air. "Thank you," I managed.

The next day Miss Garfield drove me to Kingwood. She chatted pleasantly, sticking to light topics. But my stomach was churning, and I kept wondering how many people saw me leave with the school guidance counselor.

If anyone finds out, they'll know. I'll be branded forever. They'll think I'm a hypocrite, going to Bible meetings and refusing to cheat in class, while having sex behind everyone's back, I thought.

The thoughts flew around my brain in a flurry, until I forced myself to focus. When we parked in front of the county courthouse, a forgotten scene from childhood drifted into my mind, and I remembered being on an exam table while a nurse held my arm.

"I came here for my shots," I said to no one in particular.

"Yes, the office is still here, but they're trying to get bigger quarters elsewhere," Miss. Garfield said.

We parked and then mounted wide flagstone steps like anyone else coming or going from the old stone courthouse. Except they were checking property maps or paying taxes; we were there to see if I could be diseased. Inside the waiting room, I leafed through a magazine, thankful we were alone.

"Number two," a voice called a few minutes later. "That's you. I'll be waiting right here." Miss Garfield's smile was still warm and sunny.

"Thanks," I mumbled, head bowed as I walked toward the woman with the clipboard.

Back inside the car, sunshine streamed through the windshield, warming me with its rays. I couldn't stop replaying the scene in the exam room. The nurse was older, with dark hair and a kindly nature that made me think she was someone's grandmother.

"Do you have any symptoms, Sweetie?"

What if she's the nurse who gave me my shots? What if she tells my mother?

"No, I don't think so," I folded and unfolded my hands.

"Miss Garfield said you didn't think you could be pregnant, right?"

Not since I don't have a period, no, no chance at all.

"The thing is, you see." As I looked into her knowing eyes, I suddenly realized she was an old hat at this, and felt my limbs relax. "I'm not sure what I need. I just know this guy, he started doing some things and I thought I wanted to, but then I didn't, so …"

Her head nodded in understanding. "So did he penetrate you at all?" she asked as easily as if I had a splinter.

"Yes, a little bit," I bit my lip.

What do I say? How can I tell her everything he did? We did? What will she think of me? What will she tell Miss Garfield?

"Then we should probably test you for a few common diseases, and we'll draw some blood and send it away to see if you're pregnant. But I'm sure it will be negative," she gave me a motherly smile. "Do you think you'll need any birth control?"

I shook my head hard. "No, it was just that once and I'm not going to have sex until I'm married."

Miss Garfield's voice drifted across the car and interrupted my thoughts, preventing the scene from repeating. "Today's trip will remain strictly confidential. Neither Mrs. Niles nor I will say anything to anyone, and nothing goes on your school record. The health department will contact me, but if you don't hear anything, then you don't need to worry, because that means everything is just fine."

That's when I rewound the reel inside my head, stashing it away forever.

I never told Mom about seeing the nurse.

It was another nurse who brought me out of my reverie. "Mrs. Leigh, you can go back now," she said.

We stepped into an exam room, followed by a petite, dark-skinned man. "Mrs. Leigh? I'm Dr. Mundi." He glanced at my chart, and then over at me. "There are some risks involved with this surgery, which is called a tubal ligation. Naturally, whenever anesthesia is used there's a risk of death. It's that simple. Other than that, though, there's the risk of infection."

I listened closely as he outlined the various methods of performing the surgery. "I understand," I said matter-of-factly.

"Good, but I should also tell you that usually I don't perform this type of surgery on someone your age. You're only twenty-one, and you could want more children when you are older." He smiled knowingly. "Of course, you already have four, so that may not happen. But have you considered how you would feel if one of your children died? Say, your son? Have you and your husband talked about him having a vasectomy, instead?" He glanced down at my chart again, but I wasn't sure what to say.

"It's a very minor operation compared with this one, and there isn't a risk of death, because no anesthesia's involved. Your husband would just go into the doctor's office, they'd perform the procedure right there, and he would be fine after a few days. But this surgery has a recovery period of several weeks."

I shook my head, forcing myself to find the right words. "You don't understand. I have no choice. My husband refuses to accept responsibility for birth control, and he won't let me use any, either. You're right, four kids in five years is a lot—especially for someone my age, and if there had been anything at all I could have done to prevent that, I would have. That's why I'm here now—because if I get pregnant again, I'll lose my sanity!" I expelled everything in one long breath.

I was tired of protecting Eddie, of keeping "our secret," of taking the blame for being pregnant so many times. I had to be honest. Hating that I had to give up my right to ever have children again gave me the courage I needed. It was plain and simple. Black and white.

"As for the vasectomy." I hesitated, not sure how to continue. "Well, my husband and I did discuss that. It isn't an option, at least not where he's concerned. He said someone told him it decreases a man's sex drive, and he doesn't want that to happen." At Dr. Mundi's dubious expression, I smiled thinly. "I know it's not true, I've already done the research. But try to tell him that."

"So instead, he would prefer that his wife—you—be put under anesthesia, despite this being a much more dangerous operation? It sounds like he could do with a decrease in his sex drive." Dr. Mundi shook his head. "I'm sorry. I understand what you're saying. And normally, I wouldn't even consider it. But for you I will make an exception." His smile was full of compassion.

The surgery took place one week later. I was in the hospital from early morning until late that same day. When I came out of the recovery room, I hurt from my waist to my thighs. Dr. Mundi said the pain medication would help, and gave me a prescription. He told me to get lots of rest, not to lift anything heavier than a milk jug, and to not overdue it when I began getting up and moving around.

During the days that followed, I became aware of how angry I was that Eddie had "stolen" my procreative powers, and my animosity continued to build.

It's his fault. He's such a selfish jerk. He could have had a vasectomy, instead.

At the same time, the knowledge that I couldn't get pregnant again lifted a weight from my mind, actually allowing me to begin enjoying sex. Well, some sex. With Eddie, I would never enjoy the weird sex he preferred. But it was a start, and one that wasn't lost on him. We began sharing jokes about little things, even confiding in each other, and it felt like we might become friends.

We went an entire month without a single argument, and even made a date to go camping one weekend. Mom babysat while we headed to Tygart Lake, where we made friends with a couple who invited us to join them on their motorboat. I watched, mesmerized, as they took turns waterskiing. When they offered to teach us, Eddie promptly refused, but I jumped into the water, eager to try the sport.

After donning the skis, I floated on my back and tried to relax as I grasped the rope handle with both hands. The first time, the handle flew from my fingers after I found myself being dragged, face first, through the water. The second time, I managed to hold onto the handle and was pulled into a standing position before, disappointed, I fell and sank into the water again. But on the third try, I came out of the water easily, and quickly began gliding along the water's surface, turning first one way, then another, until I could jump over the boat's wake when the small craft changed directions. By the time the day was over I was exhausted but exhilarated.

When the weekend ended and Eddie and I returned home, we both felt rested. I hoped we had been given a second chance, and believed peace would prevail.

But it didn't. It couldn't. Any newfound peace was only a temporary calm before the storm—one of many cloudbursts to come. Because in time, Eddie's job fizzled out again and he was added to the growing number of unemployed coal miners in West Virginia.

Still, we had our blessings. Slade grew rapidly, marking each developmental milestone earlier than normal. Very bright, he imitated our every word or movement. He was the happiest baby, adored by three sisters whose world he made go round, and who catered to his every whim and want.

I marveled at how a baby born into such a chaotic household could be so pleasant. I decided it was God's gift to me, for overcoming the inner struggle that had left me weeping on the bathroom floor, intent on taking Slade's little life before he had a chance to suffer like we had been suffering for years. I knew what a privilege it was, just to play some small role in my beautiful baby boy's life, and I thanked God every day: for giving me both Slade and the discernment to realize that in spite of everything, life really was worth living.

And I knew, with God's strength and guidance, I could overcome anything.

CHAPTER ELEVEN

The girls were growing tall and filling out, like the fragrant, butter-colored daffodils that grew in bunches against the hillside in our back yard.

Nearly a year had passed and my body had long since healed from the surgery. But my mind hadn't: anger and resentment continued building because of being forced to give up not just a body part, but my right to bear children. I just wasn't sure what to do about it.

It was only reasonable, especially given that no matter how much work I did, Eddie always made sure I did more. Lately he had been doing that a lot, but I wasn't sure if it was because he didn't have a job, or because our marriage was growing worse. But whatever it was, I started coming home after my cosmetic shows to find him sitting like a zombie in front of the TV, and if I asked, he refused to help me around the house with anything. He was extremely critical, so I just decided it was easier doing it all myself.

Most of the time, I did it all, too. But other times, I just couldn't keep up. Like the night I returned home following a show I'd gone to earlier that day. I expected Eddie to feed the kids, but he thought otherwise. He was already angry when I arrived, telling me there wasn't any food in the house and they were hungry.

"You're going to work before you play, young lady!" he snapped.

"What do you mean?" I sat down my case and hung up my keys.

"Just what I said. The kids are hungry and there's nothing in the house for them to eat. So you can figure out what to do about it before you do anything else."

"Eddie, there's food in the freezer. You could have thawed some ground beef and fixed burgers or even a meatloaf. You can cook, too."

"That's not my job and you know it!" His lips snarled as he glared at me.

From experience I knew he wanted an argument and nothing I said or did would pacify him. I threw my arms up in the air. "All right, you want me to take care of it? Okay, I will. I'll just go back into town and buy all the groceries we'll need for next week."

"No, you're not going back into town. You're not going to leave me with the kids all night long."

I sighed, fighting the urge to sarcastically tell him just how pleasant he was treating me. "Well then, what do you suggest I do?"

He shrugged. "I don't know. You figure it out."

In the end, I drove to a small convenience store a couple of miles away, and found something I could fix quickly. Returning home, I hugged my hungry children and hid in the kitchen, as eager to be out of Eddie's sight as he was of mine.

Then it happened: Eddie simply said he wanted to leave, that he'd wanted to for six years, and he hadn't even loved me until long after we married. His words didn't come as a surprise, but it still hurt to hear him say them out loud. Eddie's admission also freed me from the delusions I began having after the first time we were intimate together, forcing me to see the truth.

I know. I've known all along. The only thing is, you've never loved me. You don't love me now—and you never will. I just put up with it because that's what I'm supposed to do. That's what God expects me to do, I thought.

But he didn't leave. Instead, I wondered how I could ever come to terms with the many confusing beliefs that were part and parcel of who I was. If I couldn't do that, I knew I could never leave him because—unlike Eddie—I had planned it and I would do it. All in good time.

In the meantime I worried about bigger things, like staying alive. Once Eddie's unemployment ran out, we were just like everyone else we knew: stuck between a dollar and a dime, with families to support and no job to do it with. I knew it was only a matter of time before everything came spilling out, wreaking the same kind of havoc the 100-year flood had, when it devastated our county a few months earlier. It washed away houses, bridges, vehicles, a railroad trestle and even people, while leaving behind furniture, cars, broken pieces of lumber and twisted masses of metal.

Our own lives began unraveling at the seams just as the rebuilding work began taking shape, and the chaos inside our home increased, leaving behind debris of its own. We faced a growing mental strain that probably would have overtaken us all, had Eddie not found work building an addition on someone's house. But the situation worsened after Eddie came home with a shiny Ford truck. He was supposed to trade in his big old Dodge for something more reliable and easier on fuel. Instead, he walked through the door with a vehicle that left us $4,000 more in debt.

"How on earth are we going to make the payment?" I asked.

Eddie grinned. "That's the beauty of it, you see. Because I'm a coal miner and we have such good credit, we don't have a payment for three months."

I just stared at him. What planet was he living on? "What if you don't go back to the mines by then?"

It was all the fuel he needed. "All you ever do is complain and whine! Just get off my back, and leave me alone. If you've got a better idea, then I'd love to hear it!" he yelled.

"I'm just worried about making the payment. I know this odd job is supposed to last awhile, but you're only making $7.50 an hour. Besides—" I began.

"Just shut up. Shut the hell up. Don't open your mouth and say another word. You're just a spoiled little brat, who thinks it's so easy to support a family!" Eddie stomped away, slamming the door behind him on his way to the basement.

I sighed. I was always the bad guy. Just once, I wished he would grow up and accept some responsibility for his actions—instead of blaming me. During the last few months, we had gone without cleaning supplies, toothpaste, tissues and even toilet paper (although never at the same time) and other household items.

And I couldn't say a word about it. Because if I did, things would get even uglier.

By April, the tension between us was so thick I felt like I was choking, ready to pass out from the acrid air around me. I tried to find ways to scrape and save whatever I could, just to get us from one day to the next. The children always had food, even though it wasn't as healthy as I would have liked, although I sometimes went without so they could eat. The loss of a steady income was taking its toll, and it seemed the kids and I were paying the price for Eddie's mistakes. We were going to visit his parents one Saturday afternoon, when the short trip turned into a verbal abuse session. Something set

Eddie off, and he began shouting and spewing obscenities, leaving us just sitting there in silence.

Later that week he shoved me, twice, because I wouldn't stand still and listen to more of his abuse. The second time occurred when I tried to wake the children; they were still sleepy, so we curled up together in my bed. Eddie was there in a heartbeat, shouting like a madman.

"Get out of bed, you lazy bitch! I want some breakfast!" With that, he jerked me as I half-fell, half-climbed from bed, trying not to hurt the kids as I did so. Eddie stood there shouting and I heard my children's terrified sobs behind me. A minute later, he walked away. I gathered them into my arms, trying to calm them—and wondering when we could escape. I was torn between the damage they would sustain by not having a father around, and what his abuse would do to them if we stayed.

It wasn't long before my young daughters took a stand, trying to defend me after Eddie started yelling at me one day. "Leave Mommy alone!" they shrieked, which only made them bear the brunt of his violence.

In return, he kicked Gabby twice as she was trying to hurry into the bathroom to get ready for bed. Although she was only three, she didn't even cry.

She's burying her feelings, I thought. *Oh my God, just like me!*

I knew then I could no longer trust Eddie to put the kids to bed while I was away working, especially after I arrived home earlier than usual one evening. I was tiptoeing up the stairs when he began yelling. Eddie hadn't heard me, so I watched as he literally slammed, first Trista, and then Gabby, down onto the bed where Mileah was already laying, her eyes tightly closed. Not that I doubted their tales, but I knew then the children hadn't been exaggerating, when they filled me in about their evenings with "Daddy."

I swept into the room and sat down on the bed, and they jumped up and began hugging and kissing me.

"Mommy's home." "I love you, Mommy." "Will you read us a bedtime story?"

I kissed each one in return, gathering them around me as I asked what story they wanted to hear. When Eddie started to speak, I gave him what I hoped was a look that would wilt him. I'm not sure if I succeeded, but something he saw there must have caught his attention. A minute later, he went downstairs, leaving us alone, caught up in the pages of a fairytale where nothing bad happened, and all children were cherished and never got hurt.

By the time summer arrived, I felt just like those women I had passed in the supermarket aisle all my life—the ones who looked so beaten down and worn out, they barely had the energy to smile as they pushed their carts by. Or whose men dogged their very footsteps, keeping an eye out for any sign of "disloyalty" or perceived "unfaithfulness," lest their women should acknowledge a stranger's nod or greeting in public.

I realized I was emotionally battered, being repeatedly told to shut up, frequently not allowed to speak, and ridiculed and humiliated, but whenever I looked into the bathroom mirror, I didn't see that.

Instead, I saw fire in my eyes and a firmly set chin that was determined to defy the rigid rules Eddie tried to use to control me.

But it was the feelings I saw reflected there that really surprised me. I saw a woman who knew she deserved respect and honor, because she was a hard worker and a good wife and mother, who had taken his crap for years.

It dawned on me that I hadn't seen the old shame and sadness for quite awhile. I wondered why. Maybe it was because, by dressing up, and doing my hair and make-up, to sell cosmetics, I was pretending to be someone I wasn't at all: a successful saleswoman.

"Fake it until you make it," my manager once told me. From the reflection in the mirror, I knew I was well on my way to making it. Seeing that gave me an inner calm Eddie couldn't take away, not even when he continued picking fights over small things, without provocation and apparently for no reason at all.

I thought his new job might be the reason for his anger. After deciding he wasn't cut out to work construction, and with no sign the coal industry might rebound, he went to work for a family friend who owned a paving company. The pay was less than he made in the mines, but more than he did doing odd jobs. It was demanding and he worked the hours of a man possessed, but that was nothing new.

By then I was used to being a single parent. From sunrise to sunset and beyond, Eddie was gone. I often wondered what drove him. I had reached a turning point in my life, accepting that Eddie would probably always be a workaholic. I couldn't fathom why his children weren't more important to him—but then, I wasn't sure he knew, either.

I just knew he was one unhappy man. Whenever he was home, it was horrible for everyone. He yelled and sulked around, or showed his unhappiness and discontent in other ways. I tried to buffer the kids from his verbal attacks, but it was impossible. Eventually I learned to be thankful he was so driven. It kept him away from home, giving us the peace we desperately needed. For that I was grateful.

Winter came and went and the kids continued getting bigger. The only change within the fabric of our marriage, if it even could be called a marriage, was that we hardly spoke to one another by then. For years, we would fight and make up. It was characterized by a petty argument here or there, followed by a period of semi-bliss. Then the whole process repeated itself. A good month was when we only fought once or twice, but they were woefully few.

In the meantime, I dreamed of the day when I would have more time for myself. It seemed I would no sooner get up from a night's sleep than it would be time to go back to bed again, only to repeat everything the next morning. I had learned to hold my tongue, and rarely mentioned my feelings, but I still wondered if things would ever change. Surely we couldn't keep up the pretense of a happy family life forever.

Then came tax time, and things got even worse. To help cut costs, I did the preliminary work, itemizing receipts and sorting and tallying expenses. After putting the kids to bed, I worked until three a.m. trying to finish paperwork I had to take to the accountant the next day. It was almost April 15 and I had searched all over the house for Eddie's self-employment records, only to find half of them were missing. He wasn't good about keeping receipts, so it had taken me twice as long as it should have. After gathering up all the paperwork, I went to see the accountant and, at Eddie's insistence, left the kids with him. When I returned a couple of hours later, he accused me of deliberately leaving without feeding them.

I walked in the door and Gabby and Trista ran to me, flinging their arms around me. "Daddy says you're lazy. You didn't feed us, Mommy, and we were hungry." I heard their childish accusations as they hugged me. My heart sank. I had hoped he would stop putting me down in front of them, but instead it seemed to be getting worse.

Great! Now, they're repeating his nasty remarks, I thought.

I kneeled down to hug the girls, breathing deeply of their warm bodies as if they could renew my strength. "Oh you kids know Daddy gets grumpy and says things he doesn't mean. Don't pay any attention to him," I laughed.

Then I slowly stood, sat my satchel down and went to find him. He was in the kitchen, cleaning up.

"What's this about being lazy, Eddie?"

"Well, you know what they say about 'if the shoe fits.' You aren't lazy though, are you? Why you only left me four starving children to feed—why didn't you give them lunch before you left? You hadn't been gone for five minutes before they started whining to be fed."

"They did eat before I left. We had a late breakfast while you were still sleeping. And when I left, no one said anything about being hungry—or I would have fed them. Again." I sighed. "They're your children, too. What's so hard about you fixing them something to eat?"

"Only that it's not my job, that's all!"

"Oh, and doing the taxes is my job, is that it?" I could hear my own voice rising to meet the anger and sarcasm in his, but I didn't care. I didn't notice until too late that the girls were standing a few feet away, listening to our every angry word.

I forced my voice to a level of calm my emotions didn't match. "You kids go play. Your father and I are talking," I told them.

"It doesn't do any good to discuss anything with you. You never listen to anything I say. Oh yeah, you put on a good show when we go out in public. In front of them you're always 'Little Miss Goody Two Shoes,' but at home it's another matter. Well you better be careful, or I'll leave—and take the kids with me. Then you'll learn your lesson!"

My head snapped around sharply at his words.

Take my children? Would he? Could he? How dare you threaten me! I thought.

But another part of me knew he was quite capable of keeping that promise—if he grew desperate enough. Suddenly, every last ounce of energy within my body felt like it had been sucked out. I shook my head slowly, more tired than I had been for a long time. "Go ahead, if you think you need to. But while you're at it, don't forget I also stayed up half the night trying to figure out the taxes from the bookkeeping mess you left me. And then I had a meeting with the accountant. Don't forget that," I said.

He threw the dishrag across the room and stormed out cursing. I saw Mileah and Gabby run after him, crying. "Let him go," I told them.

I hope he never comes back, I thought.

The minute the front door slammed, the girls came running to me. "You made Daddy leave. You shouldn't have yelled at him," Mileah cried.

"Now he won't come back," Gabby said, smacking me on the leg.

I looked down and saw the anger and pain in her eyes, and was horrified she was imitating his bad behavior.

What next?

"Listen to me, Gabriella." I bent down and gently turned her head toward me, seeing the tears in her eyes, and the thumb in her mouth. "I want all of you listen to me. It is not acceptable to hit other people, especially people you love. Do you understand me?" I watched, observing every nuance on their faces, the way their little bodies said what their mouths would not.

Their anger is like a fuse, ready to go off any second. God help us all when it does.

I gathered them close, touching each one with a stroke on the head, or a rub on the arm. "I did not make Daddy leave, and he will come back. That much I can promise you."

Yeah, because he can't go without having his sexual needs met.

"Look, kids, I know it was wrong for Daddy and me to yell at each other and I'm sorry. It'll be all right, though, because he'll be back before long, when he gets over being angry. And then everything will be fine."

It seemed to reassure them and they were about to go and play when Trista spoke up. She was the only child who hadn't seemed bothered by his departure, and who hadn't rushed to his defense. "Daddy said one day he would hit you so hard you'd end up in the hospital," she said sadly.

I stared at my five-year-old, not knowing what to say. My mind went blank, leaving only anguish to fill the void.

Why does he have to subject us to this? Why won't he stop?

I rushed to reassure her. "Oh Sweetie, people say lots of things when they're angry. But he didn't mean it, really. Daddy was just upset." Still, a look of uncertainty filled her eyes. I hoped it didn't reflect what was in my heart. "Listen. I promise you that Daddy will not hurt me. I won't let him!"

She smiled then and hugged me tightly, before running off to join her sisters.

I sat there, wishing I believed my own words. If only I could. I looked around the room, seeing all the visible signs that told me it might only be a matter of time before he tried to make good on his threat. There was the wall opposite me, with a large, gaping hole in the drywall. In a fit of rage about six months ago, Eddie had put his fist through it. At the time, he told me it was a good thing it wasn't my face. Then there was the wooden dining room chair. Its mate became the victim of his violence on another occasion, when he threw it across the room. It had landed with a hard thud, breaking into pieces as it fell to the floor.

I absently rubbed my leg. The bruise was still visible, and I couldn't help but recall the tennis shoe Eddie had thrown at me. It happened several months ago, late one night when I had done something to displease him. I tried to defend myself, but it was useless. Without warning, Eddie stooped down and picked up a shoe, and the next thing I knew it was flying through the air toward me. When it struck my leg, I felt a burning pain. The dark purple bruise I found the next morning was about half the size of the shoe itself. It had since turned into a broken web of capillaries.

At the time, the only thing I could think was how fortunate I was that it hadn't hit me in the face. Of course Eddie claimed it was an accident. I stared at him, saying nothing.

One day practically ran into the next, and planting season was upon us. I had planned all winter for a garden. After Eddie broke up the hard ground using a neighbor's rototiller, I took the younger kids and went outside. The rich, black earth moved easily under my fingers. Mileah was in school, but Trista, Gabby and Slade all gathered around to help by dropping tiny seeds into each row. The day was sunny and beautiful. As we knelt there, working the soil, I thought how good our homegrown vegetables would taste. Spring—what a wonderful season! With it came the last remnant of dirt and dying. Everything was reborn, and I felt a strong desire to work my marriage, just as I was working the soil. I expected it to produce good results, in that Eddie and I would be happy again, and our children wouldn't face the turmoil of living in a house divided.

I stood and gathered up my gardening tools. Handing each child something to carry, we headed toward the house. I glanced back to where the sticks stood at the end of the long rows, empty seed packets hung so we would know which vegetable to expect. I paused long enough to think about the day when the tiny green sprouts would begin to poke their heads through the black dirt. Maybe, just maybe, with a jolt of hard work from both Eddie and me, our marriage would yield equally rich results. I knew then I had to try again. Harder this time.

A letter—I would write Eddie a letter and tell him how I felt. Maybe that would do the trick. I put the children down for their naps, reading them a story and trying not to think about all the things I wanted to say to him. I was too anxious to sleep myself, so when the last one began breathing easily, I tiptoed downstairs, pen in hand.

But I was unsure of what to say or how to say it. Then, suddenly, the words came pouring out. Before long, I had written two full pages. I read it, trying to see what might upset him.

May 11, 1987

Dear Eddie,

Lately our relationship has been getting progressively worse. Perhaps if I tell you how I've been feeling, maybe you will at least understand my viewpoint.

These days, all I hear from you is how tired you are, how little time you have, how much you need. Ever since the first layoff in 1982, you make sure you get your wants and needs fulfilled before anyone else's. You aren't like this all of the time, and I know you do work very hard. I feel for you when you come home late, too tired for anything but sleep. Ever since we got married, you've worked at such demanding jobs, you have nothing left for your family.

Looking back, I see you were very kind, generous and helpful—to my mom or your family, even complete strangers. But to me you were just demanding and selfish. Not that you didn't treat me with kindness, because sometimes you did.

Honestly, when we first married, in a strange way, I was happy. Then, whether by coincidence or just bad timing, our relationship quickly disintegrated when you lost your job. I was pregnant with Gabby, and very depressed, but all I heard was how my actions caused you problems. Your uncooperativeness caused a certain bitterness that has grown until now.

Three days after her birth, all I got was static—about dinners not being fixed on time, or the house being dirty. You were oblivious to what was happening, leaving me in despair.

So I kept trying harder. I read the Bible and anything else I thought would help improve our relationship. Time and again I begged you to do the same, to no avail. We seemed to get closer, but then we would end up worlds apart.

And yes, I know you don't drink, and I appreciate that. But I've put up with much more than any wife should. As far as beatings go though, let me tell you that after all your verbal abuse, a physical beating sounds mild by comparison. At least then you could see the scars. Instead, you have no idea how I've felt after you berate me—and I keep it to myself. That's one thing I've learned. I now realize you cannot possibly be interested in my feelings. Still, that doesn't mean they don't exist.

Things aren't getting better. In fact, last year you were self-employed and you still worked long hours. Now you work for someone else and it's the same thing. I've noticed a change, however, and this is what worries me. When you're around the kids now (which isn't often), you ignore them or find something better to do. Your fuse is even shorter than before, and you can't be around them for very long or you explode. And yes, you do show Slade attention—but the girls need some, too. Especially Mileah. She's at the stage where

she needs a father who truly cares about her. I can tell by
her actions and speech that she's rapidly becoming attracted
to other boys and men. I don't want that to happen. I went
down that path and it's not one I want for our children.

Gabby has shown signs that your nonchalant behavior
has affected her, too. She is very rowdy and hard to handle,
more so than usual. And I think her thumb-sucking has
increased, since she uses it as a security blanket all the time.

As for Trista, well, she's so quiet it's hard to say and that
scares me. Who knows what's going on in that little brain?
But it can't be good, and I know she's frightened by the way
you act.

Of course, Slade is too young to understand. But he will,
soon enough.

Now onto me: I can't continue this charade. I am very
lonely. I guess I need my husband by my side and this is get-
ting further and further from the way it actually is. So the
decision is yours. I would like for our life to be different. If
you want to be part of that change, Eddie, then you need to
realize our children deserve better. So do I.

—Daleen

I laid the letter down, knowing it held the potential to
make him angry, if he refused to see the good things in it.
Would he be able to see how much I wanted our marriage to
work? I hoped so. I sealed the envelope and left it on the table
for him to read whenever he got home.

I tried to wait up for him, and even called to see what time
he would be finished. After repeated attempts with no one
answering, I went to bed just after midnight.

When I got up the next morning, Eddie wasn't there. I
must have slept so soundly I didn't hear him come in or leave.
I turned over, realizing the other side of the bed remained

untouched. Maybe he hadn't come home. Maybe, maybe . . . a dozen thoughts, all of them bad, chased back and forth across my mind. Going downstairs, I looked around for a sign of the letter, but it was gone. I felt relief. At least he had come home, and hadn't driven over a hill somewhere. He must have decided to sleep on the couch. My fear and concern turned to anger.

Why didn't he wake me up? And why does he continue to play this childish game? I thought. *Doesn't he understand how much I need him? Surely he would have, had he read my letter.*

The day dragged on forever, and I divided my time between caring for the kids and wondering what I would say when Eddie returned that night. But he didn't come home. Kim called and said he was spending the night with her.

I was already asleep when he came home late three nights later. The following morning, I could see faint hues of pale bluish-yellow light breaking upon the horizon when I heard noises and went downstairs to check. Eddie had the door open when he saw me standing on the landing. I went halfway down the stairs, leaning against the banister. I waited for him to speak, but he said nothing. "Why didn't you wake me up?"

He didn't look at me while gathering up his tools. "After your letter, I figured there wasn't anything to say. Seems like you've just about said it all." He still wouldn't look at me and would have turned and left, had I not called out.

I was confused. "What do you mean, Eddie?"

He shrugged, finally meeting my gaze. "Well, I just got the idea that I have to shape up or else. And since I never could meet your standards, I pretty much know what I need to do. So I'll get out of your way as soon as I can."

"I don't know what you're talking about! I wasn't giving you an ultimatum. I was just telling you how I felt, hoping you might understand me."

"Well, that's not how I heard it," he said sourly.

"Maybe you only hear what you want to, Eddie." My voice was quiet in the large hallway.

"Yeah, it's always that way, isn't it? It's always me—never you. You don't do anything to cause problems, do you?" He snarled.

"Yes, I do. I make mistakes, and I try hard not to repeat them. I've tried to make a lot of changes, but I get the feeling you don't want to show me the same consideration." I wanted to say more, but he cut me off.

"Look, I'm already late for work. I'll see you later."

"What time will you be home tonight?" I managed to ask.

He didn't look back. "I don't know. Probably late. We're doing a government job and it's been delayed because of bad weather." With that, the heavy old door swung closed behind him.

I sat on the stairs until his truck was out of sight and earshot. I stared out the window, my mind blank, until rays of pink and grey lit up the morning sky.

What a copout. How easy it must be, to blame me for all his problems. What would he do if I wasn't here? Who would he blame then?

Until then, my thoughts about leaving him had been vague. But what before had been just a dream solidified into a concrete plan: I was leaving and my children were coming with me. I just didn't know when or how.

I slowly stood and went back to bed. The clock said five a.m. I had more than an hour before Mileah would be up for school. I closed my eyes, but sleep wouldn't come so I grabbed my journal from the nightstand and began writing.

"For years, I've thought I was a horrible person—for getting into bed with Eddie, for having sex, for letting God and my family down, and for getting pregnant. Because I believed I

was horrible, I felt like I deserved to be treated badly. That's why I always took the blame for Eddie's abuse. But something has happened that makes me realize it's not my fault he's got a bad temper. He had his temper long before I came along and anyway, he does things that make me angry— but I never take it out on him.

I don't deserve any of the things he's done to me: the bruise on my leg, the wounds on my heart, and the way he refuses to let me have any say over our sex life. And I'm tired of feeling like I'm not worth anything. Because I am, and I'm going to keep telling myself that until I know it's true ... and then I'm going to find a new life, for all of us."

I yawned. Putting the notebook down, I slid under the covers and began tossing and turning, trying to get a few minutes of sleep. Finally, just when I thought I might as well get back up, I dozed off, into a fitful sleep where the demons and ghosts that chased me were pleas and promises and ultimatums, flowing from the pages of a spiral notebook.

CHAPTER TWELVE

Making a new life for my children and I was more difficult than I imagined. My own mother had stood by her man during similar trials, following my father from the West Coast to the East, bringing her two young daughters to the perfect state for such things. She couldn't have known it all those years ago, when she drove from Wyoming to West Virginia, but that's what women here did—regardless of whether he cheated on you, beat you, or hurt your babies. Because that attitude had permeated generations of Appalachian families, it left me feeling uncertain and dubious about my own capacity for being both a mother and a breadwinner.

You know, if you're ever going to have a better life, having a job—a real job—is crucial, I thought. *It's the only way you'll ever escape, the only acceptable way.*

I knew many single mothers who lived on welfare, but I didn't want to be one of them. *Besides, I have more than enough energy and stamina to hold down a job while rearing my children.*

Still, I put off looking for work. What would I do? I was an accomplished seamstress, and had tried doing that when Eddie was out of work. I placed an ad in our local paper, which was answered by a woman who wanted me to make her a linen jacket. The garment took hours longer than I planned, leaving me little profit. So even though she raved about it, I knew I couldn't make a living as a seamstress.

Not having gone to college, all I had to fall back on were the sewing and typing skills I learned in high school. Because of being a wife and a mother, I could also cook, clean and take care of children. But none of those jobs paid well, unless I became a legal secretary. Even then, I wasn't sure anyone would hire me without legal experience.

I knew I just had to get a job—but doing what?

I continued to carve out my own time, and spent it doing all the things that made me feel proud of myself. I embroidered, baked, sewed, worked in the garden, canned food, played piano, exercised, studied all kinds of topics, and wrote—in my diaries and journals, on scraps of paper and in notebooks. I had at least four short stories taking shape so in January I queried several popular women's magazines. They were rejected, though, and all I received for my work were form letters. But I kept trying—hoping, wishing and dreaming that someday my efforts would pay off.

Perhaps all the writing and recent submissions unlocked something within me, for one day while searching for linens, I knew what I should do. Opening the door to the dining room china closet, I saw my notebooks, piled high in a tall stack. That's when it hit me: I can write.

Not only that, I'm a good writer, I thought. I remembered my high school journalism and English classes, when my teachers had nothing but praise for my writing. I wondered if I could write for a living. Like the seeds we had planted in the soil, the idea took root and began growing stronger by the day.

Before I could even try, though, Eddie and I had a confrontation unlike any other. We tried to go out on a date one Friday night, but Eddie came home two hours late, so I was already in a bad mood. He still wanted to go, so I played with the kids while he showered and dressed. Afterward, he came into the living room and stood there watching the television. I called his name twice and when he didn't answer, I picked up my keys and said I was going for a drive. I didn't even think he heard me, and was already outside when he suddenly came up from behind, grabbing the keys from my hand. He demanded I talk to him.

"Don't move. You stay right here and talk to me," he shouted, grabbing and shaking me, his hands around my throat. I managed to get loose but he came after me.

"I said get back here!" He screamed, grabbing me around the neck again as he began dragging me back toward the porch. I tried to go limp, so he would let go of me, but instead of breaking free, he drew his fist back and threatened to hit me.

"You better leave now, or I'm calling the police and getting a peace bond," I said coldly. "Do you understand me? I want you to leave. Now!"

His hands fell to his sides as I stumbled and tried to stand, before he turned away. That's the last thing I remember. I wasn't sure how I came to be there, but my hands were turning blue from the cold air when I found myself sitting on the porch trembling, hugging myself, afraid to even move. I absently reached up and rubbed my neck, which was sore and tense, and knew I should go inside.

When the door opened I froze, but Eddie walked past me without a word. He was carrying a duffel bag, and as he headed for our little pop-up camper, I prayed he would stay there. Only then did I go inside, to access the damage in the bathroom mirror. My neck was red, but there were no bruises. I thought about calling the police, but I was too embarrassed.

What would I tell them anyway? That my husband just blew a gasket and went off on me, for no apparent reason? I thought. *Would they believe me? Besides, he's not even in the house now.*

He's outside, sleeping in the camper. And we're in here, safe and sound.

When I picked up my pen long after the kids were asleep, I realized he could have killed me.

"I might be dead now, if not for risking even worse violence by speaking out for myself. Tonight has opened my eyes, and I won't close them again. Yes, I enjoy being a homemaker and a mother, but I need to feel like what I do matters. Like I'm appreciated. I don't get that at home. So I need to do something that keeps me preoccupied. I need to get busy and make that life for us, so we can get out of here before it's too late."

That incident propelled me to walk into the local newspaper office and ask if they were hiring. I was afraid of failure, afraid of being laughed right out the door, but I knew I had to try. It was a small family business, so I spoke with the publisher. He introduced himself as Fred Martin, and said a reporter's position had recently opened. He chuckled at one of the old high school newspaper articles I had brought along, before picking up the phone.

"Felecia, there's someone here I think you should meet. She's interested in the reporter's spot." He hung up and turned to me. "It's been a long time since we've seen anyone write like this. Come on, I want Felecia to see your clips."

"Thank you," I said, beaming.

We went upstairs to where a petite woman sat behind a large desk. Her long blond hair lay in soft waves around her face. She smiled generously, and Fred introduced us. "Daleen, I'd like you to meet the editor of *The Preston County Journal*, Felecia Martin, who's also my wife. Felecia, this is Daleen Leigh. She's here to see about the reporter's position."

"How do you do?" I returned her smile.

"So you've brought some samples of your work," Felecia said, taking the papers from Fred. She was soon absorbed in them and I sat there, trying to be patient, but anxious for her to finish. I relaxed as soon as Felecia started to laugh. "This is absolutely wonderful. Where did you learn to write like this?"

"Well, I took a few journalism classes in school, and I wrote for the school paper. I even wrote a few pieces for your paper, as a correspondent. I went by Berry then," I said, embarrassed. "I just love to write. I spend any extra time I can writing."

Again, that direct gaze glanced across the desk at me. "Yes, I remember your work now. You didn't go to college then?"

I started to answer, hoping it didn't affect whether I got the job. "No, I've been married since shortly after high school, and we're raising a family, so there was never any time for college. Is that bad?"

Felecia laughed, and I could see Fred smiling from the other side of the room. "No, not really. I happen to think that life experience counts for something, especially when you already have the raw talent to write. And that seems to be something you do have." She handed the papers back to me before continuing, "So, when do you think you can start?"

I was stunned. They wanted me to start working right away—and as a reporter! "Well, how about next Monday?"

"All right, it's settled then. Next Monday it'll be." It was their turn to be embarrassed, when they said the pay wasn't great.

"But your byline will appear below each article you write, which is a nice bonus," Fred grinned.

I was ecstatic and told them I'd be happy with whatever they gave me. I practically sailed out of the building, barely able to contain myself.

I'm going to work as a reporter, I thought. *Wait until I tell the kids.*

I still couldn't believe that Felecia remembered my work. I had just been a correspondent. I replayed the interview beginning with the moment I walked into the tall, unpretentious building. It looked, smelled and sounded like a newspaper office. I recalled the tall piles of old newspapers and inserts, as well as the long line of printing presses that stood taller than me. While giving me a quick tour, Fred had told me that's where everyone gathered twice a week, manually putting the sections together in assembly-line fashion, while the paper rolled off the press, hot and fresh.

I floated down from my cloud long enough to wonder how the kids would react when I left for work each morning. I wouldn't know until I tried, but I also knew it would depend on how I presented it. I tried to think of various approaches, but finally settled on telling them that I needed to be able to work at a job so I would feel better about myself. That was certainly true. Making a living as a reporter would be good for my self-esteem, too, as long as people enjoyed what I wrote.

And we could use the extra money, because even though Eddie's new job was steady, we were still separated and he only gave me as much money as he thought the kids and I needed to get by on. Which was the point: I had to learn how to be a breadwinner for the kids and me.

In the end, it was much easier than I imagined. The girls were excited and Slade was too young to understand. They danced around the living room happily, and told me we should have a party. All they really understood was that our friend Tammy would babysit them while I was at work. That was a bonus, since it gave them someone fun to play with.

The following Monday, I practically ran up the stairs to my office. There it was—my desk—with an Apple computer on it, waiting for me to begin writing. I took off my coat and hung it up, going over to the computer. I lovingly stroked it.

"Good morning," a voice said.

I was so engrossed, I didn't even notice when Felecia appeared. I turned around and grinned. "Oh, hi Felecia. I mean, good morning."

She laughed. "Why don't you give me a few minutes and then come back to my office and we'll decide what assignments you should start on." She disappeared and I sat there, nervous at the prospect of having my first talk with the boss.

I walked down the corridor. Felecia's door was open, so I went in. She was on the phone, but gestured for me to sit. Her desk was buried beneath piles of paper: opened and unopened letters, photographs, and two huge mounds of newspapers stacked so high they might topple over any minute.

"I'm so happy we hired you," Felecia grimaced as she hung up. "See this mess? Now maybe I can get you to sort through it, so I can find my desk again. Here, you can help me by taking these papers and looking through them. Just look for anything that looks like it could tie in to a local angle." She handed me a large stack.

"How long has it been since you've seen your desk?" I smiled as I took the papers.

"Oh, at least a month. It seems I can never get ahead of the game." She laughed. "They're from all over the state. Normally I go through them to keep abreast of what's happening. But I haven't had time to do that for, oh . . . "

"Let me guess, about a month?"

"Yes," Felecia spread her arms wide. "Now all of this can be your job. I'll let Lou know that from now on when the papers arrive, they're to go to you. But I have to warn you, they're habit-forming, and you should exercise care they don't take over your desk, too," she laughed.

"Now, let's see, Marianne—our photographer—she's been covering the sheriff's office, but why don't you handle that? That will free her up to do more photography. And we'll let you report on local city and county government meetings, once you learn the ropes. Concentrate on settling in and after you've done that, start with getting the police news. How's that sound for starters?"

"Wonderful. Oh, and Marianne's a distant relative."

"Great, that's even better. You shouldn't have any problems then," Felecia said.

I was hesitant to show my ignorance, but knew I had to ask. "Do you have any pointers about collecting news from the sheriff's department?"

"Yes, you can either call or run across the street to pick up any accidents or crime reports. Try to go in person whenever you can, or just hang out there. It's a great way to pick up a lead on a story you might not get otherwise. As for what to get, check with the sheriff or the dispatcher, if the sheriff's not in. Find out what's happened overnight, and ask them to direct you to the right people. Write down all the vital information, and then type it into the computer," Felecia's smile was full of confidence. "You'll do fine—you have a natural instinct for what makes a news story. Just remember to answer the five W's in the first paragraph or two of each story: who, what, where, when and why. Try to explain "how" after that. And don't use too many big words, because no one will understand them."

"Okay," I nodded.

"You'll pick up ideas as you go along, and when you do, come on in and we'll talk about them before I give you the go ahead. I think that's about it."

As I left Felecia's office, I realized I was eager to get started. But I also had a small case of the jitters, and self-doubt was starting to creep in.

What if I make a mistake? I thought. I squared my shoulders. *I'm not going to.*

Back at my desk, I grabbed a phone book and found the number. "Hello, Preston County Sheriff's Department," a male voice said.

"Hi, this is Daleen Leigh. I'm with the *Preston County Journal*. I'm calling to get any news you might have."

"I'm afraid we don't, just a small car fire from last night," the voice said. He gave me some details to jot down, and when I hung up I was pleased: I knew at 10:30 p.m. the night before, a 1984 Chrysler LeBaron owned by Rick Sanders caught fire outside Billy's Place, a local tavern. I knew the Kingwood Volunteer Fire Department responded with six firefighters, and they put the engine blaze out in less than thirty minutes. The cause was still under investigation, but initial reports indicated faulty wiring. I began typing, amazed to see the words appear on the screen as if by magic, almost faster than I could type them.

These are my words, and this is my very first news story, working as a reporter for the Preston County Journal, I thought. Nothing could have tickled me more, and I felt like I'd finally found my niche.

I read the words again and saw some things I wasn't satisfied with, so I began editing the short piece. I had no idea anyone else was in the room until I heard movement behind me. Turning around, I saw Marianne.

"Hi there!" she said, placing her camera bag on her desk. "So, how do you like our little newspaper crew?"

"Marianne, hi! Everyone is great. I hope you don't mind sharing your office with me."

She shrugged slender shoulders and smiled easily. "You'll be fine as long as you remember that Fred's the boss. Felecia's a piece of cake, really sweet and easy to work for." She winked at me.

I watched Marianne unload the film from her camera. "I'm going to the dungeon. That's the darkroom; have you seen it yet?" she asked.

"Just briefly, when Fred gave me a tour."

"Fun place," Marianne winked again and was gone.

Fred was right, for when my byline appeared in newsprint, I felt an excitement that surpassed anything from my high school days. I was helping put the paper together in the production room, where several thousand copies of the article I had written for that issue were rolling off the press. When I sat down later to look over a press copy, I turned to page two and saw my first article, and felt a budding sense of pride in my work. The next time was even more exciting, because my byline was on the front page, above the fold.

Four weeks later, I was putting the final touches on a humorous piece I had written, loosely based on a recent shopping experience with my family. I gathered up my courage and took it to Felecia.

"I don't know if this is something you can use, but I was just killing time and thought you might want to see it." I nervously handed it to her, and a small voice told me she wouldn't even like it. Then I squared my shoulders and thought: *what do you have to lose? Besides, even if she doesn't think there's any place for it in the newspaper, you know it's good—and it's funny.*

Felecia was immersed in writing her editorial, but told me to leave it on her desk. An hour later I heard her laughter, just before she appeared at my door. "This is great. Do you think you could write more like this?"

"Yes. I have others at home, written after one of the kids did something really funny or really awful, that made me grab my pen and notebook, so I could jot it down."

"You don't have a computer?" she asked.

"No, just a typewriter. Money's been tight with all of the mining layoffs."

"Well, we're upgrading the office computers, so maybe we can give you one of the old ones to use at home."

"Thank you; that would be great." I said, unable to keep a huge, silly grin off my face.

She turned to go. "We'll run this in the Saturday edition. Why don't you come up with a name for your weekly column and have it to me by Friday morning?"

That was how "Vintage Daleen" was born. Loyal readers wrote to tell me they read every column, eager to see what new and daring escapade my brood had gotten into. Usually I wrote about their childish antics—how they interacted with each other, with me, and how utterly rotten they were. Not bad, just mischievous. Readers loved it.

One month later, Felecia sent me across the street to the courthouse, so I could begin covering county commission meetings. I was green, nervous, and self-conscious. Instead of meeting the snarky, highly competitive people who worked at other news outlets, I met fellow reporters who were helpful and kind. Before long, we were a loosely-knit group, banded together in a small corner of the room, trying to find stories were there were none, figuring out how to make sense of complicated issues such as solid waste or school bond money that arose during the often tedious two-, three- or even four-hour meetings. Sometimes we just turned to one other, to keep from laughing at the absurdity of what took place.

Two months into the job by then, I knew I loved my work and would stay there forever, if I could. I lived to go to the office each day, where I made phone calls, got the latest police reports or court documents, and turned my notes into articles that would appear in print. I knew Felecia trusted me, or else she wouldn't have given me more and weightier assignments.

I felt a sense of joy and self-confidence like never before, as people learned who I was and began stopping me in the street, commenting about an article I had written, or offering me a news tip for a story I would then scoop, beating out the competition. I felt like I had finally found my place—and the feeling buoyed me up and kept me floating, even when things at home threatened to overwhelm me.

That was happening less often, though, because I was keeping so busy with work, and the new, positive experiences were crowding out the older, negative ones. I also found myself using what I learned in the workplace at home.

For instance, I interviewed a mental health clinic director, who spoke about the family stress that comes from unemployment. I also interviewed several people who were out of work. Their experiences verified what the director told me—marriage and family suffer, when the breadwinner loses his job, his income and then his self-esteem.

As I reviewed my written notes, I underlined the most significant elements of the interviews, and starred the quotes I wanted to use. I was amazed at the number of people I knew all around me who were without work. I pictured them all, living like my children and I had been living, walking on proverbial "eggshells," in an effort to keep the man of the house from taking out his anger on his family.

Equally eye-opening were the interviews I conducted for an article about a local counseling center for abused women and children. The center director told me people mistakenly think a woman has to have bruises to be abused, and I wrote down her words verbatim. She also said if a man threatens a woman with bodily harm but doesn't touch her, that's still abuse. I wrote as fast as I could.

"Then there are the mind games," she added. "That's where the men manipulate these women—even though the women are intelligent and articulate."

I couldn't write fast enough, and I was fighting to keep up, as I saw mental images of similar scenes from my past. I returned to the office with mixed feelings, having just learned what I was: an abused wife. I knew it was true, just as I realized I'd been trying to hide that awful, ugly truth for a very long time.

The months flew by as I settled into my new routine. Each morning, I got the kids ready for the sitter, then dressed myself and left for work. Once there, I made my daily rounds, going first to the sheriff's office, then to the state police barracks. Back at the office, I checked my messages and returned phone calls, saving the best for last: I sat down at my computer and wrote my stories.

By then I had developed a rapport with the police, and found other community figures candidly answered my questions. I allowed my natural curiosity to determine if there was a story and then tried to show both sides. My techniques weren't aggressive, which worked in my favor, since people told me I was easy to talk to.

At least one or two evenings a week, Felecia sent me to cover a local town hall meeting somewhere in the county. Before long, I began taking one or two of the kids with me when I knew the meeting wouldn't keep them up too late on a school night. It gave us more personal time together: I heard about their day at school, and they got a chance to see me in action. The small-town politicians loved having them there and if the kids didn't bring their homework or something to play with, the town council members usually supplied them with paper, markers and other office items that kept them preoccupied throughout the meeting. Just having children in the room seemed to lighten everyone's mood and once the meeting ended, they would tease the kids or compliment them on their good behavior, or even offer them candy or a soda pop—endearing themselves to my little ones. They, in return, would color pictures and present them as gifts, which were accepted and taped to the walls as if the childish drawings were of great value. All of the positive attention made their little faces positively glow with happiness. I loved being able to give them that time away from home, with me and other adults who treated them with kindness. Whenever I couldn't bring them, the politicians would express disappointment at not being able to see the children, which made me proud.

I was also secretly glad my meetings steered them away from the path of their father, who never failed to lose his temper during the times he had agreed to babysit for me, taking his anger out on them. I wished I could take all four of them with me every single time, but that would prevent me from focusing on my work. Besides, I knew having my entire brood tag along would be unprofessional. Instead, the kids would clamor over whose turn it was "to go to work with Mommy." I knew they were eager to be rewarded with the special treat I always promised them—usually an ice cream cone—for being on their best behavior, after the meeting.

The job was making me more socially conscious, too, which helped me use what I was learning—not just by writing about in my columns—but by applying it in my own life. After reading about two babies who died inside a car when the temperature rose to 150-degrees, I became outraged. The father admitted he hid the car behind his barn in the sun, because police were searching for him. I lambasted the father, writing a diatribe about parents who neglect or abuse their children, only to get a slap on the wrist. My growing awareness about such things had tapped a vein within me, providing an outlet for my own simmering anger, which I then released through my writing.

By early July, I recognized my anger for what it was: pure, righteous outrage that people would commit such violent acts in the name of love. That's when a local man was charged with killing his 56-year-old wife while she slept on the sofa, after she had refused to fix his dinner. Or so he claimed. It was the first fatality I covered. Ironically, it occurred the same week Eddie moved out, after I found out he was seeing another woman. As I interviewed Deputy Joe Stiles, an investigator with the sheriff's department, I found myself thinking about what went on in my own home.

That's when I started feeling differently about myself as a woman. Felecia sent me to cover a press conference at Ben-edum Airport, about an hour away. The West Virginia Air National Guard was bringing in a C-130, and wanted to demonstrate its features for the media. Felecia told me to call Brad Jansen, a part-time photographer we had recently begun using. We hadn't met yet, but I had seen some of his shots, and knew he did good work.

When we met a week later, I was completely unprepared for Brad. I was sitting in my car when his black truck pulled up beside me. The man I assumed was Brad jumped out, looked at me and smiled, his white teeth flashing in the sunshine.

Oh brother, please let him not be obnoxious. The good-looking ones usually are, I thought.

"You must be Brad."

He took my extended hand and smiled that beautiful smile again. "Yes, and you must be Daleen."

I laughed. "Yes, I am." When he turned to get his camera equipment, I couldn't stop thinking how he looked just like a Greek god. His short, wavy hair was blond and he had lovely, sea-blue eyes. He was tanned, and I could see muscles rippling under his cotton shirt.

If he isn't a bodybuilder, he's certainly missing a good chance.

"That's it." Brad hopped in the passenger side and closed the door. "It's a gorgeous day for a flight. I'm really looking forward to this."

"Actually, I've wanted to meet you. I mean, we work for the same newspaper, and until today we didn't even know each other," I smiled wryly. "Besides, you do great work."

"Well thank you. So do you. I've read several of your articles and wondered if we would ever meet. So this was a good idea."

"Yes, it was." I looked across the car and smiled at him, wondering how many women hit on him during any given day.

Driving to the airport, Brad told me how he came to be a photographer and I shared my experience about working at the newspaper. Since he was freelance, Brad said he usually just went on assignments when Felecia or Fred asked him to. He developed the prints in the darkroom basement at the office, but it was usually long after everyone had gone home, so he didn't really know the staff.

"Well, here we are." I maneuvered the car into a parking space and we jumped out. Walking into the airport, I kept fidgeting with my pantsuit. White, with a large black rose pattern, it was cool and comfortable, but with the heat I was also afraid it was showing every bulge.

I turned to see Brad grinning at me. "Do I look all right?"

His look was mixed with humor. "You look great, really."

I felt my face turn red. "I wasn't fishing for a compliment; it's just that this thing tends to cling sometimes."

"I know you weren't. And it isn't. It's fine." He laughed and I immediately felt comfortable.

After a short media briefing, we were led to the C-130, which looked like a large green bumblebee. Brad and I found two seats and snapped on our seatbelts. After takeoff, we donned what seemed to be a serious-looking harness and then made our way to the cargo door at the rear. It had been opened to the daylight outside, so we could see the terrain a few thousand feet below. The rushing wind, combined with the noise of the huge engines, was so loud it was almost impossible to hear one another.

Brad leaned over and yelled into my ear, "Why don't you stand near the edge and I'll get a shot?" I looked at him like he was crazy, but he was so taken by the idea that I took his advice. A few minutes later I was peering down over the edge, my harness the only thing keeping me from blowing away, as the wind whipped against me.

"This must be what it feels like to skydive," I yelled. "It's incredible!

Brad flashed a huge grin and gave me a thumbs-up sign, before snapping several more photos. Then it was his turn. I marveled as he leaned toward the opening, camera in hand, clicking away. Brad seemed fearless, standing much closer to the edge than I had.

After the flight, our group was walking back to the airport when we saw the pilot and some of the other military personnel waving. I waved back. "They like you." He grinned.

"I'm sure they're waving at all of us," I laughed.

"Maybe, but in that outfit, they're probably waving more at you. I know for sure those eager waves aren't intended for me," he laughed, "or at least, I hope not!"

I realized he was teasing me, and felt myself blushing.

As we left the airport building, Brad held the door open for me. The gesture made me think of Eddie, who never did. "It's nice to know chivalry isn't dead, after all. Thank you."

"You're welcome. I do it for my wife all the time."

"She must be happy to have you around. What's her name?" I asked.

"Connie. We have a two-year-old son, Jason."

"That's great. I'll bet he's a doll baby," I smiled.

"I think so." He grinned. "What about you? Is there a Mr. Leigh?"

"Well, that's not an easy question to answer," I paused, "since we're separated."

I saw the curious look Brad gave me. "Just trying to work out a few details, that's all," I shrugged.

We talked easily all the way back, making me realize how good it felt to have someone listen who wasn't constantly criticizing me. It also felt different from my professional interviews, where I merely asked questions and took notes as I listened to someone else talk. But with Brad, I was doing all the talking, and somehow the topic had come around to writing.

"So I thought I would tie in the angle about the planes being used to carry military cargo. That should make it a little more interesting. But I'd like to do some more research before I write it up. Who knows, there may be something else I'll learn before I'm done."

"You're very good at what you do. It's obvious you do your homework before you write a piece."

"Well, I've learned from prior experience that it can't do any harm to ask questions," I said, nodding, "and usually it results in a much better story."

He smiled. "You're a terrific writer."

I blushed again. "Why thank you, Brad. That's very nice of you."

"No, I really mean it. You have a way with words," Brad

said, his expression serious. "Just give me a ring anytime you need my help with a story."

"Thanks for coming along. I couldn't have gotten any prints at all without you, and besides, I'm sure your pictures will be much better than mine," I said as Brad got out of my car. "It was nice meeting you, and I'll call if I need you to do anything else."

"I'll look forward to it." He smiled and waved goodbye. As I watched his reflection in my rearview mirror, I thought about how good it felt to receive such sincere compliments.

I could use a lot more of that. It's so different from the usual put-downs I hear.

Our shared experience, high in the sky, created an instant camaraderie, and during the next couple of months, I learned Brad's friendliness was genuine: he had no ulterior motives. He quickly became an invaluable friend and co-worker. We worked together again at the Rowlesburg Ox Roast, an annual country fair held each Labor Day weekend. We chatted as we walked around the fairgrounds, deciding what shots to take. Suddenly, Brad stopped dead in his tracks. "You have four kids?" His look was incredulous.

"Yes, although sometimes it seems like twice as many." I laughed at his reaction. It was the same one I got every time anyone learned I had four children.

"Wow! You don't even look like you've had one—much less four."

"Brad, you are so good for my ego!" I laughed. "You know, if you don't knock it off, my head is going to swell to twice this size."

"No, really, I mean it. Do you mind if I ask how old you are?"

"I just turned twenty-six."

His hand went to his forehead, sweeping his hair back in a familiar gesture I was beginning to recognize. "You're only three years older than me." He shook his head again. "And you have four kids. Man, have you been busy."

I blushed and he added, "I'm sorry, I just meant—"

"It's okay; I get that all the time." We began walking toward the amusements. "Why don't we get a picture of the Ferris wheel?"

"Sure. Come on, we'll get one from the top." Brad ran ahead and I hurried to catch up.

"You mean ride it—together?"

He glanced at me sideways, giving me that silly grin. "No, we'll go separately and I'll take pictures of you riding it. Of course we'll ride it. What better place to get a picture than from the air? Besides, we can enjoy ourselves at the same time."

"All right, I'm game." We handed over our money and sat down, rocking gently back and forth as the carnival worker lowered a metal bar across our laps. As the bucket seat began rising higher into the air, we could see the river from across the ball field. The air was warm, the sun was bright, and billowy soft clouds floated overhead, making it a perfect day.

"Looks a lot different, doesn't it?" Brad asked, snapping some pictures of sights below.

"Yes, it does. The park is lovely. I think the town's much prettier now than it was before the flood."

"I think so too. I mean, it's a shame so many people lost their homes, but the whole town looks much better now. This park is great." He leaned over to take some more shots of the new playground equipment.

"So tell me, Brad, who watches Jason while you and Connie work?"

"My mom keeps him."

"That's good. You know, two is a great age. I sometimes

wish I could have kept my own kids at that age—except for the terrible part of those years, that is."

"We're pretty fortunate. Jason hasn't reached that stage yet," Brad put his camera down.

"What does your wife do?" I asked.

"She's a pharmacist."

"Sounds like a good job," I said.

"Yes, except for the long hours. But it gives Jason and me some time together. He's with my mom during the week, but Saturdays are for us," Brad spotted something, and picked up his camera again. "Look at those kids down there."

I looked in the direction he was pointing, to two girls eating ice cream. "You sound like you're very proud of him." I smiled, recognizing the paternal pride in Brad's voice.

"I am." He turned to look at me and I was once again struck by how handsome he was. I thought how easy it would be to let myself get lost in those blue eyes and that beautiful smile.

The sudden thought startled me. You're married, my inner voice reminded me.

Our bucket came to a gradual stop and as we got out, Brad turned to give me his hand, helping me up. As I took it, I felt a sense of loss. For what, I didn't know. Maybe for never having experienced such kindness. And now that I was, it wasn't with someone I could have an intimate relationship with—the kind I should have within my own marriage.

Wouldn't it be nice if Eddie treated me like that? I thought. *What a joke! Now that we're separated, the chances of that happening are more remote than they ever were.*

"Well, I need to head back to the office, so I can get this film developed," Brad said as he turned to go.

I waved as I drove off, and wondered what Eddie would think, if he knew I had just spent two hours in the company of another man. Granted, it was two hours spent working, but it was with another man, nonetheless. I realized he'd probably be pretty angry, not to mention jealous. He never wanted me anywhere around another man if he wasn't right at my side.

He probably judges all men by his own, unfaithful standards.

Then it hit me: Eddie wasn't there, because he had tired of sleeping in the camper and had moved in with his sister. I felt a wonderful sense of independence, like a bird being set free after having been held captive since birth. It was exhilerating!

Not only did Brad teach me techniques to improve my own photography, but on a personal level, working with him was great for my self-esteem. Men had always given me appraising looks, so that was nothing new. But I knew Brad saw the real me: someone with a head on her shoulders, who cared about people, and who had things to say that mattered. I also knew that, as a colleague, Brad found me attractive. But more important, he talked to me in a way that made me feel pretty. Pretty in a wholesome way—not like Eddie always made me feel, since my husband only saw me as a sexual toy, good for his own gratification.

Not long after Brad and I began working together, Cathy Ford disappeared. The Grant County woman's body was never found, but the authorities charged a sheriff's deputy with her murder and succeeded in getting a guilty conviction. Felecia summarized the case for our readers, but I pored through everything I could get my hands on, reading every detail about Ford and the blood police found throughout Paul Ferrell Jr.'s mobile home.

I wasn't sure if the articles contributed to my nightmares becoming so vivid that I had only recently begun to remember them. They had been occurring a couple of times a week for a few years, and were always the same: I was wearing a wedding gown, running through a long building, trying to escape my knife-wielding husband.

But it had taken my becoming a reporter and seeing other cases up close, for me to finally understand those dreams: I was afraid Eddie would kill me. I began writing down all my dreams as soon as I woke up, trying to piece together anything my unconscious mind was trying to tell me. My relationship with the local police continued to grow, but I remained tight-lipped about what went on in my own home, never talking about it to the "men in blue" I saw every day.

Suddenly, a year had come and gone. I loved my work and looked forward to each new story, but Eddie and I had recently reconciled, so he was hassling me again. At first, he told me how proud he was I had gone to work as a reporter. But not long after, he quit his paving job to return to the coal mines. Then he began making snide comments, pressuring me to quit. Determined to do anything but that, I went to see Felecia.

"I think we might be able to work something out. Why don't we talk about it and see what we can come up with?" she suggested.

I was thrilled when she said I could write my stories at home, as long I met my deadlines. "You know, you're so good at this. Everyone raves about what a terrific job you're doing and it would be a shame for you to lose all of that. Besides, you've been such a godsend for me. You can't imagine the amount of work you've taken off my shoulders," Felecia added.

"Have I really helped that much?" I sounded incredulous. I knew she liked my work, but I had never realized how much.

"Absolutely! You have such a way with words, and your writing skills are improving all the time. Not that they were bad when we hired you. And your column, it's terrific. Oh, here, a letter came for you in today's mail." She handed me a postmarked envelope, one of several I had recently received. Usually they were filled with praise for my column, but occasionally there was a complaint. I wondered which one this letter contained.

I left Felecia's office feeling better than I had in days, and more secure in the knowledge that she valued me. I was so thankful, because anything else would have seriously endangered my goal of saving enough money so I could leave Eddie and support my children.

And seeing my plans derailed in that regard was the last thing I needed!

CHAPTER THIRTEEN

I knew the day when I would leave Eddie was not far off, but in the meantime, it was impossible living as we were. He was always yelling at one of us, and in turn, we were always living in fear of doing something that would trigger his anger. Not knowing how long it might be before I could make my escape, I suggested we go to a marriage counselor. I thought it might give us some peace and quiet, or at least teach Eddie how to manage his anger. As it turned out, I was the one who had something to learn.

I casually suggested it one evening when Eddie was sitting at the dining room table, flipping through the pages of an auto magazine.

"We seem to have the same problems, over and over. I thought maybe we should consider seeing a counselor," I said, hearing the hesitancy in my voice.

He shrugged nonchalantly. "Whatever you think."

"If you don't want to go, Eddie, just say so. But I can't stand to see things go on like they have been, either," I said.

"Okay, I'll try it. But I'm not making any promises," Eddie grunted.

He went back to his magazine and I went to the kitchen for a glass of water, before going upstairs to bed. As I passed him, I stopped beside his chair. "Thank you, Eddie. It means a lot to me."

He didn't say anything.

We met Trudy Shaffer during our first session one week later, in a large upstairs room of a private psychology firm. The room was light and airy, with watercolor prints hanging on the walls. It was a pale ivory, and decorated sparingly. A thriving ivy plant sat in the center of a wooden Quaker table under a window that overlooked the street below. There was also a fireplace and a bookcase, filled with books on a variety of psychology-related topics.

It was a lovely, soothing room, and I instantly felt at ease. Trudy's short dark hair bobbed as she offered us seats. She told us she specialized in family counseling, and seemed really nice and down-to-earth. Eddie even seemed impressed. We didn't go into too many details, just told her why we had come, and she asked some general questions about our jobs and our children.

"We need to keep a written record, kind of like a game plan, so I'll know what progress we're making. Now Daleen, you said you feel that you and Eddie have stopped communicating, but you still love each other. Is that how you see it, Eddie?"

He thought a moment before answering. "Yeah, I guess so." From where he sat, in a chair across from both Trudy and me, it was hard to read Eddie's expression. But I could see a bit of humor there, as if he thought our visit was amusing.

"Do you see any other problems? Daleen said she'd like for you to work on your temper, but does she do anything that bothers you?" Trudy asked him kindly.

"Oh no, the problems are all mine. Everything's always my fault." Eddie seemed to slump down even further in his chair, his arms crossed in front of his chest like a belligerent child.

"I see." Trudy looked from Eddie to me.

"That isn't true, and you know it," I chided him.

"Well that's what you always tell me. That if I didn't cause so many problems everything would be just fine," he shrugged.

"Eddie, I know I have problems I need to work on, but I feel like I'm trying, and you're," I paused, adding, "well, you're not."

Trudy turned to me. "He's what? Not trying, you mean?"

Eddie answered instead. "Yeah, that's what she always says. But why should I try, when she's so perfect and nothing I do is good enough for her?"

I could hear the sarcasm and anger in his voice and I was embarrassed, but I wasn't backing down. *The sooner Trudy sees how things really are, the better,* I thought. *We might as well get it all out in the open now.*

"That's not true, either," I said. "I'm not perfect, and I don't pretend to be, and as far as accomplishing things—you know whenever you do something, I tell you how wonderful it is."

Eddie remained silent as Trudy watched us. "See what I mean? She knows everything, so why do you need me here?"

"Eddie, you sound like you don't want to be here. Do you?" she asked.

He looked up from the floor the first time. "No, not when it's not going to do any good."

I was feeling annoyed and knew it was beginning to show. "That's the problem. You never look at the bright side. You only see the negative. Of course it won't help if you don't believe it will," I said, frustrated.

Trudy was writing in her notebook and when she was finished she set it down.

"I'm going to give you some homework: I want you each to try to give the other person two compliments before you return next week," she smiled broadly. "Can you try that?"

We both nodded.

"Good, then I'll see you next week."

The weather was cold and rainy the following week and Eddie and I had argued on the way into town, making us a fine pair once we found ourselves again confined in the closed space. As soon as we entered her office, I knew Trudy sensed all was not well. Her short dark hair bobbed as she offered us seats. I really liked her. She was candid yet kind, and very intuitive.

"Hello, how are you two?"

"Fine." I managed a small smile. "Well, actually, we had a fight on the way here."

"About coming here?" Trudy looked concerned.

"No, about—oh, numerous things. You name it, we covered it." I looked at Eddie, who remained on the couch, staring stonily down at his feet, his body language saying he was trying to get as far away from us as he could.

"So Eddie, do you want to talk about it?" Trudy turned to him.

"No, let her. She's the great talker in the family." He wouldn't look up from his tennis shoes.

There was a brief silence before Trudy smiled and turned to me. "Well, Daleen, did you think of two compliments for Eddie?"

I felt myself blush. "Yes, but I forgot to tell him."

She nodded. "And, Eddie, what about you?"

"No, I didn't."

"You didn't what, think of two compliments, or didn't tell Daleen?" Trudy smiled.

"Neither."

I glanced sideways at Eddie, sitting on his corner of the couch. He appeared to be pouting. Again.

I guess we're going to be blessed with his monosyllables for the hour's duration, I thought.

Suddenly the entire scene seemed hilarious and I fought hard to suppress the laughter that threatened to erupt at any second. I knew if Eddie saw any sign of amusement, he would have a fit. He couldn't stand it if I didn't have a frown—like the one he always wore—on my face.

"All right, then you can both work on that again for next week." She looked at the notes she had taken during our first appointment. "Why do you think you have such a hard time communicating, Daleen?"

I sat there trying to come up with an answer. I didn't really want to get into the details about Eddie's infidelity, but I didn't know how to get around it. It certainly was part of the problem. "Well, I guess it goes back a few years, to 1987."

"What happened in 1987?"

"Eddie had an affair." I saw Trudy shake her head slightly as I peered past her, out the closed window. "I forgave him, and we reconciled, but he never really treated me well afterwards, and I get the feeling he thinks it was all my fault. So—" I shrugged my shoulders and looked at her, "we don't talk much."

"I see. What do you have to say about all this, Eddie? Do you think it's Daleen's fault? The affair, I mean?"

"Well, first of all, I think it's something that I'm never going to be able to live down, and second, no, I don't think it's her fault. I don't know why I'm not very nice to her. I just—" his words trailed off.

"I'd like to say something." I decided to be bold.

Trudy looked at me. "Go ahead, Daleen."

"I think that's unfair, Eddie. I said I forgave you, and I never bring it up, but right after I told you I wouldn't file for divorce, you began treating me terribly. That's very hard to get used to. Besides, I shouldn't have to—you just shouldn't do it." I stared at him, hoping he felt my pain.

"I take it Eddie was gone from the home for a time after this affair?" Trudy's voice was gently prodding.

"Yes, he moved out for a couple of weeks, until I decided

I was willing to try and save the marriage. But he's been gone some since then, too."

"You mean out of the home?" Trudy asked, taking more notes.

I shook my head and looked at Eddie, trying to give him a chance to explain. There were, after all, answers I needed from him, about why he continued to act so petulant.

"Eddie, would you like to say something about that?" Trudy asked him quietly.

He pulled the tip of his baseball cap up so we could see his eyes. "Not really, but I guess I'll have to." He stopped. "You see, I never meant for anything to happen. I'm probably as hurt by it all as Daleen is. But it happened and you can't turn the clock back, but I just get the feeling that Daleen hasn't really forgiven me, even though she says she has. And it's like she's always watching me, trying to see when I'll make the next mistake." He looked at me squarely. "But there won't be a next time."

"Does Daleen say anything to make you feel like she doesn't trust you?"

"No, not exactly. It's just a feeling I get, that's all," Eddie shrugged.

"I see," Trudy said, taking more notes.

"I don't think Eddie believes I've forgiven him because he's never forgiven himself, and he feels guilty about it," I offered.

"Is that right, Eddie?"

"Yeah, I guess so."

"Let's get back to what you mentioned earlier, Daleen. You said that Eddie still leaves sometimes. What do you mean?" Trudy asked.

"He just gets angry and takes off in his truck and doesn't come back for a day or so. Usually he goes to his sister's, but I never know until I've called around, hunting for him."

"And has this been going on for a long time?"

"No." I closed my mouth, and then realized something. "Well, actually, if you want to get technical about it, he's been doing this ever since we were first married."

Trudy's eyebrows went up. "Really?"

"Yes, he has," I said thoughtfully. "Over the years, whenever he's gotten angry—but not every time—he would take off and I wouldn't hear from him for several hours, sometimes not for a couple of days. The first time it happened, we'd only been married a few months."

"I see." Trudy looked at Eddie. "You seem to be content to just listen, Eddie. What do you think? Do you know why you leave?"

He gave Trudy his classic shrug. "I dunno. I just do, that's all. I guess I get tired of hearing her complain."

"I complain because you're never home long enough to fix anything that needs fixed, and when you are there, you're glued to the television screen, or to some porn magazine, and then you get angry when I ask you for help with the kids," I said coldly.

I felt myself begin to fume, but fought to stay in control of my feelings. I couldn't understand why, when I felt like I was trying so hard, nothing was working out.

"I see." Trudy made a few notes, before speaking in that soft, even tone of hers. "I'm sorry, but it's almost time for my next client. But before you go, I want you to try to do something for me. Do you two ever go out on a date?"

Eddie smirked. "What's a date?"

"Has it been awhile?" Trudy laughed, looking at each of us. "All right. Eddie I want you to ask Daleen out sometime this week, and then I want you to arrange for a sitter. Next week you can tell me how it goes. Are you two game?"

Our heads shook in unison, and I wanted to laugh: it was the first time we'd agreed about anything since we met Trudy.

But neither of us was thrilled about her suggestion. I could just picture us going out on a date. If it went anything like the last hour, we were in for a major waste of time.

Friday rolled around soon enough, and even though Eddie hadn't officially asked me out, I was still mildly excited about our "date." I wasn't expecting too much for our first trial run, but I hoped an evening together might improve our relationship, even if just a little.

I was getting dressed when Mileah came into the bedroom. "Where are you going, Mommy?"

"Daddy and I are going out tonight, Honey."

"Who's staying with us?" Mileah asked, watching me button my blouse.

"Pam."

"Oh goodie!" She ran off to tell her siblings. I could hear them making plans, and talking about how fun Pam was.

It had been awhile, and as I slipped on my shoes, I stopped to think about just when Pam had babysat for us. I couldn't even remember when, much less why, we had gone out.

I guess Trudy's right; we do need some time alone together, I thought.

The phone rang, breaking into my thoughts. I heard the mad rush as the children ran to answer, fighting over it. "Do not fight over the telephone. Tell whoever it is I'll be right there."

I ran downstairs to find Mileah talking to Eddie and I took the receiver she held out. "Eddie, where are you? Pam will be here in thirty minutes."

"I just finished fixing a piece of equipment they need on midnight shift tonight. I'll be there shortly. It won't matter if we're late, will it? You didn't have anything special planned, did you?"

"No, but I would like to eat before too much longer. I'm starved already." I glanced at my watch, which read 5:30 p.m.

That meant he wouldn't get home until after 6 p.m. I wasn't paying any attention to what he was saying, but I could tell by his tone of voice he wasn't worried.

"That's all right, Eddie. I'll just grab a snack until you get here. But please hurry."

"Okay, see you soon."

I turned to the kids as they tore through the house. "Hey now, you four, don't think you're going to turn this place upside down just because your father and I are going out, because you're not. I already wrote Pam a note telling her you have to clean up any messes you make before you watch television."

I went into the bathroom and began putting on my make-up. When the doorbell rang twenty minutes later, I yelled for the kids to get the door. "Tell Pam I'm in the bathroom, please."

I heard the sound of jumping. "Pam-my! Pam-my! You're our favorite babysitter," they chanted.

I stepped out of the bathroom long enough to see them fighting over which one would get the privilege of sitting on Pam's lap. "I left you a note on the table, and there's some leftovers in the oven, in case you haven't eaten. Why don't you go ahead and look over the note, in case you have any questions."

"All right kids, let's go read your mom's note."

I finished brushing my hair and went into the kitchen for a snack, to keep my growling stomach from protesting any louder.

I was still there when the front door opened and the kids ran to greet their father, whom they dragged into the kitchen. Eddie had returned to the mines a few months earlier, and came walking in carrying his metal miner's pail, amid the cries of "Daddy, Daddy!" He hugged each child and then looked at me. The whites of his eyes looked bright against his coal-blackened face. His clothes were black, too, and I had given up asking him to hold off hugging the kids when he first came home. They always ended up with coal soot on them, but I had long ago realized it wouldn't kill them. I figured that's what the bathtub was for.

"My, don't you look nice?" Eddie said, noticing the pale blue blouse and new jeans I was wearing.

I smiled, happy that he noticed I had dressed for the occasion.

"Thank you. Now if you expect us to get to town before the stores close, you better get on the ball." I teased him.

He saluted and the kids squealed with laughter, while I gritted my teeth. He knew I hated that, and he only did it to irritate me. "Yes, Maam!"

After Eddie showered and changed into clean clothes, the kids ambushed us at the door when we tried to leave a short while later. They all wanted kisses and hugs, and each one had a special, last minute request. When we finally made it into the car all alone, the quiet that surrounded us was practically deafening.

"So, where to tonight, kid?" Eddie asked, evidently letting me choose our destination.

"I hadn't really thought about it, but pizza sounds good. What about you?"

"Can't go wrong there. What then?"

"I haven't gotten any farther than that in the planning stage. Don't you have any ideas you'd care to contribute this evening?" I asked. I wondered if he would have even remembered we were going out on a date, without my reminder that morning.

"Well, I know one thing we could do that might be fun." A sideways glance told me just what he meant.

I turned my head so he wouldn't see me grimace, wondering if sex was all he ever thought about.

"They're having a live radio show at the mall. Why don't we go there?" Eddie suggested.

"Okay, but let's eat first," I said.

"Sure. You name the place."

"I think the pizza parlor over on Fifth Street has the best crust. Let's go there."

I was mildly surprised when Eddie asked about my day while we ate our dinner. Usually he never asked, but he seemed to be following Trudy's suggestion that he show more interest in my daily routine.

I told him I was working on a story about the statewide teacher's strike for the next edition. By the time I started working on the story, teachers in forty-six of fifty-five counties were on strike. Teachers were fleeing the state to find work elsewhere, and local educators were predicting a "mass exodus" if things didn't change. They believed the state government was immune to their plight and that of their students, allowing them to subsist on substandard conditions both in the classroom, and in their weekly paychecks.

That very morning I had crossed a picket line to interview teachers at the school our children attended. I found myself facing a battle line—one that included teachers with seniority who refused to cross, and some newer teachers fearful of losing their jobs if they didn't go back to their classrooms and their students.

Eddie knew about some of this, because I had mentioned a couple of things in passing earlier in the week, but as I talked, he didn't seem to remember anything I had said. I shrugged it off and tried to ignore his seeming indifference. By the time I finished, though, I knew he had only inquired about my day because Trudy assigned him to do so. Nor did Eddie tell me about his day, shrugging it off as "just another day in the pit."

Later, as we stood on the sidelines of the music show, I asked Eddie if he wanted to dance. "No, you know I can't dance. Especially not in front of all these people," he looked at me like I was crazy.

"You do so know how to dance, you just don't want to. If you tried it, you might like it," I pressed, giving him my best smile.

He shook his head. "Nah, I don't think so. I'll just watch—if it's all the same to you."

I gave up trying, and a few minutes later his expression told me just whom he was interested in watching: the voluptuous blonde across the room. It wasn't that he looked at other women that bothered me—it was the way he looked at them, as if he'd like to devour them, or like he was trying to figure out what their measurements were. I turned away in disgust, walking over for some refreshments.

While waiting for my drink, I casually glanced around the room. Many of the men were inspecting the blonde as intently as Eddie. They were openly gawking at her as she gyrated on the dance floor. Some men were more discreet than others, but they were just as interested in watching her as the men who weren't trying to hide their leering looks.

Standing there, I began looking at the women with those men. Some of them were average looking, but many of them were very attractive. Some of the women even wore an expression of forced happiness, as they pretended their husband or boyfriend wasn't favoring the beautiful blonde. I gave myself a mental shake, trying to comprehend it all. I had seen it in high school, when the jocks dated the prettiest and most popular girls, but then (behind their girlfriends' backs, of course) continued showing interest and even flirting with any other girl who showed them attention.

This was a long way from high school, though, and some

of the couples I saw were much older than me, and even older than Eddie. All around that room, I sensed a resigned sadness behind the women's fake smiles, as if they were used to being treated disrespectfully, and they had just decided to live with it. I wondered how long it would take, for me to wear that same look of resignation.

I think I'd die first, I thought. *I'll never get used to such inconsideration and rudeness.*

Drinks in hand, I went back to Eddie, noticing the way he tried to tear his gaze away from the blond before I noticed.

"You're too late." I sipped my Coke calmly.

"What do you mean?" His stare was blank.

"Too late to keep me from seeing you stare at her," I said, grinning wryly.

To his credit, Eddie pulled off a realistic puzzled look. "Her? Who on earth do you mean?"

I nodded towards the blonde bombshell on the dance floor.

"Why on earth would I be watching her?" He sounded flabbergasted.

"Oh I don't know, Eddie. Why do you stare at any woman who comes within a fifty-foot radius?" I smiled politely, hoping it looked like we were having a pleasant conversation.

"Look, I don't know why you're upset, but I wasn't staring at her."

"All right, I guess it was probably the male DJ who caught your interest, right?" I heard the sarcasm in my voice, a clear indication we were on our way to a fight, but I couldn't seem to stop myself.

"Well, I can tell another evening is spoiled. Come on, let's go."

He took off toward the exit, and I had to fight back the urge not to run after him and apologize for spoiling things, for overreacting, for everything.

It's not your fault. He caused this. If he wants to leave then, fine, let him leave. You certainly don't get to enjoy yourself, having to police him whenever he's around other women.

I forced myself not to run to keep up with him. We rode for the first fifteen minutes in total silence, until I tried to ease the tension. "You know you've always had a problem in that area, Eddie. I don't know why you just don't admit it and then work on it. Instead, you try to deny everything and accuse me of being paranoid."

"Oh, so now we're back to that! I wondered how long it would take." As his anger increased, so did the car's speed.

"Do you mind to slow down some, please, so we can get home in one piece?" The speedometer still didn't slacken though, and I knew he wasn't listening. We made it home safely, but I felt a sense of loss because the evening had turned out badly, and we weren't going to have any progress to report to Trudy. I wondered if it was any use to continue going to her.

We kept on trying, though, twice a month. Sometimes our sessions seemed beneficial, as if Eddie and I were both trying very hard to make our marriage work, but at other times I felt I was the only person putting forth any effort. That usually happened after Eddie began talking about something that had happened in the mines, which then dominated most of our session. I felt like the time we should be using to iron out our marital problems was being shortchanged. So I never mentioned it to Eddie, knowing that it would be therapy suicide if I did. That would be all it would take for him to stop going completely, and I didn't want him to blame me for that, too.

Nor did I need to speak up, because Trudy did it for me, gently suggesting we try to focus on relationship topics during our sessions. And for a while, we seemed to gain ground. But for every inch of progress we made, we seemed to slide backwards two inches. We eventually got into the habit of having lunch together after our appointment, before Eddie had to leave for work, which allowed us to continue our session privately. Those lunch dates became something I looked forward to, knowing it was one of the few times we usually didn't argue. Because we had just paid for an hour's worth of therapy, and an argument immediately afterward would have seemed like a waste of money, we usually managed to get along.

About the same time Trudy entered our lives, a Valentine's Day mystery occurred, when a local man simply vanished into thin air. It was the first of four disappearances—and what would ultimately culminate in ten murders—to occur in our sleepy little county during an 18-month period. The crime rate soared, making more work for the police and media alike. At the same time Robert Barlow disappeared, another local man from a neighboring county was shot a few hundred feet from where we lived on Swan Street in Newburg.

By then, I had been on the job two years, and local cops would offer me stories and news tips willingly. They would even give me a scoop, providing details about ongoing investigations in return for holding a story until it wouldn't compromise their investigation. I had learned that ours was a mutual relationship—we needed each other—so I was willing to work with them, because it ultimately meant getting a story.

Deputy Charlie Haney investigated the Swan Street shooting. Haney was Joe Stiles' sidekick and sometimes partner, and the pair had put on a good cop, bad cop display for me not long after I started working as a reporter, which initially left me nervous about talking to them. Before long, I learned they were some of the biggest jokers—and best cops—in the state.

Whereas Barlow had been murdered, the Newburg shoot-

ing wasn't fatal, and was an accident. Apparently, an overanx-
ious neighbor fired off a round when he heard noises outside,
hitting the victim by mistake, wounding him just enough to
send him to the hospital. As I listened to Deputy Haney and
took notes about what happened, I realized I was becoming
less sensitive to the details involving such crimes, which I took
as a good sign.

And when I sat down with Joe to get details of the latest
news about the Barlow case, I realized I was becoming less
afraid of Eddie. I wasn't sure what had happened to cause it,
but wondered if my growing rapport with the two deputies
had anything to do with it. Somewhere in the back of my
mind, I think I knew all I had to do was pick up the phone
and call them for help, and they would take care of Eddie in
a heartbeat. They wouldn't stand around and let any man beat
on his wife. Besides, I knew they liked me, they respected me,
and they knew I was a woman—not a doormat.

Just two weeks later, Lynne DeBerry disappeared after
leaving his Kingwood home. He was related to two other
men—Dennis Powell and Tommy DeBerry—who disappeared not long after that. Tommy walked to and from his job
at the local Pizza Hut. The youngest of the three men (and a
nephew to Lynne) Tommy vanished after he left work during
the early hours of March 11. By the time Dennis Powell
became the fourth man to disappear on March 24, county residents had gotten the jitters. Powell vanished after last being
seen at a restaurant in nearby Reedsville.

Rumors flew as Prestonians eagerly leaned across their
fences or met at their mailboxes, gossiping about the body
people heard the police had discovered. In the meantime,
Felecia and I worked together on the Barlow story, one of the
biggest of the year. People in West Virginia probably went
to bed a little easier the day his body was found in a remote

wooded area, a week after he disappeared.

Deputy Stiles spent hours interviewing Richard Knotts, who was later arrested. He was charged with stabbing Barlow, in a crime that turned out to be a love triangle. By then, I was only too familiar with covering violent crimes, but the day Sheriff Jim Fields invited me to join Stiles and several other officers for a diving expedition was quite exciting. The group met with dogs and divers at Bull Run, a local hangout for swimmers and whitewater rafters alike. They found the Cheat River not only a challenge to maneuver in their small, narrow kayaks, but also deep enough to jump from the rocks that surrounded the popular swimming spot.

The police didn't find any bodies in the river or anywhere else, although authorities believed a local drug dealer who was later sent to prison on felony drug charges had killed them and dumped the bodies somewhere. To local residents, "somewhere" meant they had been dumped down one of the many shaft mines scattered all over the county, but police searched those, too, and still couldn't locate the three missing men.

By the time Trudy suggested I attend a weekly Adult Children of Alcoholics meeting, we had been seeing her for several weeks—with little progress. I really liked her. She was candid yet kind, and quite intuitive. When Eddie and I left Trudy's office, all was well, but by the time we returned the next week, we just seemed to rehash the same problems all over again. ACOA was for anyone who had a friend or relative with a drinking problem, and Trudy said she thought it might help me, due to the alcoholism in my family.

When I told my friend Shirley about the meeting, we decided to go together, since she had grown up in an alcoholic household, too. Although we both felt awkward at the first meeting, by the third one, we were beginning to feel comfortable. I could identify with many of the people who spoke up and talked about how alcoholism had affected them. Then came the fourth meeting, when a young woman started talking about her childhood.

"Hi, I'm Debbie. I'm an alcoholic."

The group responded in unison. "Hi, Debbie."

"I'm also a victim of child sexual abuse," Debbie said, telling us how her father had molested her when she was just a girl. Debbie said she felt dirty and worthless, as well as powerless to stop the abuse.

As I sat and listened, something deep within me began to feel very uncomfortable. The more I heard, the more I realized she was telling my story, too.

Except with me, it wasn't my father. It was Eddie.

It was the first time I had actually heard anyone talk about a personal experience with sexual abuse. I had kept my story to myself, dissecting it only inside my own mind. But after Debbie's initial comments, I didn't hear another word she or anyone else said. When the meeting ended, Shirley and I went to the car.

Victim . . . victim . . . victim. That's what I am.

I heard Shirley's words through a distant mist. "Boy, if I had been her, I'd have killed her old man. Can you imagine that?"

"Yeah, terrible, isn't it?" I vaguely replied, my mind a thousand miles away. When we arrived at her house, we sat in the car talking for a few minutes, but I was distracted.

"Daleen, are you all right?" Shirley asked.

"I don't know," I said. "That girl Debbie—I think the same thing happened to me."

"Your dad molested you?"

"No, not Dad. Eddie. He started forcing me to have sex with him when I was thirteen," I forced the words out.

Shirley was outraged. "Do you realize that's how old my

daughter is? You were a child. Does your mom know?"

I shook my head.

"You need to tell her, and you should also tell Trudy," Shirley said.

The car was silent for several seconds. "I was raped, when I was eighteen," she said quietly. "But you were so much younger. It's probably affected you in ways you don't even know."

I told her how it had happened, and the more I told her, the angrier Shirley became. "He should be castrated!" she practically seethed.

We sat there talking for what seemed like hours, and as I was leaving, Shirley looked over at me. "Don't blame yourself for what he did to you. It wasn't your fault."

The next few days felt like a daze. I could hardly grasp what was happening. Like a broken needle on a record player, I kept replaying everything: from the first night I crawled into Eddie's bed when I was thirteen, to the last time he crawled into mine, even after I had gotten pregnant with Mileah; from the day Carla accused Eddie of fondling her to my three subsequent pregnancies; and from the ACOA meeting to Shirley's parting comment. I wondered what to do. I knew I needed help, but I had no clue where to find it.

CHAPTER FOURTEEN

The answer came during our next session with Trudy. "So, how was your week?"

I was on the couch; Eddie was several feet away in a chair. For once, I didn't want to say anything. Neither did Eddie, but that wasn't odd.

"I see," Trudy nodded, speaking volumes, but still smiled kindly. "Is that why you're sitting so far apart today?"

I nodded, looking away from the window for the first time. "Yes."

"You seem preoccupied, Daleen. Would you like to talk about it?"

I drew a deep breath and took the plunge, knowing it was now or never. I steeled myself not to be afraid, knowing he couldn't hurt me anymore than he already had.

"You may have noticed how Eddie and I always have small issues we bring in, disciplining the children, paying the bills, housework, and so on." I began cracking my knuckles and twisting my fingers, and felt myself becoming tense. "Well, I know you've said they're a symptom of something bigger, but neither of us could figure out what." I stopped, looking out the window again. It would be so easy just to keep looking out the window, and to never leave the safety of Trudy's little room again. To not talk about anything at all, ever again—especially about that.

I steeled myself to say what had to be said, and looked directly into Trudy's eyes. I had to see her expression, and wanted her to know I was sincere. On some level, I had to read the reaction in her eyes, to discern whether she believed me—or whether she thought I was crazy.

"Well, I know what our problem is now," I said, my voice unusually calm.

"What is it?" Trudy asked, her own tone neutral and inviting.

"Eddie raped me when I was thirteen." I broke off, only to hesitantly continue, afraid if I didn't say it now, I never would. "And sometimes, he still forces me to have sex," I blurted it out.

There, I thought. *There it is on the table, in front of us all.*

I could feel myself drawing into a little ball, emotionally. I felt so far removed from the other two people in the room.

Trudy was silent, but the expression on her face never changed. She still looked as caring and concerned as she always had. "Eddie, do you have anything to say?"

He shrugged. "I don't know."

"Have you ever forced Daleen to have sex before?"

"Yeah, I guess," he shrugged.

"I see." She made some notes and looked back up, thoughtful. "Well, it's been my experience that women who have been raped have a lot of issues, and a lot of anger, to work out. I think it would be better if I could see Daleen by herself awhile, until we get some of these things resolved."

"How long do you think it will take?" Eddie was five feet away, but his voice sounded like it came from another galaxy.

"I don't know. Maybe quite awhile, but it depends on the progress Daleen makes. In the meantime, maybe we could work out a schedule so you two could come together once a month, and Daleen could see me once a week by herself, if you both agree to that." She turned to me, and I forced myself to quit staring at the potted plant behind her shoulder.

"That's fine with me," I offered.

"Well, this will probably be the end of our marriage now. I might as well just throw in the towel." Eddie looked like a sulky child, I noticed while peering at the wall beyond him.

Oh yes, Eddie, it's always about you, isn't it? I thought. *Let's make sure this is about you, too, why don't we!*

"If I wanted to end the marriage, I would have done it already. I only mentioned this because I need help—and so do you. But right now I think I need to get this thing worked out before we can make any progress as a couple." As I talked, I felt the anger growing within me. As far as I was concerned, I had just announced to the world that my husband of ten years had been raping me. Yet I was the one consoling him—very weird!

"She's right, Eddie. The little issues you've been bringing in here have been masking this problem, and now that Daleen has opened up, she's ready to work on it. And, it could very well be the reason for all your other problems," Trudy carefully explained to him.

"Well, I'll do whatever it takes to fix things. I don't care what it is, I want her to get the help she needs," Eddie offered.

"It's good you feel that way, Eddie, because in all likelihood it's going to take quite awhile to sort things out. In the meantime, feel free to call me if I can help you, but anything Daleen and I discuss will remain private, unless she decides to talk to you about it."

We left the office in silence, and the drive home was equally quiet. When we went inside, Eddie began packing his lunch and went straight to work. He didn't say one word to me, and I suspected he was angry with me for telling Trudy the truth.

"It's about time," I muttered to myself.

The next couple of weeks were hellish ones to live through. I tried to pretend nothing had changed on the outside, but inside the sensations I had begun to recognize as flashbacks were increasing. They were the same scenes from the past that I'd been having for years, of actual sexual situations I'd been in with Eddie.

With the exception of the kids being more rambunctious than usual, due to sensing the increased tension in the air, everything else stayed the same. Eddie began working even more overtime, and when he was home, references to my "revelation" were rare.

A week later, during my first solo session with Trudy, she said "highly possible unresolved anger toward Eddie" had caused my depressive episodes. Trudy said I needed to decide where I wanted to go from there, and she would support my decision, whatever it was.

"I don't really know. I just know that things can't keep going like they have been or I'll go crazy," I said, uncertain of what to do or how to do it.

"I know, it's not healthy for anyone involved," she nodded knowingly.

Trudy gently moved me along at a snail's pace, as we began talking about how his sexual abuse had begun.

"You know, for years I believed that what happened between Eddie and me before our marriage was my fault. Or at least I thought I was partially to blame. I mean, he always told me that," I shrugged, trying to figure it all out.

"What did he tell you?"

I was embarrassed, so it took me a few minutes to answer. "He always said, whenever we had sex, that if I wasn't so pretty, he wouldn't have to do it. Or because I caused him to get aroused, it was my fault," I laughed mirthlessly. "He also said he would be in a lot of pain if we didn't have sex."

"That's a common line among certain types of men," Trudy shook her head. "So tell me, what usually happened during the times you were together? You mentioned his apologies; did he always do that?"

"No, not really. Usually, if I was at his house, I would go into his bedroom—to talk to him—and he would end up telling me to get into bed with him. He always promised not to touch me, but—" My words trailed off and I found myself separating from the present, beginning to drift away, to another place and time.

"But he did." Trudy's soft words brought me back to the present.

I felt tears welling up behind my eyes. "Yes, he did. And you know what? I blame myself to this very day, for being so stupid. I mean, what was wrong with me? Why did I keep going to his bedroom? Why didn't I just stop? Why didn't I stop wanting to have anything to do with him?" I angrily wiped at my tears, willing myself to stop crying.

"Daleen, it's very common for young girls to look for a father figure when their own father is unavailable, either physically or emotionally. But no girl of thirteen is ready for sex, or wants sex. All she wants is love and attention, and even if she threw herself at him, any decent adult man would kindly tell the girl that's inappropriate behavior," Trudy stopped, as if trying to let it all soak in. "From what you've told me, and I completely believe you, that never happened—which left you in a pretty awkward situation. Based on my professional experience, you kept going back because you wanted the love and attention you thought Eddie was giving you. Children and teens need that attention. But you never wanted sex. Try to think back; do you remember how you felt?"

I stared out the open window, blocking out the sounds of early morning traffic coming from the busy street below.

Slowly it all came back. "Yes, I went to his room because I thought he loved me, and was interested in me—as an equal, as a friend. I kept going back because I always trusted him, because he said it would never happen again."

"And as things progressed, what happened? You mentioned the rapes didn't always happen at his house," Trudy asked.

I shook my head, not wanting to shake the dust off the disturbing scenes from my past. "No, as I got older, he began coming to my house to spend the night." I stopped, incredulous, looking at Trudy. "You know, I still cannot figure out why my mother let him stay there. I used to lay in bed at night, torn apart by my prayers. I prayed she wouldn't find out what was going on, but I also prayed she would, so she could stop him."

"But didn't Eddie help around the house, doing odd jobs for her?" Trudy asked.

"Yes, he was always doing some chore or another. Sometimes, when we didn't have any money, he would even help pay for things like car repairs or firewood."

"So I imagine your mom also felt somewhat indebted to him. Not that it explains her letting him stay overnight when she had a teenage daughter in the house. What else do you recall?" Trudy stopped writing long enough to look up.

"That he came into my bedroom in the middle of the night, and insisted on having sex. I always told him to go away and leave me alone," I said, feeling aghast even as I said it, "but he never would."

"So this went on for how long? A couple of months?"

"About six months, then. That's when I got pregnant," I said sadly.

"I see," Trudy was taking notes again. "Tell me, were there other times, away from both of your houses, when those things happened?"

"Yes, they did," I said, thinking about *Gone With the Wind*.

"Whenever we went somewhere alone together, he would try to get me to have sex. Sometimes I could make him stop, but not always," I looked up at her. "That's what I don't understand. If I could make him stop then, why not all the time? Maybe if I just would have tried harder, I could have. I just don't get it," I shook my head, still not understanding.

"Daleen, that's an unfortunate myth among rape and incest victims, and the fact is, you're not just a rape victim—you're an incest victim." Trudy stopped, giving the words a chance to sink in. "Victims are often made to believe they said or did something that caused the rapist to stop, when in reality, the rapist, or molester, stopped himself. Think about all the times Eddie didn't stop. Did you react any differently than when he did?"

I shook my head.

"No, I'm sure you didn't," Trudy's smile encouraged me to trust myself, and to trust her explanations. "So you see, it wasn't your fault. You neither controlled him or his actions. Only Eddie had the power to do that. And he took advantage of you by making you feel like you were responsible, which is another thing child molesters and rapists do to their victims."

We sat in silence for a few minutes. I shook my head, feeling more tired than I had in a long time.

And I wasn't even sure how, but I knew I would be okay.

"We need to stop here today. If you're comfortable with that, this is what I want you to work on during the next week." Trudy's homework assignment included looking at my children during their play times, while thinking about how innocent they were. She told me to look at other young girls, too, who would be about the age I had been when the abuse began, and observe how they acted.

We would discuss my findings during our next visit. And finally, since I'd been keeping a diary for years, I might even want to review those journals, to see what I could glean from what I'd written there.

"I have a hunch you've sensed this has been the real problem all along, and your journals may just hold the key that will help you make sense of this," Trudy said, giving me a big hug as I left.

We continued working together, and during the next few weeks I took time to watch my children as they sat playing on the floor with their toys, pretending, or reading their books. I was sitting with a cup of hot peppermint tea while journaling in the living room, curled up in my favorite old chair. Mileah and Trista were stretched out on their bellies, reading and coloring, while Gabby ran around the room chasing Slade. They seemed so young, so childish. Granted, they could be mean, or even manipulative—but sexual beings they weren't. They didn't know what sex involved, the risks one took, the trust you needed to have, or the way it changes your life. Nor did they have the emotional maturity to desire a sexual experience.

I began writing and stopped, thinking about them as I watched the steam waft away from my teacup, leaving a trail of peppermint behind.

It's so odd: you see the same thing day after day and never realize what it means.

I had been a mother for ten years yet in all that time I never looked below the surface, where I was finally seeing myself in my children. It brought a wistful smile to my lips. It took having daughters of my own to make me realize I had been a child, too, and there had been little or nothing I could have done to prevent what he did to me. As a mother, I saw the innocence in their faces, in their voices and in the actions of my own little girls. At that moment, I knew I had been just as innocent.

Even though Mileah was almost ten, I needed to see older girls, just in case something changed dramatically in three years. So I watched thirteen-year-olds, to learn how I might have behaved when I was their age. What I saw was so different from what I had always believed, about myself at thirteen. While some of the girls would flirt with the guys, more often than not, I noticed a shy hesitation in how they handled themselves when around boys. Many girls weren't even around boys. They were too busy riding bikes, or sitting in their yards talking about girl stuff. Watching a neighbor girl named Shelly gave me a huge sense of loss as she got down on her hands and knees and played with my children, or sat and read them stories. I told Trudy about her during our next session.

"You know, while I was doing my housework, I watched a neighbor girl who comes over sometimes. She played with my kids like she was their age. I don't remember ever being like that. In fact, I don't remember being much of a child at all. Why is that?"

"It's probably because you weren't. Children of alcoholics are so busy taking care of their family members that they forget to have fun, or else they don't have time," Trudy explained.

"I see," I said, and I really could: that was exactly what happened to me.

"I remember you telling me once that you began handling the bulk of the household chores at an early age," Trudy's pen was again moving across the page.

"Yes, when we moved to Martinsburg and Mom was pregnant, I did some of the chores. I helped out in the café we ran, too. But I also made candy and sold it at school, and I babysat on the weekends. Oh, and I had a paper route before that."

"What a big responsibility. How were your grades then?" Trudy asked.

"Oh, A's and B's, but mostly A's. I usually got good grades, and never had to work very hard at it—until high school. Something happened then." I looked away, lost in my memories.

"Daleen, what's happening to you now? Where are you?" Trudy's voice carried me back into the room.

I shook my head. "I don't know. I guess I was just thinking about how I lost interest in school after—after what happened."

"No, not after what happened. After what he did to you. See if you can say it."

After what he did to you. After what he did to you. After what Eddie did to you, I tried to grasp the concept.

"I lost interest in school after what Eddie did to me." As the words came tumbling out, I heard how monotonous they sounded, and wondered if I had always felt so numb.

"That's good. Now, what about telling anyone? Did you ever try to tell anyone at all?"

I quickly shook my head, aghast at the idea. "No, I was too afraid of what they would think of me. I was afraid Eddie would stop loving me, too." I looked at Trudy, full of shame.

She recognized the look. "It's all right. You have nothing to be ashamed of. What happened was not your fault. Now, do you remember what you saw while doing your homework?"

I smiled, thinking about everything I had witnessed. "I saw how immature they were. How much they need to be protected. How much they want to be loved. They would do anything for that love."

Trudy sat across from me, shaking her head in agreement.

"You know, watching Shelly was amazing. If anyone would try to tell me that it was her fault for being in a sexual relationship, I would say they're crazy. That girl has no more desire for sex than the man in the moon."

Trudy looked relieved, as if she was worried I might not have seen that. "Exactly! And you were just like her. You didn't want sex: you wanted love. But you did not want to be involved sexually. I bet your body wasn't even ready for sex," she said.

I looked past her shoulder, staring into the past. "No, I hadn't even started having my period yet. It was awful. I still feel like I could die of embarrassment and shame. I just can't get over those feelings."

"I know. But some day you will. You may not realize it, but you've already come a long way and I think you're doing great!" Trudy's smile was so bright it allowed me to hope she was right.

We ended the session a few minutes later, and I left less confused than before, but with so much more to think about.

I didn't want to think—thinking was the last thing I wanted to do. I wanted nothing more than to put it all behind me and get on with my life. But Trudy warned me that my life, my feelings, had been on hold for far too long. As I walked down the street to my car, I knew there was no turning back. I was going to have to see it through to the end. Even in the blinding spring sunshine, I knew it would be painful. What I didn't know was just how painful.

Because I wanted to make progress, I began looking back over all the journals I had been keeping. If I had had any doubts about the truth of my life, reading those pages late into the night set me straight. I saw exactly what had happened, and was amazed how accurately I had recorded my thoughts and feelings. I went from blaming myself, after the first time Eddie raped me, to gradually growing more and more confused, about the role I had played. By the time we had been married for several years, I was openly writing about how bad the violence was—instead of continuing to gloss over the facts with a form of varnish that would fill in the crevices and smooth out the rough spots. In a way, those diaries seemed to act as a conduit between my waking, conscious state, and the unconscious one that had been trying to break free of its mental prison for years.

So it was no surprise when our marriage kept crumbling. Either Eddie couldn't understand what I was dealing with, or he didn't care (despite his firm assertion otherwise, the day at Trudy's office when the dam burst). Whichever the case, Eddie worked more overtime, came home after I was already asleep, and rarely spoke to me.

I knew he was angry, and while it bothered me at first, the more my therapy progressed, the less I cared. Finally, the day came when the tables turned, and my anger was directed at him.

It was one of the rare occasions we were both in bed together and still awake. I saw how bitter my revelation had made him. "I suppose we'll never have sex again, will we?" Eddie asked sarcastically.

I was nonchalant about it. "Oh, I don't know. Maybe one of these days we will."

"You don't even care, do you? But then, you've always been frigid!"

I glared at him. "How dare you call me that? If I've been frigid, it's your fault. Why aren't you more concerned about how I'm doing than your own sexual satisfaction? Is that all you can think about? What about me?"

"You seem to be doing just fine. You and Trudy probably say all kinds of terrible things about me behind my back. Every time I see you, you won't say a word to me." He whined, full of self-pity.

"Did you ever consider that I don't want to talk to you? I've been trying very hard, and considering everything, I think I've done really well. I mean, hey, I haven't even kicked you out of bed yet." I heard the sarcasm in my own voice.

"I guess that means you plan to. Hell, you might as well just divorce me now and get it over with," Eddie sneered.

I turned over and stared at the wall, unwilling to answer. Long gone were the days when I would rise to that bait, or feel compelled to comfort him.

Instead, I focused on my feelings. "The only problem is, I can't feel any anger. I know I am angry, but I can't express it like I should," I told Trudy during our next session.

"That will come, in time. Actually, depression can often be a form of buried anger."

"You mean that could be why I've been depressed all these years?"

"Yes, it could very well be. You have a hard time getting angry, don't you?" Trudy asked, pen in hand.

I thought about her question. "I guess so. I know my mother never got angry. At least, we rarely saw it, if she did."

Trudy had that look in her eyes, the one she got whenever she was making a connection.

"You think I got that from her, don't you?" I smiled, knowing she was right.

"Maybe. You said she took a lot from your father. And you say she rarely got angry with him. Was anger something that wasn't allowed in your household? I mean, did your religious beliefs say it was wrong?"

I had to stop and consider her questions. "No, it wasn't that it wasn't allowed—in our religion, that is. It's just that it was always suggested there were better ways to deal with things. But I can remember going over Bible verses that talked about how God gets angry, for righteous reasons—such as when widows and orphans are mistreated—so I know we weren't taught it was wrong. Maybe just that it could lead to wrong behavior, though—like when Eddie used to punch holes in the wall."

"I see. So you don't get angry, either."

"I do, but not often. Eddie is the screamer in our family. Sometimes, I'll yell back, but mostly, I hate fighting, so I just don't respond. I would rather keep peace." I shrugged.

"Old habits die hard, huh?" We both laughed.

"But you know, anger can be productive, when used in a healthy way," Trudy added, "and if it doesn't get out, you can turn it on yourself, like ulcers, or—"

"Depression?" I asked.

"Yes, exactly. Now, I want to change the topic for just a minute. If you can, I want you to think back to some of the times when Eddie forced you to have sex. Do you recall how you felt at the time?"

I thought back, trying to remember my feelings, but I kept drawing a blank. "No, I just remember hoping he would get it over with."

"Okay," Trudy was taking notes. "Did you ever leave? By that I mean, in your mind?"

"I think I must have, sometimes. But I don't remember clearly. I do remember how much I tuned in, to whatever he said when it happened. When I did that, I didn't have to think about what was going on."

Trudy nodded, and I could tell she understood. "That's called disassociation. It's a common tool used by incest and rape victims. It's a coping technique, and it helps you get through the trauma you're experiencing. You disassociate— separate from what's happening to you physically—by leaving the scene emotionally. By going to, or thinking about, anything that feels safe."

I absorbed everything, as a dawning awareness occurred to me. "That explains why I was always tracing the ceiling tiles."

"Exactly," Trudy said. "Now do you remember what kinds of things he would tell you?"

"Usually he told me how good it felt, and that if I wasn't so pretty—"

"Which just reinforced your own belief that you were to blame?" Trudy asked.

I shook my head, finding it hard to look at her.

"I want you to write a letter, telling him how you feel about what he did to you. He won't see it and it will help release some of your feelings. And while you're at it, write one to your mom and tell her how you feel about her not doing anything to stop the abuse. Can you do that?"

I sat there pondering Trudy's suggestion. It was going to be very hard. "I don't know. But I'll try."

Trudy smiled. "Great. Then bring them in next week when you come back. Now, what are you going to do for the weekend? Something for yourself, I hope?"

"Actually, I'm taking the kids to visit some friends we haven't seen in awhile. Eddie was supposed to join us, but with the tension level being what it is, he opted not to go, and that's fine by me."

"It sounds like fun, and you certainly deserve it," Trudy patted my shoulder fondly.

The kids and I pulled out of the driveway the next evening an hour later than scheduled. I called Martha, telling her we would be late. She told me not to worry, because she was still a night owl. As we started out, the usual nitpicking was missing. In fact, everyone was getting along admirably. Gabby was reading a story out loud, Slade was working a little handheld game, and Mileah and Trista were playing with their Barbie dolls. It felt so good to get away from everything for a couple of days. But mostly, it felt good to be leaving Eddie. I couldn't understand, but no matter how hard I tried, I couldn't make myself love him—either physically or emotionally. Our sex life had ended the day of my big announcement in Trudy's office, and soon after I realized my love for him had died long ago.

It was something that had gradually taken place over time, when the wounds were being inflicted at a greater pace then they were being allowed to heal—a compilation of verbal stabs and physical assaults in our bedroom—until finally, any feelings for Eddie were gone.

That's why I was considering another separation. I knew it would be hard on the kids, but it would give me some time to pull myself together. I just didn't know if it was the right thing to do. I hoped the weekend reprieve would help to clear my mind, and perhaps provide an answer.

When we arrived in Martinsburg four hours later, my brood was sound asleep. I had been so alert throughout the drive, running the recent events through my mind, that I wasn't even sleepy when we got to Mark and Martha's house. As if on cue, the kids woke up when I took the keys from the ignition. I picked up Slade and carried him to the porch, my three sleepy daughters tagging behind.

"Hello! It's so good to see you!" Martha hugged me and looked down at the kids. "We didn't think you would ever get here. Let's see, this must be Mileah. And you're Trista." She patted Gabby's head.

"No, she is. I'm Gabby Bopper Leigh."

I laughed. "Our nickname for her."

Martha laughed. "I'd say a pretty good one, too. Well, you all come in. You can't sleep on the porch, can you?" The kids struggled to beat me through the door, wide-awake and excited to be there.

Martha gave us a quick briefing: Mark and Stephanie, their eight-year-old, were in bed, and Stephanie was dying to have one of the girls sleep with her. I would share a bedroom with one girl and Slade would have his own bed in my room. Martha showed us to our rooms and I got the kids ready for bed, helping Slade brush his teeth. When they were all tucked in, despite any pleas to stay up longer, I issued a firm "goodnight" and went downstairs to see Martha. I was anxious to talk to her; I hoped she could tell me what she remembered about me being a teenager when we lived in Martinsburg. After all, she and my mom had been good friends, and we had gone to her house the night Dad had been arrested.

We sat down to a cup of warm tea, talking about old times across the kitchen table. "Remember when your mom and I used to take you kids skating at the park in the wintertime? Oh, we had a blast! Kathy and Rhonda loved to go skating there."

"How are they? It seems hard to believe they're all grown up," I laughed. "You probably feel the same way about me."

Martha laughed. "I do, I do. I still can't believe it. Why, you weren't much older than Mileah when your family moved here. Anyway, the girls are fine. Rhonda works as a receptionist at a law firm, and Kathy's getting married to this young man she's been dating for about a year. His name is J.R., and you'll get to meet him while you're here. He's a real sweetie."

"Martha, what do you remember about me? Was I a good teenager?" I wanted to wait, and explain how I needed to know more about that time period, but something made me plunge right in.

She stared at me, surprised. "Good? What on earth do you mean? You couldn't find a better kid. I still remember when your mom worked in the café and you helped her after school. Then you sold all that candy so you'd have your own spending money. Why girl, you were probably one of the few teenagers I knew who never got into trouble. I don't even remember your mom ever saying you talked back to her."

I laughed. "No, that was Carla's department. She was always back-talking to Mom."

"How is she anyway? She was always such a happy-go-lucky child."

"I wish I knew, Martha. But the truth is, I hardly ever see her. She rarely visits and then, it's just for a few minutes. She's always busy running off somewhere."

"No children yet?"

"No, she and Wayne keep hoping. They've even talked about adopting. I don't know, I sometimes think she runs around to keep herself from thinking about not being able to have children."

"You mean they can't?" Martha asked.

"I don't know, she just said they've both undergone all kinds of tests, but so far, nothing's turned up. I really feel for her," I sighed.

"I know. Children add so much to your life. Of course, they can make it a pain sometimes, too, but—" she laughed, and I remembered how that bubbly, contagious sound used to warm me as a child.

We talked until well after midnight, but when we began yawning, we decided it was time for bed. I was starting to feel tired, but when I laid down, all signs of sleep fled. I kept hearing our discussion, and all of the things Trudy and I had talked about kept running through my mind. Without realizing what I was doing, I picked up my journal from where it lay on the nightstand, and tore a page out. "Dear Eddie," I began, and stopped.

I had no clue what to say.

But suddenly, the words began pouring onto the page. My energy hadn't abated when I finished, so I started my second letter. An hour later, I had two lengthy letters composed. Of course, neither Eddie nor my mother would ever read them. It was probably just as well. Some pretty strong feelings had come out through my pen, and as I turned out the light, I felt a sense of release from my past. It was a small victory, but a victory nonetheless.

Throughout the weekend, those feelings gained more ground, giving me a courage I never knew I had. Martha and I went shopping, and the entire family, including Kathy and Rhonda, put together a picnic Sunday afternoon. Martha had asked some friends over, and one young couple who had no children were busy keeping my brood occupied while I filled their plates. As I called for the kids, I couldn't help but smile. They were climbing all over Ted, who didn't seem to mind at all. When they came running, they all fought over who was going to sit beside him and Mark. I looked up at Martha, who shrugged at me. "You decide, Mom."

I made a decision I hoped would keep everyone happy and as we sat down to eat, I kept thinking about my children's father. Eddie was always too busy working to take time out for them, yet perfect strangers realized how much joy and happiness they could provide. They weren't bad children—they just needed more love than one parent could give them. And there I was, back to the old dilemma: was it better to stay married to Eddie so the kids would have a father, or was it wiser to part, leaving them fatherless, so to speak. As I ate my hamburger, I watched them enjoy Mark's easy banter and Ted's friendly teasing. I still wasn't sure what to do.

Sunday afternoon we pulled away amidst yells from Martha's family. "Don't forget to write," "Have a safe trip," and "Don't wait so long to visit next time." My four yelled back, waving happily out the windows.

I was happy, too, but I needed to go home. Part of me

wished we could stay longer, but another part yearned to return, to continue on the private journey I had begun—even though I didn't know where it would lead me. As I headed onto the interstate, pinkish rays of sunlight were visible behind the trees.

I love this place. How I wish we had never moved away. Because that's when I became his pawn, when his abuse began. The molestation. The rapes, I thought.

I looked around at the kids, who were dividing up the cookies Martha sent with us. I smiled, feeling grateful.

But it hasn't all been bad. I got four beautiful blessings out of the deal.

CHAPTER FIFTEEN

The day was dreary when I next met with Trudy, the sky grey and ominous. I took my letters, which were tucked inside the pages of a notebook.

"Did you get your letters written?" Trudy asked brightly.

"I did."

My words hung there between us only briefly, before she beamed at me. "Wonderful! And how did it make you feel?"

"Honestly? Like killing Eddie."

"And your mother, did you write one to her?"

"Yes. It was harder to write, for some reason," I said.

Her nod was empathetic. "I can understand that. Would you mind reading them?"

I pulled them out of the notebook, fumbling with the pages as I did so, trying to slow down time. "Out loud?"

"Yes."

"I don't think I can." I felt like a schoolgirl who was about to be punished for refusing to do an assignment.

"That's okay. May I read them?"

"No, go right ahead." I handed her the letters and sat back, wondering what she would glean from them.

As Trudy read, I recalled what I had written. I began by telling my mother how much I loved and respected her, especially during the times when she was a single parent without Dad around. But I also said that resulted in there being not enough supervision, which contributed to the amount of time I spent with the Leigh family. I talked about all my 'what ifs,' knowing it was useless, since the past couldn't be changed.

Then I said I knew she didn't realize what was happening to me, because she would have stopped it, if she had—that I wanted to tell her the truth, many times, but I was always afraid she would think I was a terrible person. I told her how, at thirteen, I thought I knew everything and was totally grown up. How I had been smart, gotten good grades, and how all my teachers liked me. That was when Eddie really began getting involved in our lives, and I mistook his interest in me as another sign he cared about us—like he did by helping her with household repairs. How it took me years to realize he was only acting that way for selfish reasons—so he could get to me, by using her. I talked about how guilty and ashamed I felt, and how I came to believe it no longer mattered—how I stopped caring, believing I was to blame. And besides, I told her, Eddie reinforced that, telling me it was my fault. I also said that even when I tried to tell him 'no,' or make him stop, it didn't always work.

I related how I had learned, by looking at my own children, that I was never mature enough to make such a decision, or to take part in the sex he insisted on. That I had trusted Eddie because he was like the big brother I never had, and I really believed he cared about me. Only a child, I wrote, would have accepted what I did and endured it quietly, without saying a word to anyone. And in the end, borne all the guilt, as well. I told her I was tired of feeling as if I was to blame, and I thought maybe if she had been watching more closely, she might have seen what was happening. That maybe she could have done something to make it all stop. That's when I urged her to take precautions with my two sisters and brother, who still lived at home.

Then I ended the letter. "If this has helped you in any way, let it be in that none of them have to experience life as I did. I love you."

Several times while she was reading, I saw Trudy shake her head briefly, as if in agreement, and at times I could see a thoughtful look on her face. When she was finished, Trudy handed them to me.

"They're very well-written."

I felt myself blushing. Accepting compliments was still difficult. "Thank you. So, how did I do?"

She smiled. "There was no right or wrong way to do this. But you expressed yourself well, by telling Eddie how he made you feel, how it changed your life, and the anger you have because of that."

"I said I hated him." I grimaced, feeling slightly guilty. "We're supposed to forgive people who hurt us."

"Yes, and maybe someday, you will. But it's too soon for that. You're entitled to your feelings of anger or hate, and then some." Trudy paused before continuing. "The letter to your mom is really touching. It doesn't sound like you're angry with her about not doing anything. It sounds more like your letter is pleading with her to be more cautious with your younger siblings."

"Yes, I'd hate for anything like that to happen again. And it could, so easily."

"How did you feel when you wrote the letters?"

"I felt sad, mostly. But angry, too; really angry when I realized how Eddie took advantage of me at such a young age."

"I know. And remember, these letters are just for you. They're not to send, unless at some point in the future, you think you want to."

I shook my head. "I know. But right now, I don't think I ever could."

"So, how did you feel when you were finished?"

"It felt like part of the pain was gone."

Trudy smiled. "That's good, Daleen. You're doing great. You've come a long way in a short time. I'm so proud of you." Between her heartfelt words and the hug she gave me as I turned to go, I was beginning to feel proud of myself, too.

As I began to feel more—fully experiencing a wide range of emotions that ran the gamut from frustration and pain, to anger and longing—I found some things were still the same. Instead of being able to concentrate on a work assignment, I would find myself remembering. It was a fight to stay focused and do my job.

Then there were the men. I had always noticed, in a peripheral sort of way, how some men looked at me, but I gradually came to see their glances in my direction. Where I once thought their looks had to be sexual, one day I realized the looks came my way for a variety of reasons—and not all of them related to sexual thoughts or fantasies. I struggled to work through the issues from my childhood and teen years, and felt like I was morphing from a caterpillar into a moth, so I could finally fly free.

Little by little, I learned to be patient and long-suffering with myself. I still forged ahead, taking on more and more work assignments. It helped me keep working on my personal issues, but at the same time, it protected me from facing everything at once.

Everything in its own good time, I thought.

By pouring myself into my job, using my mental energy to focus on news events that distracted me from what happened at home, I could deal with the dichotomy of my life. In one way, I felt like my life was fraying at the seams, but in another way, I felt stronger and more empowered. It was as if I was a detached stranger, looking in on the person I had been, and the person I was becoming.

I only had one question: *Who will I turn out to be, when it's all over?*

As I walked across the street to get news from the sheriff's department one morning, it hit me: the time I'd spent around men and women who worked in law enforcement had been good for me, imbuing me with the type of courage I hadn't had before. I would never want to keep a loaded weapon in my own home, but during my interviews, sitting across from the desk of someone who carried one for a living, gave me a sense of safety. It was as if, after seeing all those police officers at work, protecting the public, I realized that if I really needed them, they would be there for me, too.

But it was other stories, about other women, which gave me a sense of personal empowerment. One such story occurred when Hilda Heady received the Susan B. Anthony award. I interviewed Heady and the nominating committee. Heady received the award because of her work with the Preston Birthing Center, and because she stepped into what had traditionally been a man's role, after being hired as the hospital's administrator. As I spoke with Heady, I realized that being a woman didn't necessarily restrict you from having the same things a man had—namely, recognition and accolades. Her achievement helped me see what was possible for a woman, and taught me we aren't only caretakers of our men and our children. We can be much, much more.

That's when I remembered Dad telling me that a woman can do anything a man can. After interviewing Heady, and seeing all her achievements, I finally knew my father was right.

While I came to recognize that professional career women can help make great advancements in their community and in the world, I still held onto the Bible stories that had played such a large role in my own life. There was Sarah, who had left her luxurious home in the wealthy city of Ur, to accompany her husband, Abraham, when he asked her to live the rest of her life in tents. And Abigail, who proved to be the perfect wife, who helped defuse a tense situation involving her husband, Nabal, when he nearly got his household killed after refusing hospitality to King David. There was also Esther, a young Israelite woman who ended up saving her entire nation.

These women were the same ones I had been hearing about since I was a little girl, and their examples had been imprinted on my consciousness with a branding iron, as examples of good women, good wives, who ran households while supporting their husbands' efforts.

So all the while, a battle waged within me, and I found myself torn between work and home. Work gave me confidence, but being at home took it away. With my marriage at the breaking point, the wedding dress dream became a daily ritual. Every night, I tried to escape the man hunting me with a knife, intent on killing me. Those nightmares were so real I often woke up in a cold sweat, my heart pounding, and scared to death. Or maybe it was because, by then, I was really seeing my life for what it was, and I was beginning to separate from the abuse.

I truly had no idea how traumatic waking up to the true state of my life would be. It was a blessing, but in another way, it was a terrible curse, which I learned from—of all things—a broken washing machine.

Mom's was on the mend, so she was doing her laundry at our house. "Daleen, you didn't find any extra underwear in your washer, did you?" she called to ask the next morning.

"Uh, no," I laughed. "Why, don't you have any?"

"No, it's not that. It's just that Jackie went through the laundry baskets looking for clean panties and she can't find any. I thought maybe they got mixed in with some of yours," Mom said.

"I'll look and see. I washed a couple of loads last night, but they haven't been folded yet."

"Okay. Call me if you find them."

As I folded the clean clothes, I kept an eye out for any unfamiliar underwear, but I found nothing that wasn't ours. I asked all of the kids and even Eddie, but no one had seen them. Eddie said he had no idea what I was talking about, but he checked the washer and the dryer again, to see if they had mysteriously remained behind, even after I washed our clothes.

The mystery remained exactly that until a couple of days later, when Mom called and asked me to drop by. It was a Saturday and Eddie was at work, so I took the kids with me. Mom, Jackie and I were chatting over coffee with some of my mother's delicious coffeecake, when I saw an odd look pass between them.

"I think we better tell her, don't you?" Jackie tried to smile but still looked uncomfortable, and I felt like an actor coming on stage in the middle of the final act.

"You tell her."

I looked back and forth between them, wondering what was going on. "Tell me what? What's wrong?"

"Well, do you remember the missing panties?" Mom asked.

I shook my head, wondering why they were still an issue.

"Jackie and I think maybe Eddie took them," Mom said, looking into her coffee cup.

I sat there. I heard the words, yet they made no sense.

"Last night when we came home, Jackie went to her bedroom and found her lingerie laid out all over her bed, very neatly. The only explanation we can think of is Eddie."

I remembered that Eddie had been there the night before, repairing a broken bathroom faucet. Still, some internal force, fueled by years of habit and fed by an equal amount of denial, kicked in, causing me to try and shield my husband. "Are you sure? I mean, maybe there's another explanation—" The excuse sounded weak even to my ears. I stopped, unable to finish.

"We already asked Michael, but he's here all the time and if he was going to do something like that, it seems kind of odd that he would do it the very same evening that Eddie was here," Mom said.

I shook my head slowly. "Besides, Michael wasn't here last night, was he? Didn't you say you all went to the mall?"

"Yes," Mom said.

Jackie, who had been silent throughout the exchange, spoke up. At fourteen, she already showed signs of the beauty she would become. "When I saw the things laying there like that, I went to the dresser and looked through my drawers. He had taken the bras and panties from there. I could tell by the way it was all messy, not neat like I keep it."

My heart went out to her, because I knew how she felt: violated.

I hate you, Eddie Leigh! I thought. *How dare you try to hurt Jackie with your perverted desires?*

"I can't stand him. He gives me the creeps." Jackie made a disgusted face as she spoke.

"That's true," Mom nodded. "For some reason, Jackie has been uncomfortable around Eddie for a while now. She doesn't even want to be here when he's working around the house."

"She has good reason," I said, all desire to protect him gone. "Mom, I told you what he was like. Don't you remember what happened with Carla when we were all together at

Bruce's the summer Eddie and I got married? You know, when we were going on our honeymoon?"

Mom looked puzzled for a moment, then I could see the dawning in her eyes. "Oh that. Well, I just thought that was Carla's way of getting attention."

I stared at my mother in disbelief, not sure if I heard correctly.

Wake up and smell the coffee, Mom!

"Mother, she didn't do anything wrong. Eddie touched her inappropriately on her derriere and she decided she wasn't going to take it anymore. And from what she said then, that wasn't the first time he had tried to touch her." I grew indignant, for both my sister and myself, as I recalled the scene.

"Yes, I guess so. I just don't remember that much about it. It all happened so long ago," Mom responded vaguely.

I gave myself a mental shake, as I tried to comprehend why my mother wouldn't remember something so important. But I didn't have time to sit there and dwell on it—I was going to find Eddie.

"Jackie, I want you to tell me if you remember anything else weird that's happened. I'm very sorry he did this to you. It's a violation and it's wrong. If he says or tries to do anything like this again, you tell Mom or me immediately." I said, squeezing her hand.

Jackie smiled and I knew she felt as bad about having to tell me, as I did about what he'd done to her.

I'm going to kill him. If he doesn't knock it off, I swear I won't be responsible for my actions.

As I drove home, I promised myself as soon as the kids were tucked into bed that night, Eddie and I would talk. That is, if he came home. But as chance would have it, he arrived just after I finished the dinner dishes. The kids had been asleep for only a short time. After a brief greeting, I placed his dinner plate on the table. As he was eating, I glanced casually through a magazine I was reading, feeling anything but the outer calm I wanted him to see.

She's a victim. Jackie's another victim. First me, then Carla and now ... Jackie. When will he stop? Who's next?

Then a colder, more chilling thought came to me as forcibly as if I had been struck: *Mileah. Trista. Gabby. What if he tries to hurt them?*

I won't let him. I'll kill him if he ever touches my babies.

"Eddie, do you remember the missing lingerie Mother asked us about?"

Eddie smiled as he ate. "Yeah, did she find the stuff yet?"

That's it, Eddie. Put on a good show. Act all innocent.

"No, as a matter of fact, she didn't. But I think I know what happened to it." I continued to flip through the pages of the magazine calmly. "Yes, I know where it went. You took it." I looked directly at him, staring long and hard.

Suddenly I remembered Abigail from the Bible, who tried to get her husband to listen to reason, but who refused. Ultimately, she acted with discretion, apart from her weak and selfish husband, and gave food and water to King David. Abigail saved not only herself and her household, but was chosen to be one of David's wives, after her own foolish husband died.

Abigail had been a courageous woman, and I knew her story could help me find the courage to do what I had to do next.

Eddie's fork stopped in midair. "I took it? Why the hell would I do something like that?"

"Oh, I don't know. Probably for the same reason you went through Jackie's dresser, and then laid her lingerie out on her bed while you were working there last night." There it was: my ace, on the table.

"Daleen, are you sick or something? I don't have the slightest idea what you're talking about. And I want you to know I do not like being accused of something I did not do." He had gone from angry to innocent to defensive in a matter of seconds, and I was far from finished with him.

"Then let me remind you of all the things you have done, Mr. Leigh. You touched Carla inappropriately when she was just thirteen-years-old. You made a pass at our babysitter, Angie, who was fifteen at the time. You were involved sexually with your neighbor, Vonna, who was also thirteen. You had an affair three years ago. And that doesn't even begin to take into account what you did to me before we were married, or what you've done to me since then." I could feel anger seething from every pore.

"I can't stand you!" I spit the words through clenched teeth.

Eddie acted like he hadn't even heard me. "Well, if you want to bring up past events, I think you better take a good look at your sister. Carla was always throwing herself at me—"

I cut him off short. "Oh yes, just like Vonna, right? They all—no, we all—teased you so much, didn't we?"

He sat there, his arms crossed in front of him, staring stonily at me. "Yes, as a matter of fact, Vonna did tease me."

"Give it up, Eddie. It's a lost cause." I stood up, unable to be near him a moment longer. "Well there is one thing I can tell you for a certainty. Jackie did not tease you, did not lead you on, did not throw herself at you. That much I am certain of, because she can't stand you. In fact, she doesn't want to be anywhere within a 50-mile radius of you. As for her morals, you can't find a teenager with a better reputation than hers. Everyone who knows Jackie knows that. Why don't you just accept the fact that you're a sexual pervert and get some professional help? Give us all a break, why don't you?" I gave him one long, last look of disgust, before turning and walking out of the room.

I was filled with fury at him or any other man who used

women for their own base, selfish desires, only to then try and turn the tables, by saying the women (or in this case, the young girls) had brought it upon themselves, that the women had somehow seduced them. If it wasn't so deadly serious, it would be a joke—that a big, brawny man was powerless to the wiles of a mere woman. Why, in every other area of their lives, they made it clear they were the boss, so why not when it came to sexual desires, too? Why not just admit that men who chose to use and abuse both girls and women were weak, and deficient in some way?

My sixth sense told me that admitting such a thing would deeply wound their already fragile egos, leaving them unable to function in a culture that had trained them to look at women as sexual objects whose sexuality lured them in, like bait on a fishing line. I wasn't sure how or where other men—normal men who had been reared differently, who had been taught to respect women as equals—were, but I knew they were out there. Men like Brad, Fred, and deputies Stiles and Haney, whom I had come to know and respect.

But I wasn't with a man like that—I was still stuck in my prison cell, with a man who would never look at a woman as his equal, who instead saw me in the only way that mattered: as a tool for his own sexual needs.

And I soon learned the price I would pay, for being bold enough to suggest that very thing to Eddie. Yes, he made sure I paid dearly for my act of bravery that day.

CHAPTER SIXTEEN

For the next few days, Eddie was very cool toward me. He never admitted what he had done with Jackie's missing panties, but Mom told me that they had suddenly turned up. Their equally mysterious reappearance wasn't surprising, but they turned up in a place where they couldn't have been—at the bottom of Mom's dirty clothes hamper. If I'd had any doubts that Eddie was to blame, which I didn't, his guilt would have been sealed when the missing lingerie made its comeback.

Right on the heels of that episode, something else happened that I couldn't ignore. A grand jury had convened that morning, consuming most of my day as I took notes about each case that was going to be prosecuted. It was almost midnight when I left the office. The drive home seemed much longer than fifteen miles and I had to roll down the window and turn up the radio so I could stay awake.

I let myself in the front door and heard sounds from the bathroom. Eddie was probably showering. Turning on my computer, I went into the kitchen for a snack, hoping it would keep me awake while I wrote. When Eddie came out of the bathroom a few minutes later, I was typing.

"Hi, when did you get home?" he asked.

"Just a few minutes ago." I avoided eye contact with him, hoping he wouldn't grill me like he usually did. "I thought I could get this done at the office, but finally realized I'd have to finish it here."

Coming over to stand beside me, he read the computer screen over my shoulder. "I thought maybe we could go to bed together for once."

My heart sank, and I felt a return of the feelings of disgust. "It's already 1 a.m. I'm not going to feel like making love because I'm already exhausted. I'm sorry." Not wanting to make him angry, I hid my disgust and tried to let him down gently.

"Well, I don't mind waiting."

I kept typing, trying not to break my concentration. "Eddie, you might as well go to bed, I don't really know how long I'll be."

He settled down in front of the TV. "Okay, I'll just watch TV. If I doze off, you can always wake me."

I sighed. It was no use; he wasn't going to go to bed until I did. I stared at the computer screen, trying to make sense of what I had written. I went back and forth between my notebook and the keyboard, trying to make sure every sentence was accurate. I glanced up at the clock above my desk, which said it was two-thirty in the morning.

"Eddie, you need to go to bed," I spoke loudly in his direction.

His eyelids fluttered open. "That's okay, I'll wait for you."

Well, I've got news for you, I thought. *I barely have the energy to write, much less for sex.*

I turned back to my notebook. My own eyelids were so heavy I knew I would have to proofread the article after I got some sleep. Turning off the computer, I glanced over at Eddie. I wanted to let him sleep there, but I knew he would have back pain the next morning, so I took pity on him. "Come on, Eddie, it's four o'clock. I'm going to bed."

I prayed he would realize I was too exhausted for anything

as, all my energy depleted, I climbed the stairs. I hated working so late, especially when the kids would be getting ready for school in a few hours. I threw on a nightgown and crawled under the covers. Eddie leaned over to kiss me goodnight. "Good night," I murmured, turning over. I was almost asleep, but I could feel his kisses on the back of my neck. "Eddie, stop it," I tried to move away.

I felt him tugging at my nightgown, and I came awake enough to snap at him.

"No! I have to get up in two hours, I'm exhausted, and I don't want to have sex."

"Just lay back and go to sleep, if you want. But I'll bet I can make you want to stay awake." I heard him, his voice all silky, and I punched my pillow and tried to turn towards the wall. But he held me tightly against him, and I knew any resistance was futile, and would only serve to fuel his arousal.

Somewhere a loud, shrill buzzing noise wouldn't stop. I pulled the covers over my head, trying to hide from the sound. When it wouldn't, I opened my eyes and saw the alarm clock. I had to get the kids up for school. I turned the clock off and turned over. Eddie was still asleep. I started to get out of bed when I remembered what happened while I was semi-asleep, just a short while ago.

I used my foot to nudge his leg several times. "Eddie, wake up. Time to get the kids ready." He moved a little and I poked a finger into his back. "Come on, you kept me awake, so you get up now and let me sleep."

He looked at me like he was in shock, and I couldn't resist a bit of sarcasm. "Don't tell me you're sleepy? Why, you got at least three more hours sleep than I did. So it's only fair for you to get up with the kids."

"Do it yourself," he growled. I resisted the urge to place

my foot against his back and kick him. The mental picture of him falling to the floor with a great thud made me laugh as I crawled out of bed, feeling as tired as I had two hours earlier, when I had crawled into it.

When Eddie got up later that morning, he found me in the bathroom. "What do you have planned today?" he asked.

I finished brushing my teeth, but said nothing.

"Hey you, can you hear me?" he grinned.

"You raped me last night," I said flatly.

His brows shot up. "I what?"

"You heard me," I said, brushing past him on my way to the kitchen. "You better never touch me again, or I swear I'll press charges. Do you understand?"

Eddie didn't move a muscle. He just stood there, staring at me like I was from Mars. The next thing I knew he was gone and a few minutes after that, his truck roared to life and I heard the rubber peel off his tires.

Two days later, I knew it wouldn't work. We had been fighting since the night he raped me. The abuse, the effect it had on the kids, the roller coaster lifestyle; all if it was too much for me, and I was finding it more and more difficult to concentrate on anything. Moreover, it was tearing me apart to see my children suffer because of having an unhappy home life. They would often run to me, cowering, whenever Eddie was angry. Or they would wait until he had stormed out of the house, slamming the door behind him, to say anything. Then the tears flowed down their soft little cheeks.

"I hate him! I hate him!" Mileah managed to say as huge sobs racked her small body. Her words took me back to that night on the stairs, when I was just eight and had said that very same thing to my own mother.

I wept inside for Mileah, my heart breaking. I had felt the

same way a few weeks earlier, when our family outing turned into an excuse for him to abuse Gabby. I was still weighing my options, unsure what to do, and unaware of how dramatically—and how quickly—our lives would change direction.

My breakdown came just four days later. I had been in a bad mood all week. I kept thinking about the rape. Since then, I had consciously decided I wasn't going to live like that anymore. The realization that my husband had really and truly raped me opened the valve, and a free-flowing stream of consciousness began flowing inside my mind. During the next few days, similar acts of violence came to mind, leaving me with more memories than I knew what to do with. I felt dangerously close to a breaking point, but I still couldn't let my guard down, afraid of what my family and friends would think—if they knew the real truth about my life—so I pasted on my usual smile and went my way.

It was a slow, sunny day when I picked up the kids at school, and we went out for burgers. I promised to take them to a nearby playground before our Bible meeting. I had just parked the car when I realized I didn't have the energy to move. I asked the kids to just sit quietly and read while I took a short nap.

"Then we'll get out and play," I promised. But I was so tired, I felt like I'd been drugged.

But they wouldn't sit still, and began arguing with each other.

"All right, you four. If you don't quiet down, you won't have to worry about playing or going to Bible study, because we'll turn around and go straight home." My threats earned me some much-needed peace—until someone began crying.

"Mommy, Trista hit me in the stomach," Mileah cried.

"I did not. She pulled my hair," Trista pouted.

I swung around to face them. "Look, is it asking too much to be able to take a short nap? Don't you understand that I'm tired?" I felt like my nerves were about to snap, and I just couldn't stand the noise and confusion.

"Look, Mommy, Brandon and his sister are here. Can we go over and play with them?" Gabby asked, spotting some friends.

"No!" I yelled. "You can't. If you kids won't be quiet and let me get some sleep, I am not going to let you out of this car!"

"But it's hot in here."

I couldn't listen to another word, and I was beyond caring. I just wanted to get some sleep, so I rested my head against my arm and tried to tune out their chattering.

But sleep eluded me, and I just stared out at the children on the playground, not really seeing them at all. I was startled by a knock on my window. It was Brandon's mom, Cindy.

I rolled down the window.

"What are you doing here?" She laughed and I tried to return the laughter, but the most I could muster was a small smile.

"Hey, what's wrong?"

"Oh I'm just tired, that's all," I told Cindy, opening my door and getting out. The kids took off for the playground before I could tell them to behave, but I didn't care. I somehow managed to keep the conversation going for a few minutes, before Cindy's husband yelled for her, and they left.

I sat down at a picnic table and stared at my children, who were divided equally between the swing set and the sliding board. Normally, I wouldn't take them to the playground dressed up in their best clothes on a Bible study night. But the day had been anything but normal.

Finally, I called for them to come to the car. "It's time to go, or we're going to be late," I said. Several minutes and much yelling from me later, and they were all inside, buckled up.

We drove across town to our Bible meeting, but I couldn't concentrate on what the minister was saying.

What's wrong with me? I wondered.

I felt like I was going to explode. I was angry: with the kids, for not listening; and with myself, for being so impatient with them.

Why am I so angry? What's going on?

Suddenly I felt tears well up behind my eyes. I swallowed hard, trying to hold them at bay. But it didn't work. As I sat there, my vision grew blurry from the tears and I kept sniffing, trying to hold them back. Finally, I couldn't stand it. When the tears began streaming down my cheeks, I left my children sitting there and fled to the women's restroom. Once inside, I leaned up against the stall, trying to figure out what was happening. But I already knew: I wasn't angry with my children or myself—I was angry with Eddie—for what he had taken from me. I was angry with him for not giving me any say over my own body—and for the first time since then, it was all beginning to sink in.

"Daleen? Daleen, it's Shirley. Are you all right?"

I turned the lock on the door and left the little stall. Shirley took one look at me and knew something was wrong. "What can I do?"

"I—I don't know."

Shirley looked at me closely. "Did something happen? Did Eddie hurt you again?"

I nodded as sobs wracked my body. I couldn't even talk.

She just held me for a few minutes, before saying anything. "I'm so sorry. Can I do anything?"

"No."

I heard Shirley's voice, but I couldn't follow her words. I tried to focus, but I couldn't. The only person I really wanted was Trudy—and she had long since left her office. "Why don't we go out to the lounge and sit down. I'll go get Butch and we'll decide what to do."

I sat down on the couch and when she returned, I was still sitting there. The tears continued falling, unabated. "Daleen, we want you to come home with us. I thought, with the kids, it might be better if you didn't drive right now. You're so upset. I wish I knew what to do." Shirley put her arm around me and held me, letting me cry until I could cry no more. I don't have any idea how much time passed, but the next thing I knew she was helping me into her car.

"What about the kids? Where are they?" I was present enough to notice their absence.

"It's all right. Butch is going to drive your car. They're with him. He'll follow us home."

"Are they all buckled in?" I managed to ask.

"They sure are. I did it myself."

"But they—they have school tomorrow. I don't know if I can take them, or how they'll get there."

"You let me worry about that. Don't you think about it at all," Shirley said.

I looked out the window, fastening my seatbelt automatically. As we drove, I didn't think about anything. I was completely calm, as if the tears had washed away all my pain and anger.

"I know you'll want to wait until we get home, but is there anyone else you need to talk to, Daleen?" I saw Shirley glance over, but she didn't say anything. I'm sure she suspected Eddie was behind it.

"Just Trudy, but her office is closed now."

When we reached their house, Shirley told me to go inside and she helped Butch get the kids. After they came in, they were so excited about sleeping overnight they didn't pay much attention to me.

That's good, maybe they won't notice.

I was wrong, though. One by one, they came over and sat with me, giving me hugs and kisses, or just patting my hand. Their small childish faces told me how worried they were, so I tried to smile. "I just don't feel very good right now, that's all. I'll feel better tomorrow, I promise." I didn't know if I would or not, but I hoped for their sakes I did.

"Daleen, do you feel like talking?" Shirley sat down beside me.

"I'm sorry, I'm just not thinking real clearly right now. No, I don't mind telling you. I just can't stand to live like that any longer. He's never going to stop, no matter what I say or do."

"What did he do?"

I looked away, ashamed and humiliated. "He forced me to have sex again. I was so tired and had worked about twenty hours, Shirley. I could hardly stay awake, but he didn't even care." The tears began again and I shrugged them away, wondering how anyone could be that selfish.

Shirley looked disgusted. "You've got to get some help. You can't go on like this."

I nodded. "I know. I broke down and told Trudy a few weeks ago." I felt like someone had thrown me into an old-fashioned washer and pulled me through, wringing every last ounce of energy out of me.

"What did Eddie say when you told her?"

"Well he wasn't too happy, but he did admit to molesting me for years before we married."

"You're kidding? I can't believe he would ever admit it. Not knowing what I know about him, when he used to work for Butch."

"I know. When I first told her what had happened, he confessed to doing it. That's when I began seeing her by myself, without him there. We've been working on it ever since."

"Daleen, I know this is none of my business, but how often has this been happening? If you don't want to tell me, that's all right."

I sat there, mentally calculating how often Eddie forced me to have sex with him. "At least once a month. Usually more."

Shirley sat there, shaking her head in amazement. "That's horrible. Is there anything I can do to help? You and the kids are welcome to stay here as long as you need to."

I managed a weak smile. "I appreciate that. I need time to get my head together, to decide what to do. I just know there's no way I can go back to him again."

"It seems you have grounds to leave. I mean, look what he's done to you. I think you have every right. Why, he's endangering your health—and your life. Not to mention the welfare of your children. How have they been handling all this abuse?" Shirley asked.

"It's been hard, and they hurt for me, but they're doing better than I expected," I managed a slight smile.

Hours later, when I was all talked out, I found myself in a big, warm bed, with layers of blankets on top of me. Shirley told me she would put the kids down for me. Even though I was exhausted beyond belief, I laid awake for hours. But I was more at peace with myself than I had been for a long time.

Still, I had no answers. In time sleep gradually overcame me, after I poured out my frustrations in my journal:

Two and a half months ago I came out of an Adult Children of Alcoholics meeting and my whole life changed. Something there caused me to stop living with a secret that I had not, until that night, spoken out loud to another person—other than Eddie, who was very much aware of the secret.

I am a victim of child sexual abuse. Unfortunately, I married my abuser and that abuse has continued in the form of rape. For years I have not been able to speak about what happened before we were married—it's only been recently that I realized it myself. That's because I blamed myself for what happened—I was, after all, told I was to blame. Eddie made sure I felt responsible.

Somewhere along the way I conveniently "forgot" a lot of things, including my feelings at the time. But I do remember other things since that time—bits and pieces come back more and more often. Mostly, I remember all of the times I said 'no' and he didn't listen.

I married Eddie because I felt I had been used—and no one else would ever want me. I also married him because I felt like what happened was my fault.

Since then, I realize I wasn't the woman I believed myself to be. At thirteen, not yet through puberty, naive in the extreme, I knew nothing. I was but a child. As a child, it was easier for me to hold myself responsible for what went on than it was for me to believe another person could behave in such a way, could do such things to me. As a child, I trusted Eddie. Had I opened my eyes to the truth at the time, it may have been too much for me to bear.

Since we married in 1980, things have continued as before. My husband has repeatedly said I deny him his sexual due, while I know I haven't. The truth is, there probably have been times when I wasn't interested in sex—now I know why. But most of the time, I participated in that aspect of our life, at least partially.

Then there have been all the other times—when I was ill, pregnant and uncomfortable or just plain exhausted or upset, when I said "No." Those were the times that come back to haunt me—because it didn't matter what I said, and he rarely listened. Most of the time, Eddie raped or physically forced me to have sex.

During the past several years, I have come to accept this kind of behavior. At first, I can remember fighting, kicking—nothing worked—and I also remember the bruises. There haven't been any physical bruises for ages. I guess accepting that it's going to happen no matter what made me less inclined to fight back.

But the shame: it's still there, from all those years ago, from never saying anything, keeping it a secret for so long. Now I understand why I hated to hear him talk about sex, and didn't want to remember anything. Apparently, I did a good job, since there are still things I can't recall.

I understand all that now, and more. I understand why certain places along roads we used to drive make me nauseated, why certain words and looks he gives me makes me withdraw, why I often can't stand for him to touch me and feel like I'm suffocating when we're in bed.

Yet, more importantly, I understand why I have slowly been going crazy. Why for years I've battled with depression, why I would sit and do nothing but stare into space for hours, why I've considered suicide as an escape, why I "run away" all the time by trying to get involved in anything that will take me away from home—from him. For someone who is an optimist, and tries to see the bright side of things, I couldn't understand why depression plagued me so unmercifully. I couldn't understand why I couldn't get my act together. For someone who grew up amidst turbulence and distress—I couldn't understand why I couldn't cope with it better. Finally, I couldn't understand why I never forgave myself for what happened before I got married. Now I know it was the shame—and having to keep it locked up and buried for so long.

There is so much I understand now.

The next morning, I woke up wondering how I could keep things as normal as possible, so the kids didn't have to experience any more changes than necessary. I forced myself to get ready to take them to school, but Shirley was worried when I told her I was returning to the house for their school clothes.

"Do you think that's a good idea? What if something happens?" she asked.

"He'll be dead to the world and besides, he won't dare bother me with the children around," I said, trying to be brave.

It was an outer show of bravado, but inside I was devoid of all emotion. It was one of my many skills, honed during our worst times with Eddie. Besides, I wanted—even if only for a little while longer—to pretend all was well. Shirley was silent, but she still looked worried.

"We'll be in and out in a few minutes, and he won't even know until it's too late," I said, secretly hoping I was right.

CHAPTER SEVENTEEN

From the intersection where I turned until several houses beyond ours, Swan Street was straight, so I saw Eddie's truck long before we got there. I drove slowly, inching down the street, and felt myself growing nervous and clammy. As I drove, I warned everyone to tiptoe inside and back again, and to be as quiet as mice while they dressed and gathered up their backpacks. I turned the key in the lock ever so slowly, and the door fell open without a single squeak. I said a silent prayer, and once inside, I wrote a rushed note to Eddie, telling him we would be staying with Shirley and Butch for a few days.

The kids did everything perfectly, but as we hurried back to the car a few minutes later, my heart began pounding. I was suddenly terrified that Eddie was right behind me, ready to jerk me backwards by the hair on my head. So as I pulled away from the curb, and there was still no sign of him, a sigh of relief escaped my lips. I drove a quarter-mile to the school and after parking, I walked them inside the building. I silently prayed their day would be peaceful.

They'll be safe here. He won't hurt them. I know he won't. He just wants me, that's all.

After taking each child to a classroom, I went to the office to see the principal. Anna, the school secretary, gave me a big smile. "Good morning, Daleen. How are you?"

"I'm fine," I told Anna. "I just need to see Mrs. Onestinghel for a minute."

"She'll be right over," Anna smiled.

I had interviewed Pat Onestinghel and her husband after learning he proposed to her at a football game. She loved the feature story I wrote, but more than that I knew she would want to keep my children safe.

"What can I do for you, Daleen?" Pat asked.

"I thought you should know we've had some family problems and under no circumstances are the children to go with their father. Anywhere," I said firmly. "We're staying with friends until we get some things worked out."

"We'll keep a close eye on them," she promised, "and they'll be fine, so don't worry."

"I know, Pat. And I don't think he'll give you any problems, but I just wanted to let you know," I assured her.

"You let me know if there's anything else we can do." Pat had wise eyes, and I wondered how much she had already guessed. But then again, I had never been hesitant to blame their father's anger, whenever one of the kids acted out at school after Eddie had thrown his own tantrum at home.

As I left the building I ran down the front steps, trying not to break out in a run. I was just inches from my car when I heard the noise that made my heart drop into my stomach. It was a loud, familiar roar I would know anywhere. The next instant, Eddie's truck came speeding around the corner. He slammed to a stop behind my car, where he jumped out and practically leaped over to where I stood. I froze, my pulse racing as I saw the rage in his eyes.

"Just what the hell do you think you're doing leaving me this note?" His words were as cold as steel.

He won't do anything, at least not while we're on school property. Stay calm, Daleen. Don't back down now. You know Pat's office overlooks the front of the building and there are at least a few people who, at a moment's notice, would come running to help.

But I refused to cower before him, and matched his icy tone. "I'm doing exactly what I said in the note, Eddie. The kids and I are staying at Shirley's for a few days."

The vein in his throat was throbbing so hard it looked like it might explode. "You're coming home this minute. Do you understand me?" He towered over me, yet I managed to remain calm.

"I'm not going with you, Eddie. I need some time to think. Now please, just leave and don't make a scene. The office staff is watching."

I hope they are!

His mouth opened, but he said nothing and instead wheeled around. "If you leave now, don't bother coming back," Eddie yelled before his truck roared to life and he pulled away, spinning the tires and tossing gravel everywhere.

As I slid into the driver's seat, my hands were trembling so much it was all I could do to get the key in the ignition. Ordinarily I would have left the car running, but I couldn't take that chance. Eddie would have taken my keys, if he could. I just knew it. And then, just as the key slipped into place, I glanced over at the school. Mrs. Onestinghel stood in plain view.

Thank you, God. Thank you for watching over me.

I put the car into gear and prayed Eddie wouldn't be waiting around a curve somewhere, trying to force me off the road—or worse. That's when I knew I had always feared this moment. I was afraid he would become so overwhelmed, his frustration would get the better of him—and he would finally kill me, just like he kept telling the kids.

Within seconds of leaving the school I found myself gripping the steering wheel, and realized my head was pounding because my teeth were clenched together so tight. As I drove, I tried to convince myself Eddie had gone home. That he wasn't somewhere waiting to confront me. Fear gripped my chest like a vise, and I wondered if I would be able to make it back to Shirley's. The entire drive was a blur, but somehow I found myself parked outside her house, staring ahead yet seeing nothing. It took all the effort I could muster just to stand up and get out of the car, and once inside I headed straight for the telephone. Trudy agreed to see me that afternoon.

The steps to Trudy's office never seemed so long, nor her door so welcoming. "You don't look very well. Is everything all right?" As Trudy closed the door behind me, I heard the worry in her voice.

"I haven't been sleeping well, that's all." I sank onto the couch, and began tracing the floral upholstery with my finger, finding it difficult to pull my gaze from the fabric.

"Would it help to talk about it?" She asked me softly.

"I don't know." I continued tracing the pattern until I could finally look at her. "He did it again." All I heard was a flat, dull voice speaking of its own accord.

Trudy didn't need to ask. She knew what I meant. "Eddie raped you again."

I nodded, feeling the tears welling behind my eyes. I willed them to stop, but they continued until the room became blurry, and when they spilled over and down each cheek, I let them fall.

I want to cry. I want to get the pain out, I thought.

"When?" Trudy asked me quietly.

"Monday after work." I told her everything. "I just can't stand it. I have absolutely no control over my own body. I have no say! I never have and I never will!"

The voice I recognized as my own grew louder and more passionate. I stared down at the carpet, noticing a dark circular stain there, and the way the legs of the coffee table sank down into the beige tufts, hiding its feet from view. I heard the warm afternoon breeze waft through an open window, where I watched it tug at the white curtain dancing gently in its path. I noticed everything except how I felt inside. But Trudy knew that, too.

"How are you feeling, Daleen?"

"I really don't feel anything at all. Well, maybe angry and confused. Hopeless—like part of me is numb and another part is going crazy."

"What are you going to do? You know it isn't healthy to keep living like this. He's raped you again, and he'll probably keep on doing it."

"I know. I'm leaving him."

Trudy shook her head as if in agreement. "Does Eddie know?"

"No, I just decided." I realized that I had, in that instant, made up my mind. I had planned to leave three years ago, and I knew the time had come: I would not stay around and let him rape me the rest of my life.

"I think that's a good idea. And what then?"

"I don't know. I'll have to take it one day at a time. I haven't had time to think any further than that. I have a job, and I can get food stamps. I'll have to get an attorney, but I'm sure we'll get to stay in the house. I just don't know what he's going to say about it. He won't be happy."

"Daleen, didn't you say that Eddie wasn't willing to get help for his behavior?"

"Yes. I've asked him a few times since we stopped coming here together if he would get help, but he either ignores me or says he doesn't need it."

"That means until he realizes he needs help, it's up to you," Trudy looked at me squarely. "I'm not saying you have to fix him. You know you can't do that. That's up to him. But until he gets help and makes the necessary changes, you're going to have to take any action to protect yourself—and your children."

I shook my head in agreement. Just then, a picture of a child in pain suddenly flashed before me. My hand flew to my mouth. "With everything else going on, I almost forgot. It happened last Friday, as we were leaving the theatre." I went on, telling Trudy about the incident.

"It happened when Gabby began tugging at her father's jacket. We were talking, but she was excited and wanted his attention. The next thing I knew Eddie's arm came out and punched her in the stomach. It was over in seconds," I said, vaguely aware of the scene inside my head playing all over again. Gabby bent over double, clutching her stomach, unable to breathe; me catching her before she fell to the ground, and seeing the fear and pain written all over her face.

"Are you all right? There, there. You're fine. Just breathe. Come on Gabby, breathe! It's all right. Mommy has you." I was on my knees, oblivious to anything else as I held my frightened daughter, who was crying and gasping for breath. As soon as her chest began to heave, Gabby's thumb—her ever-present security blanket—went right into her mouth, while she whimpered softly.

I glared at Eddie, who was yelling about the children misbehaving.

"What on earth did you do that for?" My voice could not have been more deadly.

"She's always interrupting and I'm tired of it!"

"Does that mean you have to hit her in the stomach?" I held Gabby against me, stroking her hair. "For crying out loud, Eddie, she's a child. She doesn't have the patience you and I are supposed to have!"

"I didn't mean to—"

"Of course you didn't," I said sarcastically.

I turned toward the children. "Come on kids, we're going home." I was vaguely aware of people coming and going, and I didn't want our little sideshow to continue. We walked to the car and when Eddie got inside, he began yelling about how he always gets blamed when something goes wrong.

"Well, if the shoe fits," I told him. "You owe your daughter an apology."

"For Pete's sake, Daleen, she's fine. I didn't hurt her." He said, his face set in stone.

I was incredulous that even he could be so callous. It wasn't his wife he had struck, after all—it was his child. "Eddie, I saw what happened and there's no excuse for it, short of an accident, which wasn't the case. In any event, Gabby deserves an apology." I wasn't backing down.

Not this time, I thought.

His eyes seemed to bore into mine, as he stared even harder at me. Then he swung the car door open and got out. "You can take the kids and just leave. I don't even want to be in the same car with you all." Eddie slammed the door and walked away.

Their tears began immediately, and the kids begged me to go after him. They were afraid something would happen to him. "Shhh, your dad's just mad. Let's give him a few minutes to cool down and then we'll drive by and pick him up."

"But Mommy, what if he gets hit?" Trista asked.

That would be a blessing for everyone.

"No one's going to hit him," I said dryly.

"How do you know?" she persisted.

Because some people are too mean to die.

"Because he's smart enough to walk against the traffic, and he won't walk near the road."

It disturbed me at how defensive my children were to the very man who was so mean to them.

We passed Eddie and offered him a ride, but he refused. Remembering the same scenario from so many years ago, I drove off without asking him a second time. Back at home, I spent the evening consoling my children. As I tucked them into bed, I promised them their father would be all right. And sometime later that night, long after I was asleep, Eddie let himself in the front door, safe and sound.

When I finished giving Trudy the gory details, she sat there shaking her head in a dazed way. "It seems Eddie has a lot of anger toward his entire family. Yet, that's no excuse for what he did. I think you're doing the right thing. For you and your children."

"Yes, but I'm afraid it may be harder on them, being without him. You know, I heard a saying once, about a bad mother being better than no mother at all. I wonder if the same thing applies to fathers." I sighed, torn and unsure of myself. "But I don't think so. I believe if a parent is bad enough, more damage occurs than if the parent was gone. I guess I'll find out, won't I?"

"You will, but the important thing is, you're doing what you think is best for everyone involved. I can tell you've put a lot of thought into this already," Trudy said.

"Yes, I have. At times I wonder how much blame I should accept, for keeping them in an unhealthy environment for so long. I know it's been a bad influence. Why, Trista told me, 'Mommy, I'm afraid Daddy's going to kill you,' after Eddie got so angry he told them he might kill me one day. Can you believe that? No, I'm making the right decision, I know it."

"All right. Now, the question is, where do you go from here? Do you have a plan?"

"I'm going to stay with Shirley and Butch awhile. They've been so good to us, telling me to take as long as I need. They're like family."

"You and Shirley come from similar backgrounds, don't you?" she asked.

"Yes, she's also the adult child of an alcoholic."

"So you have a lot in common. I'm sure it's nice, being around someone who cares about you, and to whom you can relate."

I smiled, remembering how much Shirley and I had shared. "Yes, it's been really nice. When they took us home last night, she and Butch were so thoughtful, taking care of the kids so I could get some rest."

"Well, you probably have a lot to consider, so during the next week don't forget that it may get harder, especially when you tell Eddie. Be cautious, and don't rush things. Take care of yourself and don't try to do too much too soon."

"I know," I said.

"If you're feeling better, we'll stop here for today," Trudy said.

I smiled. "I'm feeling much better."

I felt as though a vacuum was sucking out all my energy during the next several weeks. I returned to the house once more, to gather up my computer and all of the journals I had kept throughout the years. I was afraid Eddie would destroy them, once he realized I wasn't going back to him.

My heart was a dead weight inside my chest as I raced from room to room, in case Eddie returned unexpectedly. I felt like a felon, fleeing the scene of a crime.

I hate this. It's so unfair, having to run away, when I haven't done anything wrong, I thought.

At the same time, I finally knew the unimaginable had happened. I wasn't returning to Eddie.

I'll never go back!

A day later, I knew it was time. I gathered the kids together and cautiously told them about my decision, trying to make sure they knew it wasn't their fault. "Mommy, why do we have to leave? Why can't we go back and live with Daddy?" Trista asked.

I took a deep breath, struggling to find the right words. "Sometimes things happen and mommies and daddies can't live together anymore. So they live apart." I waited, trying to let it sink in. "But you kids will still get to see us both. And we love you as much as we ever did."

Slade began crying. "You made Daddy leave!" he marched off, refusing to return even when I called after him. I watched him, trying to blink back my own tears.

If only you knew. If only I could tell you. How angry you are. Already. My staying this long has made you one angry little boy.

I turned to the girls. They were trying to be brave and console me at the same time. I looked into their eyes, hoping they could see how much I hated to hurt them.

"I'm so sorry. I wish it didn't have to be like this. Just remember, none of this is your fault. You kids have done nothing wrong. Do you understand?" I asked my daughters.

"Yes," they said in unison.

I tipped back Trista's chin and looked into her eyes. "Do you?"

She shook her head.

But I didn't believe her. I didn't believe any of them.

A week later, Trudy's words shocked me.

"You did the right thing by leaving, so you could protect your children," she said. "It's rare for a mother to do that, to put her children's well-being before her feelings for her husband."

I shook my head. "It wasn't really a choice; it's the only thing I could do. I know they've already been harmed enough; there was no way I was going to stay and let their father hurt them even more."

"Well I just wish more women would choose their children over their men," Trudy hugged me.

Because the violence had been so harmful, Trudy began seeing the kids to help them learn healthy ways of coping with their pain and anger. She was teaching them how to express it on paper, using crayons. They drew pictures of what went on at home, and Trudy told me their artwork was quite revealing. They were sad, mad, and afraid: that Eddie might hurt me, that we would get divorced, that they were to blame for the fighting. It seemed there was an unending well of feelings Trudy was drawing up, but it didn't come without a fight.

They balked at going, and pouted when I said they had to. I learned Eddie had contributed to their resistance, after the kids told me their father said Trudy had threatened to have him arrested. I told the kids that wasn't true, but Eddie's negative attitude rubbed off on them anyway. Eventually though, instead of hearing their complaints all the way to her office, which was happening less and less, they began coming away from the sessions feeling a little better about themselves. Under the circumstances, it was about the best I could hope for.

Once I told Felecia what had been happening at home, she was warm and empathetic, and granted me a leave of absence so I could take care of my family while getting a much-needed break.

"You deserve it, and your job will be here waiting for you," Felecia said, with an awkward hug.

"Thank you. That means so much to me," I said, close to tears.

I didn't know how I could give up journalism, because of all it had given me. I felt like a different person, and I loved taking people's stories and writing about them. I loved the boring meetings, too, because it was a challenge to find something interesting to write about that people would want to read. Mostly, I would miss being able to tell people the truth, about what was going on in their own small corner of the world. But when I walked out of the building, I wasn't sure I would—or could—ever return.

Ironically, Eddie called and offered to find somewhere else to live so the kids and I could stay in the house, the same day I went to see about obtaining a legal separation. Because there had been violence in the home, Rita Ashton, the family law attorney I hired, recommended I ask the court to grant me a protective order. But I told Rita I didn't think it was necessary, because I was sure Eddie wouldn't try to hurt us anymore—especially since he still hoped I would take him back, and he wouldn't want to do anything that might mess up his chances with me.

Rita also told me that even if Eddie gave me money to live on, I might have to file for bankruptcy. She encouraged it, since my debts outweighed any possible income I would have in the near future. Rita asked me if I had any money at all and I said 'no.' Then I remembered our savings account: I told Rita it was set aside for home improvements, but she said if I could withdraw it, I could use it to live on—if Eddie hadn't already taken it. But I told Rita I didn't want to touch any of the money if Eddie was willing to pay me enough on a regular basis, so I could make ends meet. A few days later I decided to call him and see what we could work out.

But that's when Eddie told me that since I was filing for a legal separation, he was filing for divorce. He angrily said he wouldn't give me a cent. Much earlier, his refusal would have caused me to crawl right back to him, so I knew that's what Eddie was counting on. But I wasn't the child he had married, and I had no intention of making that mistake again. I was older, wiser, and stronger. I was a woman who had learned she could take care of herself—and her children. So instead of getting angry or trying to coerce him into supporting us, I hung up.

I'll never go back to him, and I'll do whatever I have to, to support my children myself, I thought.

The next day after dropping the kids off at school, I drove straight to the bank, giving myself a mental pep talk all the way there. As I got out of the car, I knew I hadn't been that nervous since the day Eddie threatened me at the school. The bank wasn't open yet, so I took a few minutes to gather my composure, walking over to the newspaper office.

The receptionist waved at me. "Hi there, Daleen. How's it going?" Lou's cheerful demeanor was infectious, and I felt my spirits begin to lift. After I told Felecia I needed a few weeks off, it didn't take long for the small staff to learn what had happened, and their moral support was so helpful.

"Fine, I have to stop by the bank and I just wanted to say hello. Does everyone miss me?" I asked, trying to shed my nervousness.

"We surely do. It's just not the same without you. Is that husband of yours still bothering you?" she asked.

"Of course. But not for long. We're getting a divorce."

"Good for you! Good for you! I've always said no woman should have to live with a man who treats her badly," Lou was empathetic.

I shook my head wryly. "It just took me a long time to realize that's what it was."

"Well, at least you had the good sense to see it in time. Some women don't." Her expression was grim.

"Yes, you're right. Well, I've got to get to the bank. I'll stop in again. Please tell Felecia I stopped by."

"I'll do that, Daleen. Take care," Lou grinned as I left the building. I hadn't taken more than six steps when I saw him—a tall, slender man wearing a baseball cap hurrying down the steps of the bank building. His head was down and he was putting something into his wallet.

Eddie! What's he doing here?

For a minute, I thought I might faint from fear, my heart was beating so rapidly. There was no way for him to know what I planned to do, since I hadn't told anyone but my attorney.

What if . . . what if he already beat me to it?

I gave myself a mental shake.

Relax. He can't hurt you. You're in broad daylight and there are people everywhere.

I casually glanced toward the county jail and then nonchalantly back toward Eddie, and saw him staring directly at me. Half a dozen more steps and we would pass each other. Would he grab me? Would he try to force me into his car, like the man who had raped his wife at gunpoint just last year? I had covered the story and knew she, too, had left a horrible home life. He later found her and forced her into his car, where he raped her in front of their two, small children. It was one of the most poignant domestic violence stories I'd covered, and it was pivotal in helping me to see the violence within my own family.

Forcing myself to stop thinking about that story, I shook my head to clear my thoughts.

Relax Daleen, it's going to be okay. Besides, the sheriff's office is across the street. Just scream loud and long and everyone will come running—and Lou will be the first one out the door to help!

The vision of Lou beating Eddie with her bare hands made me chuckle. By then I got so tickled by the idea, I had to bite the back of my hand to quell my laughter.

"Hello, Daleen. Fancy meeting you here." Eddie spoke without malice, and I even sensed some humor. Certainly a hint of sarcasm, but nothing that alerted me to any impending danger.

"Yes, I had to stop by the office for a minute," I said, trying to act as though we were friendly neighbors meeting on the street corner.

"Oh, you're working then?"

"You know I had to take a temporary leave of absence. That's why it really would be good if you could give us some monetary support right now—for the kids' sake." As long as we were standing face-to-face, in person, I hoped the added pressure might prick his conscience.

He stood there, one hand rubbing his chin. "Well, I thought maybe you might change your mind and come back. After all, we've had these little disagreements before and we've been able to work them out." He didn't move a muscle, and managed to look quite smug as he stood there, waiting me out.

I swallowed hard, gazing just beyond his shoulder. As Eddie's words sank in, I recalled all the times in the past when money had been an issue with him—when he had used it to manipulate, subdue or control me. He had done it throughout our entire marriage, which is why I began researching relationships, and learned how money and sex cause the biggest arguments. With money, Eddie had always gone from one extreme to another. Either he spent it on things we didn't need or couldn't afford—or he abdicated his responsibility, dumping it in my lap—only to give me grief when there wasn't any left to buy his "toys," because I used it to pay bills. Then there were the times he had controlled it so tightly it hurt his family: I recalled his first layoff from the mines, when I struggled just to feed our family with the free commodities we received.

And you were too selfish to give up that stupid luxury car, which kept us from being able to get food stamps, simply because a vehicle was more important to you than we were!

Coming out of my reverie, I looked straight into his eyes. "No, not this time. It won't work."

He shrugged, and a disgusting smile crept onto his face. "Well then, I guess my answer is still 'no.' I'm not giving you a cent. See you later." Eddie turned and walked away.

I stood there staring, resisting the urge to scream, "What about your children, you creep? Don't you care anything about what happens to them?" Instead, I remained mute, saying nothing.

Some things never change.

I squared my shoulders because, in reality, he had just made it much easier for me to drain the savings account. If I'd had doubts before, he had convinced me there was no way to save my marriage, and I was better off without him.

We're all better off!

I casually glanced back and saw him turning a corner. Then he was gone. I forced myself not to run into the bank.

What if he did it? What if he just took the money? What if that's why he had that smile plastered all over his face?

I pulled hard on the bank door and walked over to a cashier. I was shaking and my insides felt jittery. I was afraid that any minute Eddie might figure out what I was doing and come back to confront me. After our little exchange, I believed anything was possible. He hadn't said so, but he wasn't giving up that easily. I saw it written all over his face.

The teller recognized me. "Hey there, girl. How've you been?"

"Oh, hi Donna." I pulled myself from my self-induced fog. "I'm sorry, I'm having one of those days. I'm fine, thanks."

Always friendly and helpful, Donna was Deputy Haney's wife.

I rummaged through my purse, trying to find my passbook. "How's Charlie?" I asked absently.

"He's fine. He and Joe are away on another of their training trips." Donna smiled and I laid my passbook on the counter.

"Yes, they're quite a pair," I smiled. "Have they always worked together?"

Donna nodded. "Yes, for as long as I can remember, where Charlie was, so was Joe."

Just then I realized we had no time to chat, in case Eddie did return. "I need to withdraw some money from savings. Actually, I'd like to withdraw the entire amount, please. The last time I checked there was about $3,700 in it," I said, praying Eddie wasn't sneaking up behind me that very minute.

Daleen, get a grip! Stop being paranoid. You're safe in here. No one is going to let anything happen.

Then another, equally alarming thought occurred.

What if he has to sign for it, too? What if it's already gone and they call the bank president? What if they try to arrest me?

Ridiculous thoughts flew through my head as I stood there, praying Donna would return with the money. I waited, trying to act nonchalantly. "How would you like that?" Donna asked, handing me a paper with "$3,718.00" written on it.

"A cashier's check. Oh, and can you please tell me what's left in my checking account?"

Thank you, dear God. Thank you.

I let out a long, slow sigh of relief, feeling the sweat droplets running down my back. A moment later, Donna returned with a slip of paper she pushed towards me. It read: $346.07.

So that's why he was here! Taking the money out of that account so I wouldn't have access to it. Well, at least he forgot about the savings account.

I thanked Donna and turned to the desk where new accounts were handled.

"May I help you?" Andie Jacobson asked.

"Yes Andie, I want to open up a savings account." I handed her the cashier's check, not feeling a single shed of the outward confidence I wanted to project.

"I haven't seen you in awhile. Have you been busy?" Andie chatted as she typed.

"Yes, I've been too busy." I signed the paper Andie pushed toward me and prayed she would hurry.

"I read that last column you wrote. It was hilarious. I swear you live my life," Andie laughed.

"Thank you. Thank you so much!" I smiled. As she handed me the passbook, I slipped it into my purse and said goodbye. I waved at Donna, who waved back. "Tell Charlie hello for me."

That was the good thing about living in a small town—everyone knew everyone else. I'd been banking there since I got my first checking account, at sixteen. That was so long ago it seemed like another lifetime, when I was a naïve and trusting young girl.

I hurried out of the bank into the bright sunshine. Eddie was nowhere in sight, and as I turned the corner I knew I was safe. I unlocked my car door and sank down onto the seat, locking the door behind me. I grabbed the steering wheel and rested my head against it.

"Yes, I did it! I did it!" I yelled triumphantly into the empty vehicle.

The next day, Eddie called to harass me about the money I took from the savings account. "Just what do you think you're going to do with that money, Daleen? It's for house repairs."

"Calm down, Eddie. If you don't quit yelling, I'm going to hang up."

"Then I'll just call back again. Who do you think you are,

taking that money? It belongs to both of us!" He yelled.

"Yes, just like the money in the checking account, which you cleaned out—so I couldn't use it to support myself." I countered smoothly.

"That's right, because I wasn't going to let you get your hands on it," he snarled through the phone line.

"Well my attorney advised me to take the money from the savings account after you said you weren't going to give me any. I have to support the kids somehow, and I don't have any income right now. Besides, you're legally obligated to support them, whether you want to or not." I wasn't backing down, and I wasn't going to play his game and give in to his angry demands.

At first, living without another adult in the house at night wasn't easy, and I heard every sound the old house made during the nighttime hours. But prayer worked wonders, usually helping me to get a decent night's sleep.

That changed after the bat. It was pitch black when I awoke to a soft whirring sound. As my eyes adjusted to the darkness, I screamed, realizing I wasn't alone in the room. I jumped out of bed and ran out, slamming the door behind me. I came awake enough to realize what I had heard was a bat. I ran to get the kids, waking them up from a sound sleep as I scooped them into my arms and carried them out into the warm, summer night. Not quite awake, they were crying and fussing, unaware of what was happening.

Returning to the house, I heard the creature flying around my room, and cold chills ran up and down my spine. I hated bats! I was afraid it was rabid, but even if it wasn't, the house wasn't big enough for the both of us. I grabbed my purse and pulled a jacket on over my nightgown, wondering how to get rid of the bats that had made their home in our belfry.

The next morning, I told myself my fear was irrational. But it seemed symbolic of all the fears we had been living with during the last ten years. And our fear, once released from captivity—just like the furry grey mammal trapped in my bedroom—wasn't going anywhere on its own. So we stayed at Mom's for the better part of a month, before I summoned enough courage to return. Once I did, I felt strong enough to face anything, even the bats. Besides, instead of running off myself, if it happened again, I would make sure the bat left. I wasn't going to be run out of my own home again.

That night was the first time I had been there after dark since we left in the middle of the night. It felt good to be back, but even after reassuring the kids everything was fine, and reading them stories until they fell asleep, I knew I wasn't as confident as I should have been when I crawled into bed. I left the nightstand light on as a precaution, but I kept worrying a bat would fly into the kids' room and terrify us all, until I finally fell into a fitful sleep.

A couple of days before what should have been our tenth wedding anniversary, I went to the car and found a letter in a sealed envelope on the front seat. With a start, I saw my name scrawled in Eddie's handwriting, and realized he still had a car key.

I need to get his key back so he can't get in any time he pleases.

I was already nervous, looking over my shoulder at the odd moment, fearful he would jump up from the back seat to assault me. I tore the envelope open, not even wanting to read what he had written.

"Dear Daleen,

I realize I no longer have any reason to hope for a favored position with you. It's not sex, really. It's the whole thing. I'm stuck off by myself without you and the kids. I really don't understand. Why did you marry me, why did you date me, why did you keep on coming to stay with Kim, why didn't you tell your mom I was molesting you—raping you if you must—when I stayed there? Were you afraid to talk, or afraid of the consequences? I'm just in the dark.

I thought about it and realized our anniversary, if we celebrated it, will be a farce—just like the rest of our marriage. Even if this situation was solved, I'm sure that if I touch you or try to make love to you, it will cause flashbacks and will be useless anyhow. Why waste our energy fooling each other, when we need something else, whatever that is?

It is so hard knowing that you did wrong and have no way of ever righting it satisfactorily. I don't even know why I'm wasting your precious time reading this junk mail.

—Eddie"

Anger, pain, disgust, and disbelief—I felt each emotion as I read and when I finished, I began to crumple it up. Suddenly, I decided it might be wise to save it. Just in case.

I was glad I had because the following Sunday, Eddie broke in while we were at our Bible meeting. He took the most incriminating piece of evidence I had against him—a letter he had written to me in one of my journals several months earlier. I had planned to use it if I had to.

The kids found the envelope first, laying near the front door. I opened it and found $160 cash inside—and suddenly got a sick feeling in my stomach. There was only one reason Eddie would leave me money: to assuage his guilt. I ran to get the journal from my desk drawer, knowing even before I opened the drawer what I would find. The entry on the first page was in my handwriting—but the six-page letter he had written was gone. He had torn it out, and I could still see the imprint left by his words, on the page that had followed his letter.

If only I had gotten the locks changed on the doors, I thought.

Trying not to cry, but shaking inside and out, I called Shirley and told her what had happened. She was just as angry and indignant as I was. I felt like I had been violated—again—and longed to get even.

I'll get you. I'll pay you back.

That was the first time I had been without the notebook, because I kept it with me wherever I went.

Why, oh why, did I leave it behind?

I had no answers, and only a growing sense of anger and injustice. The anger could have been harmful, since it would have suffocated me, had I let it. Instead, I fought back. After talking to Shirley, I made a second call, to the sheriff, who said he would do whatever he could to help. But after realizing I had already touched everything that Eddie had touched, Jim said there was no reason to send someone out to dust for prints. He told me to stop by his office and he would take a look at the notebook, to see if anything could be done.

When I walked into Jim's office Monday morning, I recalled countless other visits there. I had always come with a notebook in my hand, used to take notes as he gave me the latest news from the sheriff's department. Woven between the detailed threads about criminal matters, were tidbits about our families.

But this visit was different, because I was there as a victim. It felt different, too, leaving me vulnerable and nervous. After a big smile and a handshake, Jim got down to business.

"Let's take a look at that notebook, Daleen." I handed the yellow book across Jim's desk. He opened the cover and looked at the inside page.

"The first six pages, front and back, contained the letter.

He tore them all out. There, in his own handwriting, was absolute proof of what he did to me." I sat back and waited, with little hope he could help.

"I'm not sure what we can do. It looks like some of the print may have come off on the inside of the front cover. You can see faint markings here." He pointed at the ink left behind. "I'll have Joe take a look at it. I can't make any promises, but I'll see what we can do."

I shook my head. "I really appreciate it, Jim. If I'd just had a chance to have those deadbolts installed . . ." I left the sentence unfinished.

"What's this guy's problem, anyway? Is he a drinker?"

Until yesterday, I had never confided in Jim about my personal life, so he didn't know anything about Eddie. "No, he doesn't drink. Or do drugs. He has an addiction," I forced myself to spit the words out. "He's addicted to sex. He's been into pornography since he was a teen and in the intimate aspect of our life, the word "no" means nothing.

I wasn't sure why, but I couldn't just tell Jim: "He raped me."

"Is he abusive in other ways? To you or the kids?" I had Jim's full attention.

"Yes, that's one of the reasons I had to leave. I could take it when it was just me, but when he began abusing the kids, too . . . well, I just couldn't let them, or us, live like that." I shrugged, trying to smile.

Jim was reaching into his desk and when he handed me a small business card a few seconds later, I took it from him and looked at the number he had written on the back. "That's my personal office number. You can call me here or at home any time—day or night—and I'll do whatever I can to help you. In my book, a man who hits a woman isn't a man and I won't put up with it."

"Thank you, Jim." I stood up, ready to leave.

"Just remember, if you think he's come into the house again, don't touch anything. Just get out and call the police from a neighbor's house. That way we can dust for finger-prints and have him charged with breaking and entering." Jim stood up and came around the desk as I went towards his door. His look was solemn and direct. "You also know, unless he half-kills you, not a whole lot will happen to him, legally. That's the way the law works, and I'm just as disgusted with it as you are."

I shook my head in agreement. "I know. I remember only too well the cases I've covered for the paper, when the guy only got a slap on the wrist. But it means a lot, just knowing you're on my side."

"You bet I am. Take care of yourself, you hear?"

Outside in the bright sunlight I realized I felt stronger. I had someone who would enforce the law, or who would at least try to help me help myself. It felt good knowing someone like the sheriff was on my side.

The summer passed, sometimes quickly, other times as if it was in no hurry to go. We kept busy, which was a blessing, because I didn't have time to think. The nights were hard enough, when I would go from bed to bed, listening to each child's fears.

What if Daddy doesn't love us anymore?

What if I made him leave?

How come he doesn't come to visit us?

Mommy, you won't ever leave us, will you?

The never-ending questions were heart-wrenching, leav-ing me feeling so powerless and sad that many nights I would just crawl into bed and cry myself to sleep. In front of them, I could be strong, pretending like everything was all right, but in the privacy of my own bedroom my guard came down and their pain became mine. I knew Eddie didn't care about them. If he did, he would at least visit them. Not that I wanted him to, because I knew that was just as harmful. It had always been like that, in one of those "damned if you do, damned if you don't," ways. I thought of all the stories I had covered, where a parent—usually a father—abused his son or daughter, and then tried to excuse his actions, blaming the child for the abuse.

I thought about several girls I had grown up with, abandoned by the fathers of their babies, or who later divorced for reasons similar to mine. Those men cared more about their trucks, their paychecks, and even going out to a local beer joint, than they did their children, who were often left behind, with only a mother to tend to them. Or, as I was beginning to see more and more in our little community, for the grandparents to rear—since the mother was usually left without any child support, forced to eke out a meager existence for herself and her children, working some low-paying job. If she wasn't doing that, she was living on welfare, and it wasn't long before a stream of men began going in and out of her life, like so many worn-out pairs of shoes.

One warm evening after the kids were tucked in, I sat down with my journal and wrote about the problems, including my own vow not to live on welfare. I knew I could support my children, and that's what I was going to do. As for Eddie not taking the time to show an interest in his children, well, there was nothing I could do about that. It wasn't my fault, and it was out of my control. Besides, I was afraid to be around him, and I didn't want to take any chances. So him not visiting, or making any effort to do so, was a mixed blessing. For all of us.

But it was still hard to listen to my children and hear their voices filled with doubt, wondering if "Daddy" didn't come to visit because they had done something wrong. I tried to give them more love and attention than usual, in an effort to make up for what their father wasn't, and really never had given. I put down my pen, and prayed it was enough.

When the phone rang a few seconds later, I thought it might be Mom, checking in as she usually did each night, just to make sure everything was all right. Instead, it was Eddie.

After a curt hello, I got to the point. "What do you want, Eddie?"

"Just to hear your voice, I guess." He sounded despondent.

At one time I would have felt pity, and allowed him to reel me in. But no more, not after all he'd done to hurt our children.

"Fine, you've heard it," I said, laying the receiver back into its cradle. I wanted nothing to do with him, not even to hear his voice.

CHAPTER EIGHTEEN

When Eddie eventually called about what he'd done, to feel me out and to gloat—as I knew he would—I stood up to him, knowing I had the sheriff at my back.

"Yes, I'd like to talk to you about that. How dare you break into this house and take the pages out of my notebook. What did you do with them anyway?" I forced myself to remain calm, and not scream at him.

I could hear the smugness in the phone line before he even spoke. "I guess you could say they're ashes now. They were as soon as I took them. Did you really think I'd let you keep that letter, knowing what it could do to me if anyone else ever read it? Not on your life," Eddie said.

"Fine, you got what you want. But let me give you a word of advice, Mr. Leigh. When I left Sheriff Fields' office, he was very interested in you. I'm to let him know if you ever try to harass me again, so I'd advise you to never set foot on this property again without my permission. Do you understand me?" I heard the self-assurance in my calm words.

When no sound came from Eddie's end, I realized that for once, he was speechless. I returned the receiver to its cradle and started dancing around the room. I had rarely taken up for myself, and I realized it made me feel . . . powerful!

I'm the only person who can control my life, and I'm the one who has to make changes, I thought.

I decided I would no longer be a passive observer on the sidelines, merely hoping for more. For better or worse, I was going to fight back.

I'm going to fight for my children, for myself, and for my right to be treated with respect and dignity!

But it was going to be a long, hard battle, because my children kept expressing their pent-up pain. I tossed and turned in bed one hot, late night. Sometimes I felt it was all directed at me and I wasn't sure how much more I could take. Especially when little Slade unleashed the enormous amount of anger he had been carrying around inside. "You made Daddy go and I don't like it!" he had cried.

"Sweetheart, I didn't make Daddy go," I said, cradling him on my lap and smoothing his blond hair. "I really didn't. Daddy and I just can't live together anymore, but we both still love you and your sisters very much. That won't ever change. We just can't stay together, and Daddy knows it's better for him to live somewhere else." I pulled him close, his tears falling on my blouse as I fought hard to blink back my own.

Even in spite of my own reassurances and our weekly family therapy sessions with Trudy, Slade's accusations were becoming more frequent, not less.

I was pretty sure Slade's behavior could be explained by the few visits Eddie did have with the kids, which he was using to an unfair advantage. They returned from their father's home saying things like, "If you let Daddy come back, we'll be so good. We'll never do anything wrong again." Or, "Daddy really loves you, but he says you don't love him anymore. He said he would come home tomorrow if you would let him, but you won't." I was horrified at his emotional manipulation.

He's playing mind games with them, trying to get to me through them. How dare he do this to our children! What kind of a father is he, anyway?

I knew I needed to have a serious talk with him about it, and prayed it would make him stop and think about how wrong it was to use his children. Before I could, though, Eddie showed up unannounced at the house one day. We had gone to get groceries, and upon our return, Eddie was inside, repairing a window in the kids' bedroom. The kids grew excited when they saw his truck parked there, but I was appalled that he had gotten in, since the locks had been changed the day after he destroyed part of my journal. I knew the old house had other "entrances," including the small coal bin door, and I was just thankful that he hadn't decided to drop in during the night-time, while we were sleeping.

Eddie heard them all the way inside, and it was only a few minutes before he appeared in the doorway. The kids went running to him and threw themselves at him, and I tried to ignore him by loading the groceries into my arms. I knew I was just buying time; the sheriff had told me to call if he went inside the house again, and while a part of me wanted nothing more than to call Jim, another part of me dreaded making a scene in front of my children. Besides, I knew he would twist it to his advantage, and make me look like the bad guy, and the children would act up even worse than they already were.

I brushed by him and went into the kitchen, trying to ignore him completely. But he followed, and offered to help get the rest of the groceries. "No thank you, I've got it," I said coldly. I wanted nothing more than to berate him for what he was doing—trying to put on a good show in front of our children—but that would hardly do any good. So instead, I asked him what he was doing there.

"I knew the window in Slade's room needed to be replaced, and I had some free time, so I decided to stop by and fix it. That's all. I know the bats have been a problem, so I thought this might help. I don't want any trouble," he seemed sincere and even a little apologetic.

"Fine, but then you need to leave." I kept my back to him as he spoke, hoping I would turn around and he would be gone.

"Sure, but there's one small thing I could use some help with. I need someone to hold the window in while I anchor it inside the frame. Would you mind to help me?"

I was uneasy and suggested he get a neighbor to help instead.

"No, that's all right. I'll just do it myself," he said, and turned to go.

Disgusted with myself for being afraid, I stopped putting away the groceries and went upstairs to help him.

Why is it he can make me feel so guilty, like he's done nothing wrong and I'm a nasty shrew?

I walked over to the window, intent on assisting him as long as was necessary. I drew a deep breath, to calm my nerves. "What do I do? I just have a few minutes, because I need to make dinner," I said abruptly.

Eddie showed me how to hold the window steady, and then began nailing it in. The second it was in place, I turned to go. That's when he turned around and grabbed me.

I tried to pull away, but Eddie wouldn't let go of me. "Let go of me, this minute! How dare you?" I jerked and pulled away, trying to escape his embrace, but the next thing I knew, I was sitting on Eddie's lap on the bed.

"I'm not going to hurt you," he said. "Just hold on a minute. I just wanted a kiss, that's all." His arms were wound tight around me, and he was kissing me anywhere he could reach: my face, my lips, my neck.

As I struggled against him, a picture of a recent murder victim pleading for her life flashed through my mind, just before she was shot three times. Then I saw Tonya Wolfe, sound asleep on her living room couch, oblivious to the gun her husband had pointed in her direction. Then I saw the woman whose husband had raped her in front of her children.

Oh my God, he's going to rape me. Right here. Right now.

I tried to turn my head, hating every touch, every kiss. My heart was pounding, and as I looked at him, I saw the desperation in his eyes. They were wild with desire.

"Let go of me! Right now. Do you hear me? The kids are downstairs and if they come up here and see what you're doing, they're going to be afraid. Do you understand?" I hoped if I appealed to him on their behalf, he would stop, but Eddie paid no attention at all. It was as if the words didn't even register, he was so intent on getting what he wanted.

"You'll never be another man's. If I can't have you, no one else will, either!" He pinned me between the wall and the bed, and at the sound of those words, I became like a wild animal, fighting for my life.

"We're going to work things out. And we're going to start right now! Do you understand?" Eddie yelled at me, and I began sobbing.

"Please, please let me go," I cried.

"The only way I'll let you go is if you call the cops or if you kill me."

In desperation, I began hitting him, trying to pry his fingers from me.

"I just want to hold you, to love you," he cried.

"Daddy?" a voice from the doorway said.

We both froze, and I turned and saw Gabby hesitantly standing there, unsure of what to do.

"It's okay Honey. Daddy and Mommy are just making up,

that's all," he said smoothly. "You go run and play now, and we'll be down in a minute." Obediently, she turned and ran down the steps, leaving us alone together again.

I knew then he was going to rape me. I knew it with every fiber of my being, and it was going to be just like the woman I had written about: my children were going to come back up and see him raping me.

Only this time, I'm going to be the victim, and someone else will be writing the story.

In that minute, all the rapes I had endured during the past thirteen years flashed past, as if being fast-forwarded, through my brain, and I saw clearly everything he had ever done to me. It felt like it was happening all over again, and I began praying.

Please, dear Father, not again. Please, help me. Help us all. I beg you, please don't let him do this to me.

I knew then I wasn't giving up—not without a fight. He might have me down, but I wasn't out. Not by a long shot.

A few seconds—or maybe it was minutes—later, Gabby came bounding up the stairs again. Yelling for me. She hadn't even made it to the top, when I heard her words.

"Mommy, they're here. Mickey and John are here. They want to know if they should come inside," she said.

I was breathing very hard, twisting and trying to get away from Eddie. I had completely forgotten we had guests coming over for dinner. "Yes!" I yelled. "Tell them to come in. Now! Go get them, Gabby, please!"

Thank you, God, thank you!

Immediately, Eddie let go of me. It happened so quickly it seemed like he'd been burned with a hot iron. I just laid there, stunned and in shock, as he jumped up and off the bed.

"I'm going to kill myself. You'll never have to see me again, or worry about me bothering you," he said.

Then he was gone and I was alone. I managed to sit up, trying to smooth my hair and straighten my rumpled clothing. I needed to compose myself, but I couldn't stay there and chance Eddie changing his mind. As I neared the stairs I found myself running and crying at the same time. I had to make sure Mickey and John came inside—that they didn't leave us alone with that madman.

Somehow my knees didn't collapse beneath me as I went down the stairs and when I reached the doorway, I motioned my friends inside. They turned from talking to the kids and I saw Eddie's truck begin to back up. I realized he was inside it.

God answered my prayers. They got here just in time to keep him from raping me.

I was a mess for the rest of the evening. I told them what happened, careful my children couldn't hear what I was saying. While cooking and then again during dinner, I suddenly found myself in a daze, and heard nothing that was said. By the time dinner was over, Mickey made plans to stay with me for the night, just so another adult would be there. John said he was sure Eddie wouldn't return, but if he did, to call 911 first, then to call him. For the next few nights, different friends came over and stayed with us, offering me comfort and support, and giving me a feeling of protection, since there was safety in numbers.

It took a long time to recover from that incident, but in a way it was good, for it helped me to face the fear and anxiety that I had locked away for all those years. The bats—living in our attic, and occasionally getting free, flying around our bedrooms at night—had started me on the road to feeling the cold, raw emotion of fear. But that day in Slade's bedroom, held captive against my will in a madman's arms, I felt fear on a deeper level than I ever had before. It protected me, because I never let down my guard again and allowed myself to be in a situation with him where I didn't feel comfortable.

Eddie didn't commit suicide, either, and by then, his ploy of saying he would had grown old—helping me to see right through his empty threat. It allowed me to see him for what he was: a coward who manipulated me by making me feel like I had to protect him from himself.

A few miles away, in the little town of Arthurdale, another mother was playing out a similar scene in her own mind. Wanda Toppins was just a few years older than me. At 34, she had recently divorced her husband, a big, mean man who worked as a foreman for a local coal company. Taking her small son, she fled the big, beautiful home they had shared.

I didn't know her, but the day after I wrote about my fears, Wanda was murdered in cold blood in front of her son, a three-year-old little boy she had been so worried about taking away from his father, that she allowed herself to remain in the danger zone. Wanda had gotten caught between her concern for her child, and her fear for her own life.

I wasn't working when she was killed, so I wasn't on scene to cover the story; I heard about it from Brad afterward: a SWAT team had been deployed, because after the shooting Jerry Toppins fled, taking his youngest son with him. Law enforcement surrounded the house, blocking off all access and evacuating nearby neighbors.

Returning to work soon after, I sat down across from Deputy Stiles, who was the lead investigator. Joe told me how violent Toppins had been.

"Wanda was shot several times, up close. And even after she fell to the ground and couldn't get back up," Joe explained, "Toppins continued firing bullets into her body."

I listened in rapt attention, but I had a hard time paying attention—especially when I realized that the day before

Wanda was murdered, I had written in my diary about my fear that I might be killed. That if Eddie didn't kill me, his abuse would cause me to take my own life. Instead, Wanda was the one who was killed. Her husband, like mine, had a long history of being violent, and at least one other wife had died under suspicious circumstances.

Toppins' marriage to Wanda had been equally volatile as his others, and his son, Jerry Jr., had joined the military to get away from his father's violence. When Joe told me Wanda had warned friends that if she died, it would be at the hands of her ex, I thought about my own situation. My own life.

I thought about Wanda's children: her little boy, David, her daughter, Candy, from a previous marriage, and Jerry Jr. All of those children were going to be permanently affected by the violence. There was no way they could remain unscathed.

I considered my own children: Mileah had stabbed Gabby in the back with a fork, just a year or two ago. And at least once, Slade had chased his sisters with a knife. Too, they all argued about the smallest thing, which would then escalate into a battle, complete with hitting, pinching, biting and kicking. Our children—Wanda's and mine—had lived through a war zone, fighting for survival.

"I know Felecia's story said Wanda had filed a battery complaint against Jerry, back in May, which was later dropped. What can you tell me about that?"

Joe looked at his notes. "I can tell you the magistrate ordered him to stop abusing her, and she got temporary custody of her daughter, Candy, and their son, David, the three-year-old."

"Yes, I remember something about that in Felecia's story. It said Toppins came home, crashed his motorcycle, and told her to leave. That he threatened to take the baby and disappear. Was there anything else? What's his motive—well, other than being a jerk?" I heard the sarcasm in my voice.

Joe grinned. "You said it, I didn't. Well, let's see, you know about the new boyfriend, right?"

"Just that he was there with her, the day she was killed."

"They were supposed to get married that day. He had been Wanda's high school sweetheart. So that's one motive— Jerry didn't want another man to have what he still viewed as his."

Joe turned a page in his notebook. "That would explain the statement her fiancé gave to police, since the last thing he remembers was Toppins yelling something about 'the whore's out here. I killed her. Come and look at her.'"

I wrote it down, trying to clearly focus on what he was saying. I kept thinking back to Eddie's recent threats.

You'll never be another man's. If I can't have you, no one else will, either!

I tore myself away from that horrible day, forcing myself to concentrate on Joe's words. "These men are all the same," I muttered under my breath.

I didn't realize Joe had heard me. "Yes, they are. Batterers are all pretty much cut from the same cloth."

"Were there any other complaints filed—and how did they even end up having contact, if there was an order in place?"

Joe looked squarely at me, his blue eyes intense. "Because she dropped it when the divorce began. And according to Toppins, he killed her because she refused to let him take the boy, if he didn't give her the child support."

I must have looked confused, for he continued. "Now, I'm not saying that she did or she didn't. But that's what Toppins claims happened. We did find a check there, on the ground beside her, and while that may have been a factor, I doubt it." Joe ran his finger over his chin, deep in thought. I waited patiently.

"How often does that happen?" I asked Joe.

"It happens, a lot more than I'd like." He shrugged his shoulders. "It's leverage, usually to get the man to pay the woman child support or alimony. The attorneys recommend it, and the man is only too happy to give up money or something else, in return for having the criminal complaint dismissed."

I realized that Wanda had been in the same situation I was in—her ex used money as a weapon, to try to get what he wanted, too.

"I understand, but I don't think that's a good thing—to drop the charges in return for something else," I said.

Joe looked up from his file. "You'll get no argument about that one from me. While I was at Quantico a few weeks ago, we had a class about interpersonal violence, and discussed that very problem. The fact is, there's always some give and take, but it often makes the situation much worse, because what we're starting to see is a lot of women filing for protection, but then dropping the charges down the road, for one reason or another."

I thought about how I had never tried to file for a protective order—not even after the most recent incident, which scared me to death. "It must be hard, knowing if you file, there's a price to pay, in terms of facing his anger, and having to deal with him."

"Yes, but the order is supposed to keep him away from her." Joe gave me a weary look. "Look, I said that's what's supposed to happen. It doesn't always."

I checked my notes, asking him to give me a few minutes to see if I missed anything.

I walked down the stairs and out the front door, wondering for the umpteenth time why I had never filed for a protective order. Even my attorney recommended I get one, but I just couldn't bring myself to do it. And it wasn't from a fear Eddie would retaliate in anger, if I did. It was more from shame and embarrassment, at having to admit to the cops I knew professionally that my life was no better than the victims they saw and helped, every day of the week.

Beyond that, I still believed his violence was only an isolated event, something that happened here and there—that I could handle on my own, without a protective order. After all, my mother had handled everything on her own—raising five children, holding down a job, taking care of my father and a huge old house that required lots of work. So why couldn't I?

Aside from all of that, though, there was a single remaining reason why I had not gotten a protective order after any episodes of abuse—I was afraid to speak up, afraid of what others would think of me and, mostly, afraid they wouldn't believe me.

Ever since I began openly talking about our "secret life," and taking steps to protect myself, I felt weepy and cried a lot. After Eddie broke in and held me hostage, I had more anger and fear to deal with, and I often felt like I was coming apart at the seams as the emotions I had locked away for years started to overwhelm me. The summer heat and humidity only made the situation even more unbearable.

It feels like a funnel cloud. I've gotten so sucked into their pain and anger, I can't even see clearly, I thought.

So in late June, I packed up the kids and drove to Harrisburg, Pa., to see Bruce. He said he was glad we were coming, and over the telephone told us about all the fun activities he had planned. When we arrived at his apartment that Friday night, the kids ran from the car, yelling "Uncle Bruce, Uncle Bruce." I followed them, amazed by their devotion to him. They had no sooner reached his door than it swung open.

"Why, if it isn't a bunch of poor orphan children, come

to visit me. Won't you come in, little orphans. I'd love to have you visit for the weekend." With that, the girls whooped and yelled, laughing at his teasing welcome. They all tried to hug him at once, and he looked like he had small legs and arms coming from everywhere. Only Slade hung back, but Bruce was quick to notice.

"There—what's this? It looks like one more orphan, a little orphan boy. Won't you come in, too?" Slade acted shy and Bruce gathered him up in his arms, hugging him tightly. "How are you little boy? My, you've gotten so big. I haven't seen you for a long time. I'll bet you're about ten now. Are you ten?" Slade shook his head and held up five fingers, and everyone laughed. Bruce always knew just what to say to get the kids going.

Our five days together passed too quickly, with picnics and a visit to the nearby science center. The kids loved the hands-on science activities, and Bruce and I went from one child to the next, snapping pictures the entire time. He had bought some riding toys for them, so in the evenings after dinner, we went out to the large yard behind the apartment building.

While the kids played together, Bruce and I sat on the grass and talked about everything that had happened. Whereas I had somehow sensed Mom wasn't willing to hear all the sordid details, it was different with Bruce. He understood. He was shocked at how long the abuse had gone on, and couldn't get over the fact that Eddie had refused to support his own children, or how mean and hateful he continued to act. I told him Eddie had always been that way when we were alone, but put on a good show when my family was around.

"I don't know how you lived like that," he said, amazed. "My sister Jane had a boyfriend who was mean, but nothing like that."

"I guess you just get used to it. And besides, Eddie always

blamed me for anything and everything. I think you get to the point where you believe it yourself, and think you're not good enough for anything—or for anyone—else."

"Yes, I suppose that's true. But how terrible to live like that."

"What happened to Jane? Is she still with that guy?"

"Oh no, as soon as he began mistreating her, she kicked him out." Bruce laughed. "Yes sir, I remember her telling me she wouldn't stand for any man to treat her like a doormat."

I smiled, wishing I had been that strong. "Your parents must have set a good example for her, for all of you, when you were growing up. I really think domestic violence—which is what it is—gets passed down from one generation to the next. You end up marrying someone like your father, and you become an abused wife."

"No, my parents were never abusive. Oh my dad was a drinker, but he never hurt my mom. At least, we never knew about it." Bruce looked thoughtful for a second. "But wait a minute, your dad never hit your mom, did he?"

I nodded slowly and told Bruce the story about Dad's burnt dinner. He looked flabbergasted. "Your dad did that to your mom? I've never heard her say anything about that!"

"Yes, pretty sad, isn't it? I was eight when I told her I wanted her to divorce him, because I never wanted him to hurt her again. It was pretty frightening," I said.

"I'll bet. Man, that is just so hard to believe. I mean, I would have never guessed."

"Well, it's not exactly conversation you'd share during dinner parties, if you get my drift." I smiled.

"No, I guess it's not," Bruce said, still visibly upset by my news.

"After all, that's the way it happens. The abuse occurs and it's kept secret. No one knows, and no one talks about it. That's why it continues—and why so many women never leave. Why, except for that one discussion, when Mom knew I saw what was going on, we never talked about again. Not one word."

"But maybe it just happened that one time," Bruce said.

"Sure!" I gave him a sideways look. "That's why Mom left Dad when they were in Jordan and she was pregnant with Michael—because he threw a can of beer at her. That's the only other big one I know of, but there were others that led up to it. I really don't know that much about it, because she still won't talk about it. Only if I press her, and then it's still difficult for her to say much of anything at all."

Bruce sat there staring at me, and as I saw the battle within him, I wasn't surprised.

To believe or not to believe?

Bruce knew it was the truth, but like all family and friends, he couldn't understand why he hadn't seen the signs of abuse himself. He couldn't understand why he hadn't known what was going on for all these years in my own marriage. Even more disturbing, Bruce had just learned that his best friend— who happened to be my father—had been abusive to his own wife, my mother.

"But maybe it only happened those few times. I mean, basically your father's a great guy who just drinks too much. Of course, there were many times when he would come home late at night, drunk, and I'd wonder how your mother could be so understanding and take all that nonsense. It's different for me, because I'm single and I don't have a wife waiting at home. But still—"

"Maybe the physical violence did only happen a few times—I only saw it that once, and she told me about the beer can incident. But there was also emotional abuse. Putting her down, being critical of her, swearing and yelling when he was drunk. In the end, she ended up believing all that garbage about herself." I could feel myself getting heated up, passionate about how much harm comes from domestic violence.

Bruce appeared to consider that. "You know, you're right. That's abuse, too. It's just that most people don't look at it that way."

"No, they don't. Our society thinks abuse against women—be it physical, emotional or sexual—is okay. We might say we don't, but we show by our actions that we do. We permit it by not enacting stronger laws against it, and by closing our eyes to the fact that it happens. Yes, you have groups out there to help women and their children, shelters for them to go to, but how many times does the neighbor across the street come over and offer help? Or does that person instead say, "I'm not getting involved. It's none of my business." I stopped, spent, and decided it was time to get off my soapbox.

Bruce smiled. "You're right, you know. That's exactly what people say. Pretty sad, isn't it?"

I shook my head. "Yes, it sure is."

By September, things were much calmer and I was feeling stronger every day. A picture of me holding the plaque I had received appeared on the front page of the newspaper. It was all I needed to validate my writing abilities.

"Congratulations! You both won awards in the West Virginia Press Association's competition," Felecia had told us a few days earlier. Brad and I looked at each other, breaking out in matching grins.

"No kidding," Brad said, surprised.

"That's incredible," I finally found my voice. "Which story?"

I knew Felecia was entering our work in the competition, because she had asked us to choose our best pieces. "Your series on health care. It took first place in the investigative reporting division," she said.

Brad gave me another big smile. "Congratulations!"

"You, too!" I laughed.

At home, the kids were ecstatic when they saw my photo. "We need to have a party for you, Mommy!" Mileah said.

Trista and Gabby quickly chimed in, suggesting cake, cookies, ice cream and all the usual stuff we ate at our parties. The excitement was palpable, and I was happy my children wanted to celebrate my award. I had always tried to throw a small party for their achievements: first day of school, a good report card, winning a school competition, or just to lift someone's spirits, when they were down in the dumps. So that night, we sat down and had a party for me—and as I looked around at my lively, laughing children, the moment felt bittersweet, because I knew what I was going to do. I prayed their happiness would hold out, giving them something to hold onto, in the days to come.

Later, after everyone was asleep, I stood looking at the plaque for a long time. Then I looked at the newspaper clipping of my picture. It felt so good to receive such an award. New and exciting things were happening and I was elated, because it confirmed what I already knew. Deep inside, I knew I was a good reporter. But because I had been questioning so many things about myself for many years, I still had doubts about many of my abilities. Looking at the plaque, I felt pride that it was mine. Winning a first-place award for investigative journalism didn't just mean I was a good writer: it also meant I knew how to research the facts, dig and sift through them, and then analyze all the data to come up with an objective, accurate article.

My thoughts turned to Wanda, and how her short life had ended. We had never even met, but we shared a bond stronger than most people who lived—and loved—together. A shared sisterhood of silence, brought about by years of being abused while living in a war zone within the four walls of our own homes. Wanda might have lost her battle, but it wasn't for nothing, since her death had helped give me the fortitude to continue on my own path to peace and contentment, where my children and I would be free from fear and violence.

Eddie wouldn't stop trying to convince me to come back to him, saying he was sorry, that he would change, and he still loved me. I didn't care what he wanted, and I told him as much every time he tried to sway me with words. But his refusal to give up left me dubious, fearful and sick, that I would never be entirely free. What would it take?

I knew I had work to do, with far more abuse to process, than I could possibly do on my own. I had known that for some time. So my next step was to check myself into Chestnut Ridge Hospital in nearby Morgantown. Trudy had helped arrange for me to be admitted since I didn't have any medical insurance. Given my reduced income, single-mom status and having four mouths to feed, the hospital took me in as a charity case.

"I can't thank you enough," I said, close to tears because of her kindness and all her help. "You're a godsend, Trudy."

"It's nothing. I think it's an excellent idea, given all you've been through," Trudy said. "And honestly, you may have some deeper issues they could help you address better than I can. They have a doctor who's supposed to be great with rape victims."

It was a breezy day when Mom, of all people, dropped me off. I had been protecting her from the truth for years but after Eddie broke into the house and I felt more threatened than ever before, I told her the truth.

"I knew he had a bad temper, but I didn't know it was that bad," she said as matter-of-factly as if we were talking about the weather. I had never noticed how little emotion she expressed, when it came to life-changing topics. "Well, I guess it's a good thing you took the kids and left."

I felt an inner lightness, because of opening up to her. But I still hadn't told her about the sexual abuse that began when I was thirteen. I really didn't think she could handle it. Maybe, in a way, I still needed to protect her. That would come in time, I felt certain.

I'll tell her someday, I thought.

When Mom had gone and I was left alone in my hospital room, I began feeling weepy and missed my children. It was the first time we had ever been apart like that; visitation with their father was sporadic, and when it did occur, it rarely lasted longer than two nights.

"Mrs. Leigh?" I turned from the window to see a thin woman in a nurse's uniform standing there. "I'm Susie and I'll help you get settled in. We have to go through this checklist, to make sure you don't have anything that could be used to hurt yourself," she said with a cheery smile. "Now, do you have any nail clippers in your suitcase?"

"Really?" I asked in disbelief.

"Yes, they're contraband. You'd be surprised what people can do with them," she said.

Susie ran through her list, inspected my suitcase and confiscated my purse: "We'll keep this in a locked area for safekeeping," she explained. "If you need anything from it, just ask someone and they'll help you. Now I'll be right back with your meds."

I went into the bathroom and stood looking above the sink; my face looked distorted, like it did with carnival mirrors, only worse. I could barely see my reflection. Placing my hand on it, I knew what was wrong. It wasn't even glass.

It sobered me to realize that people who came here would try to kill themselves while they were patients. I thought they came to get better. That's why I was there: I'd been having problems with depression, and at times the old hopelessness and thoughts of suicide tried to creep back in—but I refused to let it.

That's why I'm here, I thought. *To get better. To leave all that garbage behind. In the past. Where it belongs.*

Susie brought me a hospital gown and led me into a small room, and a male doctor came in soon after. I sat there on the table, suddenly feeling small and vulnerable while he conducted a short exam.

What if he rapes me? I thought.

I had to resist the urge to jump down and run out screaming. I was terrified at being alone, partially undressed, in a room with a man.

Stop it. He's not going to hurt you. He's here to help.

If only I believed that.

I was in the hospital for two weeks, and went from feeling like an outsider to taking the lead during group therapy. I didn't care if other people knew what had happened to me, because I knew I was a good person, and the sexual abuse from all those years wasn't my fault. It was just like the poster above my bed said: "I know I'm good because God doesn't make junk." I wanted to get better, and the only way to do that was to open up, to be honest and candid. I had to make sense of my past, and talking about it was the best way to do that.

In art and relaxation therapy, though, I didn't have to say a word. The art therapist gave us all kinds of things to work with: colored stones, watercolors, wood, varnish, and glue. My first piece was a picture of a bird flying free in the sky.

"You know, many people who feel imprisoned draw birds," he told me.

Putting the final touches of blue paint on the sky, I smiled. "Yes, that's me, flying free."

Relaxation therapy was my favorite, because it taught me how to relax every single muscle in my body. Using soft, soothing music, the therapist told us to close our eyes and block out everything but our breathing. She taught us to breathe slowly and deeply, and then to gradually allow each muscle to relax. By the time I left an hour later, I was so relaxed I felt like I had taken a long, luxurious nap.

But it was Dr. Williams who helped me to release my inner pain. Using similar techniques I'd learned to relax, she helped me remember the rapes: how helpless and frightened I had felt, and how I had wanted Eddie to stop. Dr. Williams said the trauma was buried, so I had to work through it by essentially reliving it. For hours afterward, I felt emotionally raw and vulnerable, just as I had all those years ago. But by the next day I felt a little better and by the day after that, I could feel myself getting stronger.

Dr. Williams said she was certain I had Post-Traumatic Stress Disorder, and offered to see me on an outpatient basis. But I needed to think about it, because going back into such pain was, by far, the hardest thing I had done during my stay.

The day I was discharged, everyone wished me the best and I felt like I was leaving family behind. As I left the hospital, I took a deep breath and stepped out into the bright sunshine. The warmth touched my face and infused me with hope for whatever lay ahead, and I felt a sense of freedom I had never experienced before.

On the way home, I thought of the big old house where we had once lived together as a sad, broken family, and wondered what was next. Whatever it was, it was going to be better. I knew that. I didn't know how, but I knew that much, at least. I was convinced it would be better. Our future was going to be nothing like our past. I had gone from being a passive victim of abuse and rape, to facing death that day I fell apart on the bathroom floor, to recognizing I have an abundance to give to the world around me. Yes, our life as a family was going to be very different.

I went toward the house, my children, and our future. It was full of promise and possibilities.

Finally.

Later that night, I began tucking the kids into bed. I loved that time of the day, when they had toothpaste breath and warm cheeks waiting to be kissed. "Good night, I love you. Sweet dreams."

As I was leaving, Slade called out, "Don't let the bug bites bite you."

I smiled as I walked down the stairs. *They're the reason my life is meaningful,* I thought. It was a real smile, one that came from within, unlike those I once pasted there while playing out my masquerade. The kids had not left me alone for a minute the entire day. We celebrated with a party. A welcome home party for mom, they had said, complete with cake and ice cream.

I went into the bathroom—the same small room where I had planned to end all our lives—and looked into the mirror. The woman standing before me wasn't a stranger exactly, but we were getting to know each other better. And I liked her, I really did!

But if I peered a little deeper, I could see signs of someone else who had once stood there, looking at her reflection. In many ways, that woman had been afraid of her own shadow. In other ways, she had been more courageous than many women are, or can be. That woman—the one who used to be me—was slowly becoming a distant memory.

A few minutes later, I walked into the living room and curled up on the sofa, a cup of tea in one hand and my discharge papers in the other. Looking into the mirror and thinking about my hospital stay had reminded me of that day in

Dr. Towson's office in 1986, when I wanted my family doctor to give me something for my depression, but I was too afraid of being locked away in a place with people wearing starched uniforms and dispensing purple pills, to tell him the truth about just how depressed I was. If I had known how much good would come from my two-week hospital stay, I would have been admitted years ago.

It was amazing that I felt better, that I was better. I wanted to read the words, one more time, just so I could see them for myself.

"The patient denies any further suicidal ideation or feelings of hopelessness/helplessness. In fact she has actively engaged in treatment and has demonstrated leadership qualities on the unit ... depressive symptoms have resolved."

I smiled as I sipped my tea. *I'm a leader?* I thought. I had never seen that in myself before, but if so, maybe I could help other women whose lives were as chaotic and confused as my own had been.

But how? Even before the thought was formed, I knew: I would write about it, for my column. What better way to help people realize being ill—or seeking help—is nothing to be ashamed of? That it's only a stigma as long as they allow it to be.

And that's what my readers learned when they opened the next issue of their newspaper. Years later, someone told me that framed column still hangs inside Chestnut Ridge Hospital.

Felecia chose the title, "Getting help is a sign of strength," and that column led more people to share their personal stories about depression and suicide with me, than I could have ever imagined.

> *"My mom was depressed all her life."*
> *"My uncle killed himself because he was too proud to*

get help."

"Thank you, maybe other people will get help now, too."

But my favorite letter came from a woman named Jane.

"I just wanted to let you know how much I enjoy your column, Vintage Daleen. Thank you for letting your readers take a peek into your life and for showing us that problems can be dealt with a lot easier with a bit of humor.

I really appreciate you sharing your problems with your readers. It makes me feel a kinship to you since I have gone through some of the same things you write about.

Please don't quit writing. Your column is the first thing I look for when I receive the paper. You may never know what an impact you have had on your readers. I can tell you that you have helped me and maybe someday I will get to West Virginia and meet you."

I was moved with wonder upon reading what Jane had written. I knew then how powerful words can be when used to help others.

That's what I'm going to do with my life, I thought.

QUESTIONS FOR READERS

1. What is the significance of the book's title, *Sister of Silence?*

2. What importance do the initials SOS have?

3. How can you use this book to help other women in similar situations?

4. Describe what helped the author to recognize she was mentally ill?

5. What steps did she take to help herself, and/or get help from others?

6. How were her children impacted by the violence in their home?

7. What role did her children play in the author's life?

8. If there was one message you gleaned from reading this book, what was it?

9. What can we do to help make mental illness easier to discuss?

10. How did the early sexual abuse affect the author?

11. When did the author realize she was a victim of marital rape? How did this impact her?

12. Do you think other women recognize if they are victims, too? Why do you so answer?

13. What can we do to help these women?

14. Do you think society is open to discussion about marital rape? Why or why not?

15. Why do children blame themselves when they are sexually abused?

16. In denying that acquaintance molestation is a significant problem, what message does society send to the victims of such abuse?

17. Could anyone have prevented the author's abuse? Why do you so answer?

18. Why is this an important book for parents?

19. How was the author able to overcome what happened to her?

20. What message is she trying to share?

21. What is empowerment?

22. How was the author empowered?

23. Why does the author portray her experience as a journey?

24. Has this book changed the way you view child sexual abuse? Rape within marriage? Mental illness? Why do you so answer?

25. What will you do differently now, after reading this book?

RECOMMENDED READING

Dr. Jacqueline Campbell's Danger Assessment for health professionals:
www.dangerassessment.org

Perfect Daughters: Adult Daughters of Alcoholics, by Robert Ackerman

Treating Attachment Abuse: A Compassionate Approach, by Steven Stosny,
PhD

*The Courage to Heal - Third Edition - Revised and Expanded: A Guide for
Women Survivors of Child Sexual Abuse*, by Ellen Bass and Laura Davis

Self Matters: Creating Your Life from the Inside Out, by Dr. Phillip
McGraw

When Men Batter Women: New Insights into Ending Abusive Relationships,
by John Gottman and Neil Jacobson

Why Mothers Kill: A Forensic Psychologist's Casebook, by Geoffrey R.
McKee

Understanding Domestic Homicide, by Neil Websdale

Kenneth V. Lanning

Mr. Lanning is currently a consultant in the area of crimes against children. Before retiring in 2000, he was a special agent with the FBI for more than thirty years, where he was assigned to the Behavioral Science Unit and the National Center for the Analysis of Violent Crime at the FBI Academy in Quantico, VA. He is a founding member of the board of directors of the American Professional Society on the Abuse of Children (APSAC) and is a former member of the APSAC Advisory Board. He is currently a member of the Advisory Board of the Association for the Treatment of Sexual Abusers (ATSA). Mr. Lanning was the 1996 recipient of the Outstanding Professional Award from APSAC, the 1997 recipient of the FBI Director's Annual Award for Special Achievement for his career accomplishments in connection with missing and exploited children, and the 2009 recipient of the Lifetime Achievement Award for Outstanding Service from the National Children's Advocacy Center. He has trained thousands of law enforcement officers and criminal justice professionals.

ORDER FORM

SISTER OF SILENCE
BY DALEEN BERRY

Please complete the following information to order additional copies. Select one method of payment:

Visa:_____ MC:_____ Discover:_____
Check:_____ Money order:_____

Card number:_____Exp. date:_____
Card security code (3-digit code on back of card):_____

Number of copies desired: _____ @ $18.99 per copy
State tax (95-cents each):_____
Shipping & handling: $4.99

Total amount submitted: _____

Name: _____
Address:_____
City:_____State:_____ Zip:_____

Mail coupon and payment to address below:
Nellie Bly Books, 364 Patteson Drive #275
Morgantown, WV 26505

Please allow two weeks for delivery.